EXPLORING ADOLESCENT HAPPINESS

EXPLORING ADOLESCENT HAPPINESS

Commitment, Purpose, and Fulfillment

Zipora Magen

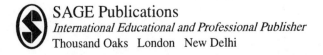

SAGE Publications
International Educational and Professional Publisher
Thousand Oaks   London   New Delhi

For information:

SAGE Publications, Inc.
2455 Teller Road
Thousand Oaks, California 91320
E-mail: order@sagepub.com

SAGE Publications Ltd.
6 Bonhill Street
London EC2A 4PU
United Kingdom

SAGE Publications India Pvt. Ltd.
M-32 Market
Greater Kailash I
New Delhi 110 048 India

Printed in the United States of America

Library of Congress Cataloging-in-Publication Data

Magen, Zipora.
 Exploring adolescent happiness: Commitment, purpose, and fulfillment / by Zipora Magen.
  p. cm.
 Includes bibliographical references and index.
 ISBN 0-7619-0730-0 (hardcover: alk. paper)
 ISBN 0-7619-0731-9 (pbk.: alk. paper)
 1. Happiness in adolescence. I. Title.
 BF724.3.H35 M34 1998
 155.5'182—dc21   98-8973

This book is printed on acid-free paper.

98 99 00 01 02 03 10 9 8 7 6 5 4 3 2 1

Acquiring Editor:	Jim Nageotte
Editorial Assistant:	Heidi Van Middlesworth
Production Editor:	Sherrise M. Purdum
Editorial Assistant:	Nevair Kabakian
Typesetter/Designer:	Janelle LeMaster
Indexer:	Juniee Oneida
Cover Designer:	Kristi White

Contents

Acknowledgments

M any individuals over the years have contributed to this work. I am very appreciative of the generous help given by several readers and critics, as the book progressed from stage to stage. Zvi Giora, Allen Ivey, and Sam Juni made an invaluable contribution by reading and commenting on the manuscript. Special thanks to Arieh Lewy, who lent his wisdom, inspiration, and expertise from the very beginning of the writing process. To Mordechai Arieli, Menucha Birenbaum, Naomi Gur, Moshe Israelashvili, Moshe Landsman, and Alona Raviv, I am grateful for your support and your helpful input and advice.

I would like to express particular recognition of the late Harry Passow of Teachers College, Columbia University, who always made me feel that he valued what I had to say and whose conviction that this book was important helped me persevere.

The initial impetus to transform my thoughts and research into a book came from the encouragement and enthusiasm I received while on sabbatical at Columbia University, New York University, and the University of British Columbia. I would like to express my special appreciation to Marion Dragoon, Martin Hamburger, Pat Raskin, Roger Meyers,

Bob Wasson, and Ishu Ishiyama. My original ideas have been greatly expanded and altered through my close professional association with these colleagues. I am also genuinely grateful to my colleagues in the School of Education at Tel Aviv University, especially Avner Ziv, Iris Levin, and Rina Shapira, whose steadfast faith and respect for my ideas allowed me to continue pursuing what was an unconventional research method.

Considerable gratitude is also due to my graduate students at Tel Aviv University, who collaborated with me on research, stimulated my interest, and spurred further methodological and theoretical refinements. In addition, many rich opportunities to clarify my thinking were made by my counseling students who participated in my courses and seminars over the years.

I owe, of course, a renewed debt to the adolescents and parents, and to the counselors and educators, who have shared bits of their lives with me over the years, increasing my sensitivity to their experiences and inspiring me to continue my search for the humanistic impulse.

To Larry Smith, who lent his outstanding editorial skills to the manuscript at various stages and to putting the book in its final form, I am deeply indebted. Special thanks also go to Toby Mostisher, whose literary talents added another dimension to the book, to Gabriella Oldham for her help in the first steps of the project, and to Alice Zilcha, for her careful typing and cheerful disposition. I would also like to gratefully acknowledge my editor at Sage, Jim Nageotte, for his support and creative contribution in reading and commenting on the manuscript at its final stage. Finally, this book would never have come into being without the editorial assistance of Dee Ankonina, who has traveled the long road from beginning to end with me in bringing this work to fruition.

As a wife, mother of two, and grandmother of six, I have been privileged with a loving family that unwaveringly cherishes and supports me. Above all, one person stood by me in writing this book from the time when the paper was still blank, giving of himself in innumerable ways in an atmosphere of love that made it possible for me to sustain the pain and challenge of writing. To my husband, Joseph, who has taught me what real happiness is, this book is dedicated.

Preface

Happiness, commitment, self, beyond self. . . . Civilization itself is a working out of the struggle of opposing forces, and the often tortured search for a "happy medium" between the interests of the individual and those of the group. Yet, it also seems that each of us in our life's work, whatever the nature of that work, may stumble on moments in which we realize that the values of the self are not necessarily isolated, and that, in fact, the real job of art and science is to uncover the essential connection of individuals to the world.

This book is the record of an empirical search for that connection. It is, I hope, a particularly credible affirmation because it takes as its subject matter, not a mature population that has over the years cultivated a sense of happiness through living for others, but in fact, the adolescent population, where narcissistic preoccupations are still developmentally prevalent, if not predominant. So, if our assumptions about happiness and transpersonal commitment are shown to be persuasive here, then it would seem to suggest some rather exhilarating universal potential for moral generosity as a function of self-fulfillment.

Throughout this book, we return to the same basic questions: what makes adolescents happy, what makes them feel good about themselves and the world, what invests their experience with meaning. Of course, as ethnographers, my colleagues and I found no better way to begin answering these fundamental questions than by allowing the adolescents to speak for themselves and to then apply the appropriate analytic tools and models.

As professionals, readers will interpret the material in those tools and models as supportable scientific data. But as human beings, readers will, I hope, also listen to the voices of our adolescents as an unvarnished record of "modern man in search of a soul."

At the same time, these voices have pointed relevance to our work as educators, counselors, and psychologists, as well as to our experience as parents. They offer a wide-ranging mirror of the issues adolescents face in their development and provide significant hints as to the values and relationships they see themselves bringing to bear as emerging adults. Likewise, the various interventions and practical solutions suggested in the book are better planned and implemented the more we hear and understand the voices of our subjects.

In all of this, or course, I had something of an agenda. It was certainly not my intention to reinforce the classic hedonistic paradigms or Hobbesian despair that has adumbrated modern psychology in its evolution. Quite to the contrary, my co-researchers and I were looking for evidence that those who commit themselves to activities beyond the self are the ones most capable of experiencing deep joy and happiness. The research studies presented in this book do overwhelmingly point in that direction; yet, it is certainly our view that neither our methodology nor our analyses were distorted because we wanted to find the result we did. As I explain our procedures at various points in the text, I hope the reader will agree.

There were so many directions in which to take our research, even as we established a link between commitment and happiness. Personality types, the impact of experience, and—a particularly difficult issue to get our hands around, but also one of the most exciting—the influence of cultural and ethnic factors were unavoidable corollary areas. After all, not only were we dealing with a population developmentally inclined toward self-involvement, we were also doing so in the Middle East, where political circumstances would seem to encourage more emphasis on self-survival and self-aggrandizement as exclusive life objectives.

Some of the transpersonal yearnings we found are probably more dangerous and destructive than the purest narcissism. But I hope the reader will also agree that many of the voices in this book suggest the possibility of moral growth and human unity, even in the most disheartening of circumstances.

—*Zipora Magen*
Tel Aviv University

Introduction:
How the Research Started

For many years I was a junior high and high school teacher and guidance counselor. As a teacher, I conveyed material and made demands; as a counselor, I got to know something of the students' feelings, thoughts, and experiences. In both roles, I was able to observe not only the problems and difficulties of adolescence, but also its glory. I met students in moments of joy, excitement, and zest for life, often revealing profound sensitivity to others and readiness to reach out and to give of themselves. Yet, at the same time, I felt that I did not adequately understand their world and needed to know it better. As a graduate student at Tel Aviv University, I came across countless books and articles, but almost all of them focused on the conflicts and problems of this age and on the difficulties that these engendered for their parents and teachers.

I felt that something basic was missing in the professional descriptions of the adolescent's inner world. What made adolescents happy? What made them feel good about themselves and the world? What made them feel uplifted? Which events had real meaning for them? What were their deepest aspirations? The professional literature at the time—in the 1970s and 1980s—had little to say about these things. Nor did the literature shed much light on the nature of the well-known dichotomy in adolescence of inordinate self-centeredness, egotism, and hedonistic tendencies, on the one hand, and the idealism of the age—adolescents' extraordinary readiness to give of themselves, their search for ideals by which to live, and their longing for commitment—on the other. It seemed to me that, although there was so much attention to the selfish end of the spectrum, what mattered more was the self-transcendent end of the polarity. I had no way of knowing how prevalent the ability or inclination to rise above the self was at this age or, more important, how it could be fostered and encouraged.

Then, almost by chance, I found a road—not yet answers, but a direction, an open door, so to speak, which might lead me to what I was looking for. In the mid-1970s, Professor Ted Landsman of the University of Florida arrived at the Department of Counseling Psychology in the School of Education of Tel Aviv University. I had the good fortune of being his student and research assistant. Ted was an illumination and opened up the rich concepts of humanistic psychology for me.

I was familiar with the writings of Rogers, Jourard, Maslow, and a few other humanist psychologists. Their faith in the essential goodness of human beings and their inclination to look at the positive aspects of human experience made a great deal of sense to me, as did the conviction, which ran as an undercurrent through much of their writings, that the truest realization of our human nature comes from our giving of ourselves. Their philosophy was particularly resonant for me because I grew up in a household that was infused with the Hasidic philosophy of life. Although my parents themselves were secular Jews, they both hailed from generations of Hasidic rabbis and leaders. My grandfather, who was always held up as model and inspiration to us children, had been an esteemed rabbi of the shtetl of Sadigura in Austro-Romania. I never met him, but his widow, who lived with us, kept his legacy alive in our home, as did the multitude of uncles and aunts who were part of my childhood landscape.

Hasidism was in its day a revolutionary movement that set out to counter what it saw as the excessive intellectualism, mechanical observance, and elitism of mainstream Judaism. It literally preached a joyful approach to life and God. God was to be worshipped with joy and delight. Its *tsaddikim*—or righteous men and women—were not necessarily those who observed the ritual laws to the letter, nor those who had the greatest learning. They were those individuals whose faith was full, whose intentions were honest and pure, and who gave of themselves anonymously, wholeheartedly, without thought of return. The spirit of my parents' home was similarly characterized by faith in people, openness to others, and, above all, the sense that every person deserves attention, care, and, where it was needed, help. In much of what we did, there was a sense of joy and elevation. Birthdays, holidays, family gatherings were all occasions for uplift and celebration. We reveled in the fullness and vigor of life.

So the humanist approach was quite close to home for me, and I like to think that I intuitively applied it in my work with students and counselees. But Ted Landsman gave me a broader intellectual context in which to work. As Landsman's research assistant, I was immersed in the systematic study of the positive aspects of humanity for the first time in my life. To be sure, Landsman was far from a lone voice in this field. Many other scholars, such as Coan, Jourard, and Maslow, as well as his students, Antonovsky, Csikszentmihalyi, and Diener (to name just a few here) were busy exploring such issues as well-being and such questions as what made life meaningful, joyful, and coherent to people.

But Landsman was my personal teacher, and, in fact, he was a living embodiment of humanistic values and being. In the 1970s, when the tensions between Israel and her Arab neighbors were at their height, Landsman understood that personal relationships among individuals could provide a basis for political understanding and discourse. He organized discussion groups of Jewish and Arab teachers and school counselors and, in the most unlikely of meetings, he somehow succeeded in bringing out in all of us the caring and positive feeling that we rarely showed each other, either as individuals or nations.

Among the most important things that he taught me was a professional methodology that mirrored his humanistic instincts. Rather than closed questionnaires with predetermined statements, where participants made ratings on discrete scales, he used open-ended questions that encouraged participants to be introspective and allowed them to express themselves in their own terms. I soon saw that this method had a better chance of revealing what people really thought and felt, was more likely to elicit what was really meaningful to them, than the quantitative approach then in vogue.

Using this subjective method, Landsman studied positive human experiences. He worked to discover those which made people feel good about themselves and the world. Landsman, like the other humanist psychologists, focused on adults, giving little thought to adolescence; some psychologists did not even seem to consider adolescents useful subjects for their inquires.

It did not take me long to realize the potential of Landsman's approach for the earlier part of the life cycle. I began to wonder what were the positive experiences of the young people I taught and counseled.

I proceeded to read his writings and the studies conducted by students under his supervision, and I gradually formulated a research proposal of my own. The proposal included not only the question of what made adolescents happy, but also the other issue I cared about: adolescents' commitment beyond themselves. I wanted to know whether happiness and commitment were dialectic polarities in adolescence, like egoism and giving. Perhaps they were related; if so, how? I also wanted to know whether these things were associated with particular personality traits, which would suggest that adolescents with certain personalities were either more or less prone to being happy. Were such adolescents more committed than those with other constellations of personality traits? Were the sources and extent of their happiness and their readiness for commitment culture-bound or universal?

To answer the last question—about the relation of culture to happiness and commitment—I chose to study adolescents from three different cultures: American Christians, representing a modern, industrial society; Israeli Arabs, representative of a traditional society; and Israeli Jews, who may be considered somewhere in the middle of those two worlds. Is the happiness of the three groups of youths grounded in similar, or different, kinds of experiences? Are the adolescents of the three cultures more or less equally prone to commitment beyond themselves?

This, in short, is how my research started. Over the course of my research, I was intrigued by the young people who were actually engaged in activities benefiting social causes and/or individuals in need, and I wanted to learn what typified them and whether they would experience life events as more inspiring and joyous. Also, do adolescents who are fortunate enough to interact successfully and meaningfully with other people develop a general desire to contribute to fellow human beings? Or does the desire for commitment beyond self, whatever its source, motivate the youngster to engage in positive interpersonal contact?

Like much research, every study I did yielded some answers and raised new questions. Each study thus gave rise to the next in a flow that has not yet dried up. These studies kept me busy over the years. This book, product of a decade and a half of research, makes no pretense of presenting every study, but it strives rather to present a comprehensive picture of adolescents' happiness and commitment.

Part 1

Theoretical and Empirical Foundation

1

The Value of Happiness, Happiness as a Value

No matter how dull, or how mean, or how wise a man is, he feels that happiness is his indisputable right.
—Helen Keller, *The Story of My Life* (1954)

Happiness, perhaps even more than beauty, is in the eye of the beholder, which probably accounts for the abundance of its definitions. No two philosophers and no two psychologists or sociologists agree on exactly what it is or how to attain it, or even on whether it is attainable at all. All we know about happiness is that we want it.

As far back as the 4th century B.C., Aristotle called happiness the *summum bonum,* the supreme good, and dedicated an entire volume, *Nicomachean Ethics,* to defining it. Aristotle regarded happiness as the reward of virtue. The Epicurean and Stoic philosophers who followed were similarly concerned with the question of the kind of life that was most likely to lead to happiness. Christian philosophers placed greater emphasis on other values, including suffering and sacrifice. In the eighteenth century, the Enlightenment philosophers once again turned their thoughts to happiness; in particular, the Utilitarian philosophers addressed the question of how to organize society and social institutions to bring the greatest happiness to the greatest number. The American Constitution went so far as to declare "the pursuit of happiness" an inherent right.

In the twentieth century, psychologists were applying the methods of their discipline to many of the issues that had previously been the province of philosophy, but they were slow to pick up the theme of happiness. Freud (1930/1982) formulated the pleasure principle as a basic motivating force, but he associated the attainment of pleasure with tension reduction and the maintenance of homeostasis rather than with happiness. "One feels inclined to say that the intention that man should be 'happy' is not included in the plan of the creator" (p. 13), he observed. In Freud's wake, for more than half a century, the focus of psychology was on illness and its cure. The ultimate endeavor was to alleviate the pain and suffering caused by the mind. It was not until the second half of the twentieth century that more than a few isolated psychologists and educators began to regard happiness as worth pursuing in itself. This idea fast gained in popularity. Since the 1970s, about 2,500 scientific studies on happiness have been published (Veenhoven, 1993).

The impetus for this interest came from the Humanist school of psychologists, who felt that there was something important missing in the traditional focus of psychology on illness and the impediments to well-being. They turned their attention to health and well-being itself. The humanists did not initially use the term *happiness*. Their central concern was with higher states of being, beyond the mere normalcy or adjustment with which traditional psychology seemed to content itself. They regarded these earlier goals as mean, as falling short of what human beings are capable of achieving. They believed that the proper task of the psychologist (and educator) was to help the individuals they worked with to develop and grow toward the best that they could be.

The humanists were also interested in special people who live on a higher plane than most of us, and in special moments when human beings are lifted above their mundane selves. They focused on the moments when, to use Jourard's (1969) formulation, a person "experiences the world in greater richness, feels upsurges of strength or accomplishes goals so untypical" (p. 205) of himself or herself. Carl Rogers (1961) developed a revolutionary approach to counseling and psychotherapy to help the client become what he termed a *fully functioning* or *high functioning* person. Rogers (1980) went on to describe a sensitive openness to the world and a trust in one's ability to form new relationships with one's environment as characterizing such people. Richard Coan's (1974) book, *The Optimal Personality*, explored what he termed the *optimal self*, marked by efficiency, creativity, inner harmony, relatedness, and transcendence. Ted Landsman (1974) wrote about the "beautiful and noble person" who is aware of himself or herself as a worthwhile individual, and who nurtures an abiding love for the physical environment and others. A central figure in these developments, Abraham Maslow (1961), concentrated his work on the *self-actualizing* person—an open, spontaneous, self-motivated, and self-aware individual, who lived life fully, honestly, and intensely—and on studying the *peak experiences* that he considered the transient moments of such self-actualization. Maslow regarded happiness as both a result and an accelerator of personal growth, and he viewed people as at their best when fueled by "growth motivation"—in other words, being pulled by pleasure rather than pushed by pain.

Happiness entered the professional vocabulary as psychologists struggled to grasp the essentials of these elevated states. Consistently, they began to view happiness as a core element of these states. Maslow (1971) referred to peak experiences as "moments of ecstasy" in which, borrowing the well-known term from C. S. Lewis, one is "surprised by joy" (p. 46). "Peak experiences," wrote Maslow, "is a generalization for the best moments of the human being, for the happiest moments of life, for experiences of ecstasy, rapture, bliss, of the greatest joy" (p. 101). Jourard and Landsman (1980) stepped down somewhat from Maslow's elevated heights. For them, "Positive experience refers to all occasions of pleasure, fun, satisfaction, completion of projects, fulfillment of hopes—the good moments of life" (p. 56). But happiness is no less essential an element. Such experiences are "significant experiences of joy, happiness, warmth" (p. 57). Ten years later, Mihaly Csikszentmihalyi (1990) put forth the tenet that the state of consciousness he called *optimal experience* is experienced subjectively as "pleasure, happiness, satisfaction, enjoyment" (p. 24).

Happiness, it should be noted, was never the only component of the elevated state or special moment as these writers understood it. Honesty and authenticity; freedom from cant, repression, and blind conformity; self-knowledge and sensitivity to others; the ability to give of oneself to both people and causes and the capacity to work toward an aim; moral responsibility, wholeness, and spirituality—such are the moral underpinnings that anchor transcendent experience.

The rather innovative idea, that happiness also defines human beings at their best, made the concept worth defining and identifying in actual experience. Happiness as a component of the peak or positive experience soon became viewed as part and parcel of life on a "higher plane." Thus, Landsman asserted that positive experiences (with an emphasis on those in childhood) contribute to the development of the beautiful and noble person. To be sure, others were somewhat more wary of asserting a direct causation, but the sense that runs through their work is that positive/peak experiences do contribute to human growth, that they somehow make one a better human being (Kelly, 1969; Landsman, 1967; Maslow, 1964, 1971; Moustakas, 1972, 1977; Otto, 1967; S. M. Smith, 1973; and others). Other thinkers and researchers also support the tenet that human development can be fostered if one allows oneself to experience events and feelings completely, responding with greater arousal and strength, and delving into a search for the deep meaning of the experience (Csikszentmihalyi, 1990; Frankl, 1988; Jourard, 1971b; Waterman, 1993).

The idea that happiness is a value worth striving for fired others, including psychologists in various fields, sociologists, and various social scientists. Happiness itself, often apart from the elevated states in which the humanists had originally anchored it, finally became a subject of inquiry. What is happiness? What makes people happy? Is happiness absolute or relative? Does it depend on outer circumstances or inner attitudes? And what are those circumstances and attitudes? Who is happy? Can people who suffer traumas, who live in want, who have handicaps, be happy? Does happiness depend on a steadiness of disposition or the ability to feel strongly?

These and other questions were raised under the assumption that, if happiness were better understood, things could be done to make people happier. As Csikszentmihalyi (1990) put it in the introduction to his book *Flow,*

The intent of this book . . . is to explore this very ancient question: When do people feel most happy? If we begin to answer it, we will perhaps be able to order life so that happiness will play a larger part in it. (p. 2)

Csikszentmihalyi was in good company. Beginning in the 1980s, Ruut Veenhoven made an enterprise of the study of happiness. Among other things, he compiled a bibliography of happiness consisting of several thousand contemporary studies on the "subjective appreciation of life" (1993); formulated a variety of operational definitions of happiness; examined perceptions of happiness in different cultures; compared different theories of happiness; and researched the personality traits and life situations of people who scored high on his happiness measure. Ed Diener started his career in the mid-1980s by examining the correlates of subjective well-being. Alan S. Waterman, in paper after paper (1984, 1990, 1993), elaborated on Aristotle's notion of *eudaimonia* (happiness) or "activity expressing virtue." In his aptly titled *Psychology of Happiness*, M. Argyle (1986) presented a systematic overview of the psychological aspects of happiness. Albert Kozma, along with M. J. Stones and colleagues, tried to differentiate the attributes of very happy people from those of the very unhappy (Kozma, Stones, Stones, Hannah, & McNeil, 1990). Other professionals who turned their attention to this most absorbing subject included Michalos (1985, 1991), Headey, Holmstrom, and Wearing (1984), Larson (1989), and Fordyce (1988).

Not surprisingly, their inquiries started with, or brought them to, a wide variety of definitions of happiness and how it is best attained. Among the more common definitions seem to be various formulations of *global life satisfaction* (e.g., Campbell, Converse, & Rodgers, 1976; Veenhoven, 1984), or satisfaction with specific aspects of life, such as job or marriage and subjective well-being (e.g., Bradburn, 1969; Diener, 1984, 1994). Some definitions focus on the affective manifestations of happiness, such as hedonic pleasure or mood (Kozma & Stones, 1980), whereas others are based on the assumption that feelings of happiness are anchored in doing things that make one happy (Csikszentmihalyi & Larson, 1984; Waterman, 1990, 1993); these definitions try to conceptualize happiness in terms of the feelings that people have when engaged in such activities. Thus Csikszentmihalyi (1990), in defining happiness, developed his theory of flow, in which one is carried away by the interaction between the self and the activity. Waterman added to this theory the idea that the *flow experience* is achieved in those activities in which the individual is most self-expressive. These later concepts differ widely both from preceding concepts of peak or positive experiences, as well as from one another. For all the variety of definitions, however, they can all be seen as expressions of a shared assumption that happiness is of sufficient importance and value to be the object of contemplation, time, energy, and study.

This assumption was not shared by everyone. Almost from the beginning, there were those who raised their voices against this focus on personal happiness and self. The first and by far the strongest protest was raised by Viktor Frankl (1966), who regarded what he termed *self-transcendence*—not self-actualization—as the essence of what it means to be human. Self-transcendence, as he defined it, is such "a constitutive characteristic of being human that it always points, and is directed to, something other than itself" (p. 97). For Frankl, the focus on the self—whether couched as self-awareness, self-development, or self-actualization—stands in stark contrast to self-transcendence. Actualizing the self and going beyond the self are diametrically opposed. Happiness, Frankl held, is thus the wrong goal. The essential goal of human action is the attainment of meaning. Happiness is a side effect of whatever reason one has to feel happy.

Frankl's view emerged from his experience in the Nazi concentration camps, where he lost all his family except his sister. His starting point was the question of what makes people want to live under such circumstances (Frankl, 1963). Meaning, not happiness, was the only answer he could glean from his own experience; and it was from this teleological perspective that Frankl rejected all views that elevated happiness—whether in the Freudian sense of pleasure or in its later formulations—to a goal worth striving for. Indeed, as Frankl (1988) argued, "Man does not care for pleasure and happiness as such, but rather for that which causes these effects, be it the fulfillment of personal meaning or the encounter with a human being" (p. 40). The pursuit of happiness is thus self-defeating. For in making it the object of one's motivation, Frankl maintained, one loses sight of the reasons that one is happy. Happiness thus slips away. The same argument holds for self-actualization, peak experiences, health, consciousness, and all the other goals that center on the self. These cannot be realizable goals, but only by-products of the attainment of meaning. Some research has, in fact, lent strong empirical support to Frankl's contentions: For example, a feeling of meaning in life was found to be strongly and negatively linked with a sense of hopelessness (Grygielski, 1984). A related criticism was articulated by Adrianne Aron (1977) from a sociopolitical rather than philosophical perspective. She castigated Maslow for failing to provide a political or ethical road map for getting from self-actualization to the good society. She objected to the fact that "the thrust of Maslow's thought is toward the individual rather than the community, the private rather than the public, the interior life of the mind rather than the exterior life conducted in the society of others" (p. 12). The result of the search for self-actualization, she argued, is the self- indulgence, the dropping out, and the lack of norms and values that marked the 1960s. Maslow may not have been a direct influence on the hippies, but his work presumably contributed to the whole sensibility of an era that glorified self-indulgence.

Hampden-Turner (1977) defended Maslow from such guilt by association—indeed, the attacks on Maslow do seem somewhat reminiscent of the Athenian elders charging Socrates with the corruption of their young people—but the sense that personal happiness and responsible social involvement are at odds nonetheless informs other criticism as well (Headey et al., 1984; Koch, 1971; D. Smith, 1973). It has even been argued that personal happiness comes at the expense of values such as solidarity, equality, and salvation (Headey et al., 1984; Isen & Levin, 1972). This attack on Maslow provoked an energetic defense. Maslow (1971) himself, who felt he had been misread, refined his early descriptions of self-actualization to explicitly include what his critics found missing:

> Self-actualizing people are, without one single exception, involved in a cause outside their own skin, in something outside of themselves. They are devoted, working at something, something which is very precious to them—some calling or vocation in the old sense, the priestly sense. (p. 42)

Waterman (1993) made efforts to distinguish his version of eudaimonia—the happiness derived from "personal expressiveness," which is attained through the optimal application of one's skills and abilities and, at the same time, the true advancement of one's purposes—from hedonic happiness, where the advancement of talents and life goals is not an integral feature. Veenhoven (1988), who defined happiness as life satisfaction, similarly distinguished it from hedonism, and in an article aptly titled "Utility of Happiness," he marshaled the existing studies on the subject to show the positive effects of happiness and to refute concerns that happiness as an end in itself weakens social contacts and isolates self-seeking individualists. "Happiness does not lead to rosy passivity or self-complacent egoism. Rather, enjoyment of living stimulates active involvement and encourages social contacts" (p. 351), he argued, adding that society is the better for happy people, who are politically more concerned, healthier, and harder working and who "weave closer intimate networks and provide their children with warmer homes" (p. 351) than their less happy counterparts. David Myers (1993) brought together in his book, *The Pursuit of Happiness,* the available research to debunk myths that happiness is related to circumstances or factors such as age, gender, race, culture, or wealth, arguing instead that it is related to inner qualities, faith, good personal relationships, and the possession of and progress toward goals.

The majority of scholars and empiricists that I have reviewed in this chapter discussed the value and attainment of happiness almost solely as the terrain of adults. In fact, Aristotelian tradition might actually preclude youth, because eudaimonia requires a contemplativeness and moral virtue that presumably develops only with age. Significantly, Maslow (1970) said he could find almost no examples of self-actualization in people who were not well into their adult years. Waterman (1990), however, raised the possibility that even the curiosity and explorations of young children are already driving the search for "personal expressiveness," which is the trademark concept in his definition of happiness. Adolescents could thus be seen as likewise undergoing experiences that will encourage the pursuit of a happiness closer to Aristotle's than to Timothy Leary's.

The search for happiness holds a special value and meaning in adolescence, when youngsters experience both considerable emotional intensity and a need for strong emotional stimulation. Although happiness at this age has been linked to hedonistic fulfillment and short-term gratification, intimate interpersonal contacts and the intense seeking out of self-identity are no less compelling stimulants (Blos, 1979; Conger & Petersen, 1984; Patterson & McCubbin, 1987).

The adolescent period is acknowledged as a critical one in development, a time to question and assess early childhood values and concepts, an age in which full identification with the values and symbols of society is attained. The quest for identity in adolescence entails many facets of the question, "Who am I?" although the answer can only be discovered through a broad inquiry into one's values, experiences of joy and sorrow, life aspirations, meaningful relationships, and readiness for responsibility (Erikson, 1968; Waterman, 1982). Significantly, to answer the question "Who am I?" is also to answer other existential questions, including, "What makes me happy?" and "What makes me feel good?" While struggling to define their individuality and to discern their own needs, desires, and goals, adolescents delve deeply within themselves, yet at the same time are confronted by a broad spectrum of physical and emotional options in the external world.

Even hedonistic drives in adolescence can be interpreted as playing a part in the formation and pursuit of a socially productive personality type. The adolescent learns about the world and about the self primarily via things that have an affective and cognitive connection. By seeking out thrills and exhilaration, through a search for a sense of being moved and touched emotionally, the teenager is simultaneously pursuing an understanding of the world and the self.

Despite the common notion that the stress-filled teen years are markedly unhappy, surveys of representative samples of people throughout the lifespan in many nations have shown that no time of life is significantly happier or unhappier than others (Inglehart, 1990; Latten, 1989; Myers & Diener, 1995; Stock, Okun, Haring, & Witter, 1983). Similarly, the sources and extent of meaning in life did not vary with age over the course of the lifespan (Baum & Stewart, 1990).

Csikszentmihalyi (1984, 1990) is almost unique in his exploration of enjoyable experiences, happiness, and moments of transcendence (flow) among adolescents. Otherwise, there is a paucity in empirical studies attempting to discover the actual sources generating adolescents' emotional excitement, illumination, and a sense of feeling good about themselves and the world. The elucidation of those life events that trigger young people's positive experiences would make it possible to identify the internal and external catalysts of their joy, satisfaction, and pleasure and would shed considerable light on the personal meaning of these events in their lives.

There is thus outstanding potential in research on adolescent happiness for modeling new interventions. Through moments of joy, adolescents are able to give new meaning to themselves and their experiences. They now see the world as a whole, trying to give it both a personal and wider meaning. The more they explore and comprehend their own experiences, the more existential meaning and personal motivation they will draw out of these positive moments. A father who suddenly trusts his teenage son or daughter, a new relationship with peers, or a successful accomplishment—any of these can clarify aspects of one's self- identity, individuality, connection with humanity, and one's future.

Examining positive experiences (in the classroom, in therapy, or at home) can thus encourage more self-awareness of values, role models, and life goals. Interventions can be constructed to tap into ways adolescents may contribute their talents to enrich the quality of life for themselves and others. Instead of just learning to cope with harsh realities, they can be helped to recapture and re-create instances of joy and fulfillment. Educators and certainly parents, who interact with adolescents for the majority of their teenage years over long daily spans of time, may learn how to expand their own awareness, sensitivity, and compassion in order to help revivify the memory and meaning of past moments of fulfillment.

The positive experiences of adolescents provide a crucial insight into various aspects of their personalities. A focus on satisfying, enjoyable, or inspiring experiences and inner musings may work as a therapeutic tool with at-risk youngsters such as suicidal adolescents. For counseling, the integration of positive experiences may be a valuable device to buttress the hopeful aspects of the adolescent's inner world and to facilitate self-awareness and growth toward personal potential. Moreover, perhaps, adolescent happiness can be viewed as the developmental predecessor of adult happiness. Elucidation of the former can serve as the avenue to help us better understand happiness in adult life and even across the entire lifespan.

2

Measuring Happiness

We should consider every day lost on which we have not danced at least once. And we should call every truth false which was not accompanied by at least one laugh.

—Nietzsche, "On Old and New Tablets,"
Thus Spoke Zarathustra (1883)

In the concept of happiness that we embrace in our series of research studies, we do not speak of the "happy person" who is content or satisfied with the overall quality of his or her life, or of a generally "happy life" that such a person may live. Rather, we identify happiness as a distinct feeling or feelings, different from the run of mundane positive emotions, and inherent in particular moments in which the individual is elevated above the usual needs and interests that maintain his or her equilibrium. This refers to moments of joy, revelation, and the capacity to deeply realize the feeling that one lives and experiences life to its fullest. We mean a powerful emotional arousal that projects the individual onto another, higher plane. We mean the ability to experience in a way that makes one feel that life is wonderful, that the world is beautiful, and that one feels good about oneself and others.

This special experience, what Maslow calls the peak experience and I prefer to call the *highly intense* experience, is marked by this quality of transcendence or elevation. People who have it are caught up in extraordinary feelings, transported above the mundane, and elevated onto a higher existential plane where they feel the spirit breathing life through the earth of the body. These intensely positive life experiences have been viewed in the literature as heralding significant, happy moments and meaningful occasions of intense satisfaction and fulfillment (e.g., Jourard & Landsman, 1980; Maslow, 1971; Mathes & Jerom, 1982; Wuthnow, 1978). As distinct from a state of simple hedonistic pleasure, characteristics of deep or intense experience include unusually intense involvement, a unique sense of special fit, a feeling of completeness, a sense of destiny, and the ultimate fulfillment in living of which each person is capable. Young people subjectively report the "happiest moments" in their lives as times of bliss, greatest joy, and illumination.

This chapter will elaborate our methodology for tapping and measuring this experience.

THE POSITIVE EXPERIENCE QUESTIONNAIRE _____

The foundation for my research is an empirical measure of adolescents' best moments: the open-ended Positive Experience Questionnaire (PEQ) developed by Landsman (1969). This questionnaire poses a single open-ended question to elicit adolescents' most joyful remembered experiences:

> Most people have in their lives experiences that cause them good feelings toward themselves and toward life in general.
>
> In this research, we are interested in learning about experiences and special events in which human beings have the feeling that "the world is good" (that "life is good"). Please tell us about an experience that caused you to have a very, very good feeling, an experience where as a consequence you felt that life is wonderful. Please try to give us as full and detailed a description as you can. That would be a great help to this research.

This is an evocative question which the respondents can answer in their own words from their own perspective, relating any experience they choose. At the same time, the short preamble is meant to give enough direction to help the respondents better relate precisely what it is that makes them feel that life is wonderful. The assumption is that the global and somewhat abstract sense that life is wonderful begins with feeling good about oneself and/or the world.

It is also assumed that the description should reflect an inner reality, the person's experience of the experience rather than simply what happened. If the PEQ is taken as a measure of happiness, the implication is that the happiness described will thus be an inward capacity rather than something induced from the outside. This conceptualization of happiness is consistent with, but more complex than, Csikszentmihalyi's (1990) later declaration that happiness "does not depend on outside events but, rather, on how we interpret them" (p. 2).

Also packed into this formulation is the assumption of humanist psychologists, that openness to experience is a defining characteristic of the high-functioning person (Allport, 1961; Bugental, 1967; Combs, 1969; Mahrer, 1978; Moustakas, 1972, 1977; Rogers, 1961). As Jourard and Landsman (1980) defined it, the concept has both passive and active components. A person who is open to experience readily accepts those experiences that "present themselves as opportunities" and "takes them, uses them, experiences them—with no denial, blocking, or suspicion" (p. 235). Passively, such people are thus able to notice and appreciate the beauty in their environment, to accept new ideas and new people. Actively, they seek out new experiences and are ready to invest the energy that is required. This notion thus assumes that people who are open to experience have richer fields of experience than others, that their experiencing is more intense, and that they find life more enriching, exciting, challenging, and meaningful (Combs, 1969; Jourard, 1971a, 1971b; Moustakas, 1972, 1977; Rogers, 1961).

Another assumption in our using this measure is that a single remembered experience can yield knowledge about a person's overall experience of happiness. A number of studies have confirmed that happy people recall more positive than negative life events, compared to unhappy people (e.g., Diener, Sandvik, Pavot, & Gallagher, 1991) and that the sense of both past and present well-being depends on an encoding of important emotional experiences in conscious memory.

Sandvik, Diener, and Seidlitz (1993) argued that the recall of remembered material must be a primary source of self-reports of well-being. As its name indicates, the PEQ was designed to gain insight into the special moments when individuals experience an unusual sense of good feeling. Yet, as I read the respondents' descriptions and calculated the results, I became increasingly convinced that it did in fact succeed as an index of overall happiness beyond its original intent. Although some research has indicated that recollections are naturally influenced by mood (for a review, see Blaney, 1986) both at the time of encoding (Bower, Gilligan, & Montiero, 1981) and retrieval (Clark & Teasdale, 1985; Forgas, Bower, & Krantz, 1984), these remembered moments, as will be shown in Part 2 of this book, also turned out to be related both to stable features of personality and to the nature and degree of commitment that the respondents evidenced. As such, the happiness that was described could represent not merely an isolated, transient event but rather a durable state indicative of the person's overall being.

THE POSITIVE EXPERIENCE QUESTIONNAIRE AND OTHER MEASURES

The PEQ differs from most other measures of happiness both in form and content: in how the measure is taken and in the conceptualization of happiness that is inherent in it. Most measures of happiness consist of some form of direct self-report questionnaire consisting of either a single item (e.g., Andrews & Withey, 1976; Kammann & Flett, 1983a; Michalos, 1985) or multiple items (e.g., Bradburn, 1969; Campbell et al., 1976; Diener, Emmons, Larsen, & Griffin, 1985; Kammann & Flett, 1983b; Seidlitz & Diener, 1993). For more thorough discussion, see Fordyce (1988) and Sandvik et al. (1993). In these, respondents are asked to respond according to some sort of scale that can be used alone or combined with other indices to yield one happiness measure. These assorted scales use a variety of dependent variables, from happiness itself (i.e., Bradburn & Caplowitz, 1965; Campbell, 1981) through such alternative concepts as life satisfaction (e.g., Diener et al., 1985), subjective well-being (Diener, 1994), and mood (Stones & Kozma, 1991, 1994).

In addition to such self-report measures, happiness, in its various conceptualizations, has also been assessed by means of written interviews, measures of daily moods over extended periods, reports of knowledgeable informants, memory measures, and forced-choice questionnaires (Sandvik et al., 1993). These purportedly objective measures were meant to solve problems inherent in self-reporting. Although the various aforementioned measures have yielded consistent and stable findings over a variety of cultures and ages (Fordyce, 1988), and the standard self-report measures have shown high convergent validity by their agreement with alternative measures and their relations with theoretically related constructs (Sandvik et al., 1993), no measure of happiness has emerged over the years as a standard reference point for ongoing study (Fordyce, 1988). Although the PEQ does not pretend to serve as such a standard, it does add uniquely to the other tools at our disposal.

The PEQ differs from the scales and other fixed-answer questionnaires because it does not require respondents to rate their emotions or attitudes and permits them to relay their experiences in their own words and as they see fit. Its results do not reflect differences in rating styles or rely on arbitrary definitions of the measures at hand. Its aim is instead to trigger respondents' memories of their most positive experiences and encourage them to render them in detail. In this, it permits systematic research into experience without losing too much of the human quality (Landsman & Landsman, 1991). In its open approach, it is similar to Csikszentmihalyi's extensive and in-depth studies on happiness, in which participants were asked what they liked doing best and how they felt when they were doing it.

Moreover, the nature of the happiness embodied in the positive experience here differs fundamentally from that defined in most of the measures. The vast majority of measures inquire about subjective well-being or life satisfaction, sometimes globally, sometimes with reference to specific aspects, and tend to take happiness to be some kind of aggregate of feelings over time. By contrast, the happiness that the PEQ probes is the happiness that is felt at special moments. It is a state characterized by strong emotions. It is not some kind of average over time and not necessarily a steady state. Nor is it unpunctuated by or exclusive of sorrow or grief (Jourard & Landsman, 1980).

The definition implicit in the PEQ also differs from that inherent in Csikszentmihalyi's measures. Those all focus on what people like doing. Their unstated assumption is that happiness derives from and inheres in activity. Such an assumption is limiting. The experience queried by the PEQ, on the other hand, can be either active or passive. There is no prior assumption about the source of happiness or the type of experience in which it is felt.

POSITIVE EXPERIENCE VERSUS PEAK EXPERIENCE

Our own measures of happiness differ significantly from Maslow's, even though, in both instances, the emphasis is on specific experiences. Maslow and his followers defined "peak" experiences as moments of rapture, ecstasy, or bliss and conceived them as illuminating and life-changing events that the person who undergoes them permanently distinguishes from every other kind of experience (Maslow, 1971). These experiences were studied by asking people such questions as "What was the most ecstatic moment of your life?" and "Have you experienced transcendent ecstasy?" (p. 168). These questions, and the descriptive questions that accompanied them, were aimed at learning about both the nature of the experience itself and the personalities of the people who had such experiences. The rationale for the approach was based on two related convictions: that peak experiences are the identifying marks of the self-actualizing person and that to understand human beings, one must try to understand them at their best.

The problem with this premise is that it tends to be highly exclusive. The questions that stem from it are formidable. Maslow maintained that most people have peak experiences and that one can have such experiences even while engaged in the most mundane activities. But most participants could not find the moments of nonpareil ecstasy that were expected of them. Peakers and self-actualizers were found to make up an extremely small proportion of any tested population. Moreover, as Maslow (1972) himself acknowledged, there are apparently self-actualizing individuals (he named Eleanor Roosevelt) who were not classified as peakers. The findings about the peak experiences of the few people who identified them thus yielded little if any information on the much larger "nonpeak" population, whether high-functioning individuals or not.

The PEQ tones down its demands. It shifts the focus from well-nigh mystical exaltations to merely positive experiences, and in place of the awesome language of transcendental ecstasy, the PEQ frames its question in down-to-earth terms of experiences that make people feel "good" about themselves and the world, and that make them feel that life is wonderful. The exuberance of *wonderful* is even tempered by the more moderate tone of *good*. The premise is that such experiences are both more common and easier to retrieve than flights of rapture and that asking about them makes the questionnaire applicable to a larger population.

The reported positive experiences were evaluated on two dimensions: the depth or intensity at which these life events were experienced, and the content area of the experience.

Intensity

The assessment of the intensity of the respondents' experiences is anchored in the view that high-functioning individuals allow themselves to experience events and feelings intensely, fully, and completely and that they respond to those events with greater arousal and strength (e.g., Jourard, 1971a, 1971b; Mahrer, 1978; Waterman, 1993). Both peak experiences and intense positive experiences occur without block or repression; the openness to experience allows a whole range of perceptions, memories, and imaginative productions and an enlarged experience of one's own possibilities and the possibilities of the world. Maslow's peak experiences are by definition intensely felt, and the people who acknowledge them must be capable of feeling intense joy. Maslow (1965) defined peak experiences as "an episode or a spurt in which the powers of the person come together in a particularly efficient and intensely enjoyable way" (p. 91). Landsman's (1969) approach goes further than Maslow's by encompassing less intense, less definitive moments of transcendental happiness. Yet, he also defined the "beautiful and noble person" by his or her passionate feelings and by the ability to welcome experiences with strong feeling and enthusiasm.

The relationship between intensity of emotion and happiness has been the subject of some debate in the literature. Diener and his colleagues (Diener, 1984; Diener et al., 1985; Larsen & Diener, 1987) reported that although affect intensity (as measured by the Affect Intensity Measure) was found to be related to both positive and negative predictors of happiness (e.g., extroversion, activity, psychological distress indicators), it nonetheless failed to exhibit a significant relationship to any of several measures of psychological well-being itself. As Diener himself explained throughout his body of work, the ability to feel strongly can be taken as a quality of temperament encompassing all types of emotions, positive as well as negative, so that the two apparently cancel one another out on the standard measures of happiness. Stones and Kozma (1991) developed this idea and suggested that more emotional people would be located nearer the extremes of a happiness continuum than calmer people and would experience both pleasurable and aversive events more acutely.

Diener (Diener, Sandvik, & Pavot, 1990) also argued that happiness is related to the frequency and duration of positive emotions, not their intensity, and that peak intensity contributes little to global subjective well-being as currently measured (Larsen & Diener, 1985). Both his findings and explanations rest on a conceptualization of happiness as the ratio of positive over negative feelings over time. Intense positive experiences, he suggested, can contribute little to overall happiness because they are very rare, whereas moderately pleasant experiences are more common. Moreover, he contended, intense positive emotions have countervailing effects that mitigate their long-term impact. Apparently, there is little sense in the work of Diener and his colleagues that intense experiences have a residual effect on future perception or that the content of those experiences serves as a lasting reference point simply by virtue of their power in one's memory. Diener (1994) did admit, however, that the evidence that subjective well-being depends more directly on time/duration of pleasant experiences than on their intensity is tentative and that further study is still required. Stones and Kozma (1994), in fact, showed that people who are inclined to experience intense positive affect do score higher on happiness measures.

Neither Maslow nor Landsman actually measured the intensity of their respondents' experiences. Without a continuous measure, Maslow and his followers simply divided their participants into *peakers* and *nonpeakers*. This dichotomous approach to personality is not only artificial but, as noted above, excludes most of the population from fruitful study.

In place of Maslow's dichotomous approach, I developed a continuous measure, a 4-point scale ranging from shallow to peak, as follows:

Level 1:   *Barely positive experiences,* which contain little, if any, emotion, such as:

My experience is I like to look at television.

When I lived in _____ we lived in a very small town and there wasn't much to do. But a year ago, my dad got transferred to Tel Aviv. So now we live in the city and there's a lot more to do.

Level 2:   *Satisfying and pleasurable experiences,* but no more, such as:

The most wonderful thing that ever happened to me was when I went hunting in Montana. . . . . I saw hundreds of miles of land with no trees, just land. I also saw Mount Rushmore with Lincoln, Washington, Roosevelt, I think Edison. I traveled all over the U.S. in a car and saw many beautiful things, such as trees, mountains, different animals.

When my brother came back from the USA, I felt very happy. He returned after succeeding in his studies and came with his wife to stay with us and to live happily with his wife in our home. When he arrived, the whole family went to the sea and spent a very pleasant time there.

Level 3:   *Meaningful and joyful experiences,* which cause some change in the person but lack inspiration or feelings of transcendence, such as:

Last summer I visited my relatives in the country and stayed there for two weeks. . . . I had a wonderful time, it was so nice and I enjoyed it. This visit left a very strong impression on me and taught me that life is beautiful. I hope for these days to return. I intend to go back and visit my family and hope to enjoy it as much as I did.

One day we went on a trip with the scouts to the city of Ashdod . . . we had a really pleasant time. On the sixth day, we went into town with the counselor to see a beautiful play. When the play was over, we returned. We passed a candy store, I stopped to buy something, and the other children kept going. They got really far away from me, and I couldn't see them. I was really scared because I didn't know how to get back to the camp. I asked a few girls about the way to the camp, and they guided me and I thanked them. When I got to the camp, I was really happy. On the next day when we went home, I told my family all that had happened to me, and they were really happy.

Level 4:   *Inspiring, exciting, and joyful experiences,* which change the individual's perception of the self, others, and/or the world, such as:

I think that the best thing that ever happened to me and changed the whole way I look at the world was when I kissed my girlfriend, who I love very much. It was a tremendous experience. You don't have to pretend. There are no masks. Everything is calm and quiet. When you love, you don't have to worry about what will be. There are no rules. Everyone wants to do the best he can for the other person. And that's the point of the entire matter. To give a lot and to get a lot. It made me feel I was in paradise. My worries were suddenly unimportant, and everything took on different proportions. The world is happy.

One of the most wonderful experiences I had happened a while back. I was playing the piano for a group of people. When I started playing, I was conscious of the people around me. But then as I proceeded to play, I just got lost in the music. Playing the piano makes me feel like nothing can go wrong. It can make you forget all your problems. It is one of the most wonderful things a person can experience.

. . . He held my hands and said he loved me. Only then did I know that he really loved me. I had chills throughout my body and felt myself blush, and I could hardly speak. I felt that life is wonderful despite its difficulties. . . . I felt that, all in all, life has great significance, and things should be viewed from their brighter side instead of getting annoyed at every little thing.

Assessing the intensity of feeling on the basis of written accounts raises the possibility that the intensity perceived by the raters stemmed from the teenagers' descriptive powers rather than from the remembered experience itself. This concern was addressed in the part of our research that examined the personality traits associated with the intensity of the positive experience. There, verbal intelligence was controlled for in the multiple regression analysis that measured the association, and the findings revealed that the other traits that were entered into the equation still remained operative. Another indication that the judges could validly discern intensity beyond the writer's expressiveness and verbal skill was obtained in studies of hearing-impaired adolescents, whose verbal resources are often limited. They were nonetheless able to express the whole range of emotional intensity, and their intensity scores did not differ from those of hearing participants.

Content

The contents of the respondents' positive experiences were analyzed to get a better idea what these experiences consisted of. In other words, what was it that made our adolescents happy? Although Maslow frequently conjectured about the types of experiences that brought people to the heights of rapture (he variously suggested listening to music, dancing, accomplishing something, etc.), he never analyzed them methodically. His exclusive focus on intensity gave fuel to Frankl's (1966) charge that his theory of self-actualization is deeply flawed because it does not encompass the reasons that people have for being happy.

Our analysis was made along three major content categories delineated by Landsman: with self, with external world, and interpersonal. These categories had been used in a large-scale study conducted by Landsman's research group on a large random population in the United States, in which about 3,000 positive experiences elicited by the PEQ from participants ranging from preschool children to octogenarians were submitted to factor analysis (Landsman, 1967). The classification was determined to have a reliability of .78 to .98 by independent judges. Subsequent researchers explored distributions of these categories in specific populations, such as prisoners, "high-functioning" women, and college students, and analyzed their content components (e.g., Fuerst, 1967; Lynch, 1969; McKenzie, 1967; Puttick, 1964; D. Smith, 1973). The categories were assessed in people of all ages; adolescents were never referred to as a distinct group in these assessments.

Landsman conceived of the three categories as stages in the growth of the "noble and beautiful person." As explained by Landsman and Landsman (1991), the criteria for the beautiful and noble person derived from the existential concept of *being-in-the-world,* which filtered down from the philosophy of Heidegger to psychology by way of the existential analysts, Boss (1963) and Binswanger (1963). Heidegger (1927/1962) distinguished three simultaneous modes of what he called *world* but which, for our purposes, can extend to define modes of *being-in-the-world.* These are: *Eigenwelt* or *own-world,* which refers to self-relatedness and self-awareness; *Umwelt,* or *world-around,* which refers to the relationship with the biological and physical world; and *Mitwelt,* or *with-world,* which refers to relationships with other people (May, 1958).

These three modes are the bases of Landsman's conceptualization of the beautiful and noble person (Jourard & Landsman, 1980; Landsman & Landsman, 1991). The first stage—or level—involves the person's relationship with the self and is described as the *passionate self.* This level is characterized by intense love of one's self, self-confidence, and self-knowledge, which, at the same time, excludes selfishness, bragging, and possessiveness. The second level, called the *environment-loving self,* is marked by a passionate love of and delight in the entire physical world, from nature and the urban landscape through music, art, and other connections with objects and belongings. The third and final stage in the evolution of Landsman's ideal is called the *compassionate self* and is characterized by deep love and caring for others, as exemplified by sharing relationships with friends, spouses, and children, by care for people who are hurt or in need, and by the readiness to take action on their behalf.

In the present studies, Landsman's classification was applied to the PEQ responses, which were evaluated by trained judges. Experiences with the self consist of *moments of intensified self-awareness,* as exemplified in the following two quotations from PEQ respondents:

> The things that give me a feeling that the world is really good are small things. When I do things that I want to do and succeed in them, I feel great—like writing poems or walking in nature. Then I see that the world is truly beautiful. When I succeed in doing something good and important, I love the world.

> The first time I got a 100 in math I was bowled over with joy. I did it! And I've been overjoyed ever since.

Experiences with the external world entail an essentially *sensuous response to nature or objects,* exemplified in the following:

> The best thing is the sight of the sea and the waves. I've seen this landscape and have enjoyed this landscape. The teacher asked us to leave the place, and we went to someplace even more beautiful, among trees and very beautiful flowers, and the air was fine and beautiful. I won't forget this all my life.

My best experience was a week ago. I have a black cat at home that my mother also wants. I got two female dogs, both my own, both at home, and their names are secret. I can't tell you them for reasons of security. But this really made me happy.

Interpersonal experiences are marked by a *dialogical connection between the self and others* (Buber, 1961). Essential to it is a heightened sensitivity to the feelings of others—an imaginative leap, as it were, into someone else's shoes. Romantic love is classified into this category, but so are other, more distanced types of relationships.

The experience that made me feel very good was when I went on our annual school trip. It was great fun and everyone enjoyed each other. But what really made me feel that the world is beautiful was when the boy I wanted to have something going with came over and talked with me. We talked a lot, and it was great. I returned home feeling wonderful.

Two or three years ago, my family and I went to visit relatives in New York in the winter. We went into my grandmother's house, and one could smell the pleasant aromas wafting from the kitchen. It was just like Thanksgiving. The whole family was there. During our days there we went sledding across the street on a steep hill near the pasture. It was very cold, but being in such company, with everyone around, and having so much fun, made it all wonderful.

In most of the adolescents' descriptions, as in life, more than one content area is naturally involved. Experiences with the self often enough involve other people, experiences with the world may trigger encounters with the self and others, whereas experiences with others may bring those who have them into closer touch with the world and themselves. The judges were instructed to categorize the experiences according to what they considered the main source of happiness in each. The category of the experience was thus determined by the content area, the way of being in the world, that did most to produce the happy emotions that were described.

3

Commitment Beyond Self

Only to the extent to which man fulfills a meaning out there in the world, does he fulfill himself.

Victor Frankl, *The Will to Meaning* (1988)

The debate about happiness—whether it is necessarily an entirely egotistical and egocentric entity or entails elements that take the individual beyond his or her hedonistic pleasure—presupposes a more underlying question: Are there any actions that are actually motivated by care or concern for others rather than by self-interest or some passion?

It's a debate that precedes the development of the social sciences in the twentieth century. Its polarities hark back to Hobbes (1651/1947) and, about a century later, Hume (1740/1896), among others. As Hobbes saw it, all people are motivated by self-interest, manifested in a perpetual striving to maximize their power in relation to others. However, because a war of all is in no one's ultimate interest, people agree to submit to the dictates of an absolute ruler who can impose law and order and protect them from one another. Individual selfishness is restrained by the threat of detection and punishment. Hume, adopting a more discriminating view, regarded self-interest as only one of many human motives. At worst, it would lead to the conflict envisaged by Hobbes. But at best it could serve as a rational force to counter the tumult of emotions such as anger, hatred, and revenge, as well as the malevolent impulses that impel people to unthinking acts and are destructive to both the community and, often enough, themselves.

Notably, neither Hobbes nor Hume spoke of benevolence or altruism as such. At best, Hobbes reduced apparent generosity to a self-interested act of distress release, as when he explained why he gave a sixpence to a beggar, "I was in pain to consider the miserable condition of the old man; and now my alms, giving him some relief, doth also ease me" (Aubrey, 1697/1982, p. 159). The concern of these philosophers was more with the minimum level of behavior that would enable people to live together in societies. Feeling the need to explain why and how inherently self-seeking individuals curb their personal ambitions, both Hobbes and Hume posited a more enlightened self-interest that took more into account than immediate gratification.

These ideas were not universally accepted either in their day or subsequently. The very term *altruism,* which the positivist philosopher Albert Comte (1851/1875) used to refer to the unselfish desire to "live for others," implies another more positive view of human nature. Nonetheless, it was the pessimistic view that eventually became the background of modern psychology.

Freud (1920, 1930/1982) viewed human beings as driven by the dual urges for pleasure and for aggression and saw the civilization imposed on the individual by family and society in childhood to curb these drives as an unnatural, antithetical, oppressive, and precarious overlay. Nothing runs so counter to the basic nature of people, Freud maintained, as the commandment to love one's aggressive, exploitative, selfish, and uncaring neighbor as oneself. Civilization exists to protect people from each other; yet, based as it is on a renunciation or sublimation of people's sexual and aggressive instincts, it is also the source of much misery and neurosis (Freud, 1930/1982). Freud substituted the concept of drives for the older concept of passions, moving the policeman from the outer society to the individual's psyche, in the form of the superego. He was clearly ambivalent about the merits of culture and civilization, but there was much of Hobbes and Hume in his thinking.

The convictions of Freud and his philosopher predecessors have permeated Western thought for the better part of the twentieth century, running through everything from economic theory to biology, sociology, and psychology. At the same time, the evidence, although undeniably strong, is not unequivocal. Every day, people do countless things that do not serve any obvious self-interest or destructive passion or drive, and often at some cost to themselves. They give up leisure or sleep to comfort their friends and listen to their problems, stop on rainy nights to help motorists whose cars have stalled, and give directions to tourists, sometimes even leading them to their destinations. Passers-by will stop when they see a crying child and take the time to offer comfort or help in finding the missing parents. People take the trouble to vote when their voice will have only a minuscule impact on the outcome of an election. There are many people who donate blood, bone marrow, or organs to utter strangers. After natural disasters and terrorist bombings, there is usually little looting and theft, and people pour out to help. There are always volunteers to comfort the bereaved, bring coffee to the rescue teams, or join them in the search through the wreckage for survivors. Rarer are the acts of running into fire or jumping into icy water to save some unfortunate, but these things too are part of the human repertoire. Then, too, there are always people who put great labor into social causes, whether conservation, social welfare, political freedom, or some other ideal. Some spend many years struggling, and some even sacrifice their lives to try to make the world a better place.

Similar acts of giving are found too among adolescents, selfish and self-absorbed as they are thought to be. Walk down the high school corridor—a place where insults are exchanged and anxious youngsters may get abused or humiliated. Yet, one youngster is also helping a classmate with math, another volunteers at the local hospital's pediatric unit, and a third plays music every Saturday at a home for the aged. You strike up a conversation with two other students, only to find that for the past several weeks, they have been paying weekly visits to a hospice, trying to cheer up AIDS patients.

These acts are of different orders in the amount of time, energy, dedication, or sacrifice they require, and they stand out against the cruelties, indifference, small-mindedness, and selfishness that are also part of our lives as human beings. But they do exist. As far as we know, they may be no less common, and perhaps even more so, than our more egotistic behaviors and certainly than the barbarities that reach our news broadcasts. Yet, for the skeptics, such acts are not counterevidence to their sweeping condemnation of humanity but require an explanation (Wright, 1994). Wright, in his book *The Moral Animal*, asserted that our intuitive moral principles have no claim to inherent truth and should be distrusted. He further claimed that helping behaviors are rooted in reciprocity, where people extend help in the expectation of help for themselves in the future.

Not surprisingly, given the diversity of human motives, such explanations abound. The crudest are the external explanations: fear of punishment or social censure, expectations of reciprocity or some other material gain. But where external motives are not to be found, internal ones can always be ferreted out. These run the gamut from avoidance of the distress one may feel in the presence of another's suffering through intangible rewards and punishments both by society (admiration, respect, approval; rejection, censure, disapproval) and by the self (pride, confidence, positive self-image as a good, kind, or moral person; guilt, shame, and anxiety). In this welter of possible egocentric motives, it is not difficult to reduce all acts on behalf of others, even ones that involve a great risk to life, to self-seeking. The prevalent assumption among personality and social psychologists is that social encounters are instrumental to self-serving ends and that people who work in *any* capacity for another's benefit are simultaneously seeking a subtle but powerful form of self-benefit and self-gratification (Aron & Aron, 1986; Cialdini, Baumann, & Kenrick, 1981; Jones & Pittman, 1982; Kenrick, 1991; Schroeder, Dovidio, Sibicky, Matthew, & Allen, 1988).

Subtly related to this pessimistic view is the very high ideal of altruism, virtually restricted to martyrs and saints, that is articulated in religious and moral texts. A particularly vivid rendition appears in the following passage by a sixteenth-century French moralist:

> The man is good who does good to others; if he suffers on account of the good he does, he is very good; if he suffers at the hands of those to whom he has done good, then his goodness is so great that it could be enhanced only by greater sufferings; and if he should die at their hands, his virtue can

go no further: it is heroic, it is perfect. (Jean De La Bru, *Characters of Personal Merit,* 1688)

As is the way of things, such an extreme sensibility generated a reaction. The reaction took the form of two related avenues of inquiry, one into what is termed altruism, the other into what is termed prosocial behavior.

PURE ALTRUISM

The altruism literature attempts to isolate "pure" altruism from acts of helping, donating, and so forth, that are rooted in selfish motives. Its basic contention is that, even if much of what goes by the name of altruistic behavior is egotistically motivated, at least some of it is not.

A leading researcher in this field is C. Daniel Batson, who in the early 1980s undertook to explore with his colleagues

> whether our helping is always and exclusively motivated by the prospect of some benefit to ourselves, however subtle. We want to know if anyone ever, in any degree, transcends the bonds of self-benefit and helps out of genuine concern for the welfare of another. We want to know whether altruism is part of human nature. (Batson & Shaw, 1991b, p. 107)

The central issue for Batson, as for those he set out to refute, was motivation. Batson rejected the view held by some psychologists that altruism requires sacrifice (e.g., Krebs, 1991), on the grounds that this requirement moves the emphasis from the intrinsic meaning of the act to its outcome, and also because Batson's interest focused on normal people, not saints.

Opting for a more modest conceptualization, he defined altruism as "a motivational state with the ultimate goal of increasing another's welfare," as contrasted with egoism, which is "a motivational state with the ultimate goal of increasing one's own welfare" (Batson & Shaw, 1991b, p. 108). In Batson's view, although a single behavior may have multiple motives, a single motive cannot be both altruistic and egotistic. Thus, he trained his searchlight on the "ultimate goal" of an action, as distinct from instrumental ones. Put simply, Batson's position is that if you donate blood so as to make others or yourself think well of you, it is an egotistical act, but if you do it *because* others will benefit and *then* you receive praise or feel good about yourself as an ancillary outcome, then it is an altruistic act. Showing that some people, under some conditions, are altruistic thus required him to dig out the ultimate goal of any given helping act.

To this end, he and his colleagues (e.g., Batson, 1990; Batson et al., 1988; Batson & Shaw, 1991a, 1991b) devised a creative array of experiments with specific, systematically varied conditions to differentiate three sets of motives: (a) the avoidance of aversive arousal (i.e., distress, worry), (b) the avoidance of material, social, or self-punishment or the obtaining of material, social, or self-reward, and (c) empathetically evoked altruistic motives, whose ultimate goal is to reduce the other person's distress.

The researchers interpreted their results as consistently confirming their empathy-altruistic hypothesis, which is that under certain circumstances, empathy evokes altruistic motivation directed toward the ultimate goal of reducing the needy person's suffering. This hypothesis is as modest and circumscribed as the research question. And the researchers' conclusions are equally so:

> If under certain specifiable circumstances individuals act, at least in part, with an ultimate goal of increasing the welfare of another, then the assumption of universal egoism must be replaced by a more complex view of prosocial motivation that allows for altruism as well as egoism. (Batson & Shaw, 1991b, p. 119)

The circumstances include the feeling of empathy and the relative absence of competing claims, such as concern for oneself. Altruism is restricted to those for whom we feel empathy, and self-concern can readily come between the altruistic motive and the altruistic act if its cost to the self is too high.

The ingenuity and step-by-step thoroughness of Batson's work has evoked a great deal of respect in the profession and made his findings impossible to ignore. But for all the minimalism of its conclusions, and despite their support by other scholars who similarly found that individuals are capable of caring about others without regard to their own well-being (e.g., Staub, 1991; Wallach & Wallach, 1990, 1991), his studies have not put an end to the counterview that we are egotistical creatures at heart.

One of the major criticisms has to do with the distinction Batson and his team drew between empathy motivation and the motive to avoid aversive arousal. The distinction is important to them, not only theoretically but also practically. If our ultimate aim is to reduce our own discomfort in the face of another's plight, then we will just as soon cross the street when we see a beggar as give him money, they would argue. There are also many questions about whether the laboratory conditions Batson set up to distinguish between the motives actually did so; the concept of empathy itself creates confusion. If empathy is defined as feeling sad when someone else suffers and happy when they are happy, then where is the line between self-oriented and other-oriented motives?

This inherent confounding of motives has led to two different sets of conclusions. One is that all human actions are, once again, egotistically motivated. Thus, Cialdini et al. (1987) contended, based on their own experiments, that the real motive for the helping behavior that Batson claimed issues from empathy was to reduce the empathic individual's sadness in the face of another's distress. Where that sadness is reduced by other means, such as drugs, they claimed, helping behavior also declines. Their view is supported by a study conducted on children by Perry, Perry, and Weiss (1986) and is consistent with that of experimental social psychologists, who continue to view self-interest, self-benefit, and reward and punishment contingencies as the chief motives for human behavior (Zahn-Waxler, 1991).

The other conclusion, diametrically opposed, is that, because the motives so commingle, helping behavior is no less altruistic because it is undertaken to reduce the helper's distress. Thus, Hoffman (1991) argued that alleviating the "empathic distress" caused by another person's suffering by helping that person cannot be considered egotistical, and Hornstein (1991) claimed that when high empathy links one person's distress to another's plight, it is irrelevant whose distress is meant to be reduced. The distinction between additional self-oriented motives and motives located in the needs of the other person also collapses. Thus, Krebs (1991) asserted that the motive to benefit oneself and the motive to benefit another are not mutually exclusive, and virtually all helping behaviors are aimed at enhancing the welfare of both self and other. And Mook (1991) stated that if we help someone because it makes us feel good, then we are still entitled to call it altruism.

The argument thus boils down to the legitimacy of internal reward for doing good. Those who see such rewards as tainting the purity of the giving see all giving behavior as egotistically motivated; those who regard them as legitimate see the same behaviors as altruistic.

PROSOCIAL BEHAVIOR

The other area of inquiry stimulated by the view of human motives as unadulteratedly egotistical was into what is termed *prosocial* behavior. Such behavior includes the helping behaviors generally classified under altruism, but it is broader in scope and extends to all the conduct (i.e., voting, telling the truth, paying taxes when there is little risk of getting caught) that enables people to live and work with one another in a community or society. The underlying question of this body of research is how the egotistical, self-interested creatures that we are presumed to be can continue to cooperate and act for either the common good or the good of specific others. As Jencks (1990) put it, "One of the classic puzzles—perhaps *the* classic puzzle—of social theory is how society induces us to behave in ways that serve not our own private interest, but the common interest of society as a whole" (p. 53).

Some of the thinking in this area is much like that to which Batson responded: that prosocial behavior is ultimately egocentrically motivated (Zajonc, 1982), that its objective is always to maximize gains and minimize costs to the self (Clary, 1994), and that sharing and caring behavior may be ultimately more beneficial to the individual than calculations of immediate self-interest (Frank, 1987).

Yet here, much of the thinking is more complex in that it rejects the notion of a single motive for multiple incentives. One line of thought, developed by Janet Mansbridge (1990) in her aptly titled book, *Beyond Self-Interest,* is that human behavior as based on narrowly conceived self-interest is too restrictive to conceptualize and that prosocial motivation also includes "commitment to moral principles, concern for others, 'we-feeling,' and readiness to cooperate when cooperation does not serve self-interests narrowly conceived" (p. ix). She contended that when people define and pursue their interests, they often give great weight both to their moral principles and to the interests of others. Like many of Batson's critics, Mansbridge rejected the polarization of altruism and self-interest. On the one hand, she pointed out that "emotions of duty, love, and self-interest are often intertwined in complex ways, and to say that an act serves someone's self-interest does not mean that it is bereft of those nonegotistical motives" (p. 137). On the other hand, as a sociologist, she argued that society must provide enough "self-interested return" for duty and love (which she called the two forms of altruism or unselfish motivation) so that they are not so costly as to discourage or extinguish the altruistic impulse. As Mansbridge put it, "If nice guys always finished last, the cost of niceness to the individual would be intolerable. Social learning would quickly extinguish the behavior" (p. 137). Meanwhile, social arrangements that make unselfishness less costly or actually make it pay in narrowly self-interested terms do not, she maintained, "negate the content of the empathic or moral impulses" (p. 137).

Jencks (1990) likewise suggested that people may be motivated by identification both with specific individuals and with a collectivity (communitarian unselfishness) to put the interests of others before their own. Elster (1990) argued that the opportunistic model fails to explain many social behaviors, including nonreciprocated anonymous giving, and that altruism, codes of honor, and long-term self-interest all enter into the equation. Separate studies found that familiarity, friendship, and genetic, racial, or national similarities were also related to a willingness to help another (Bell, Grekul, Lamba, Minas, & Harrell, 1995; Rushton, 1991).

Another line of thought focuses less on the interplay of social configurations and personal motives than on the variety of personal motives themselves. Staub (1978, 1991), for example, explored the personal goals that may contribute to the individual's desire to increase other people's welfare. Sen (1990) included the commitment to moral principles.

So did Nancy Eisenberg (1991), a social psychologist who argued that Batson's concept of altruism motivated solely by empathy is too narrow and that moral values such as justice, equality, and the greater good should also be considered altruistic. The bulk of Eisenberg's studies have related to the rich interplay between sympathy (her term for Batson's empathy), moral reasoning, and prosocial behavior. In general, her studies have provided support for the empathy-altruism hypothesis (as did an extensive review of the research that she published with Miller in 1987), while at the same time identifying many other motives that are associated both with sympathy itself and with prosocial behavior.

The picture of prosocial motives that emerges from Eisenberg's studies suggests that no single motive can be isolated in the way that either Batson or his adversaries tried to do and that, moreover, seemingly distinct impulses like guilt and sympathy tend to coexist in the same individual. Sympathy, the cognitive ability to take the perspective of others, and altruistic norms, such as taking responsibility for other people's well-being, were all found to be positively related to helping in adults (Eisenberg, Fabes, et al., 1989; Eisenberg, Miller, et al., 1989). Among adolescents, sympathy and prosocial behavior were found to be related to what she termed *high-level moral reasoning,* marked by a concern for values (Eisenberg, 1991; Eisenberg, Carlo, Murphy, & Van Court, 1995). A similar cocktail of motives was found in a study of volunteer activity described by Clary (1994). People who engage in volunteer work over a long period of time, he showed, combine their altruistic values with such motives as the wish for new learning opportunities and/or the desire to advance in their career or develop self-confidence. Along somewhat different lines, Isen (e.g., Isen, Daubman, & Nowicki, 1987) argued that the motive to help others is a motive in its own right, and she explored other motives that may support or undermine it.

COMMITMENT BEYOND SELF _____

The strong evidence for the inextricably mixed motives that go into prosocial conduct suggests that the distinction between altruism and egoism, between selfish impulses and unselfish ones, may not be an adequate framework or foundation for considering the human readiness to act for the benefit of others. Another way of looking at the matter that I would like to suggest is through a concept I term *commitment beyond self.* As I define it, commitment beyond self refers broadly to a readiness to act for the benefit of others, whether directly or through devotion to causes in society at large. It goes beyond distinct, and possibly isolated altruistic acts to the giving of oneself to a person, principle, or cause—to a giving that entails both affect and cognition, implies extension over time, and finds its ultimate expression in action. The words *beyond self* are included in the concept for two reasons. One is to distinguish what I am describing here from the many other senses in which the word commitment is used, including Parsons's (1960) normative attachment to religious, economic, or other social arrangements, and Becker's (1971) "consistent line of activity" (such as staying with a particular job), which is pursued over changing circumstances. The other reason for the usage is to indicate the relation between the self and the commitment that I have in mind. It is a commitment to something or someone outside the self, yet it does not entail the abnegation of the self or exclude benefit to the self. Among the reasons that I have chosen to look at commitment beyond self rather than altruism is to avoid the artificial either/or polarization of motives that has characterized so much of the literature. In fact, as I see it, commitment beyond self exists as a motive in its own right.

The concept as it formed in my mind was strongly influenced by the work of Victor Frankl. For Frankl, self-transcendence was the essence of existence and an inherent feature of being human. Human beings' true goal is the fulfillment of a meaning outside the self, and being human for Frankl (1988) "profoundly means being engaged and entangled in a situation" (p. 51).

Frankl has not discussed self-interest directly in his critiques of Freudian psychology. But he has argued with the Freudian view that the driving motive of all human action is to attain inner equilibrium by the reduction of somatic and psychological tension, and with the implication inherent in this postulation that the expectation of self-benefit is behind everything we do. The concept of tension reduction as a basic motive, Frankl (1967) maintained, is reductive: "There is no room left for anything such as commitment to a cause for its own sake or participation with a partner for the partner's sake" (pp. 38-39). Ideals, morality, and, with them, commitment, are essential features of what it means to be a full human being.

According to Frankl, it is a sense of meaning that keeps people alive in extreme adversity and keeps them physically and mentally healthy under normal circumstances. Without ideals and without commitments that transcend the self, the individual is psychologically sick. With them, our lives have meaning, and with meaning come self-actualization and happiness. Frankl disputed the Maslowian notion of self-actualization and happiness as proper goals in themselves but saw them rather as the natural outcome of self-transcendence, commitment, and living by ideals.

Two points in Frankl's thinking are incorporated into my concept of commitment beyond self. The first is that people have a need (which is not necessarily and perhaps not generally articulated) to go beyond themselves, to commit themselves to people and purposes for the latter's sake and not as mere means to personal benefit. The second is that this self-transcendence is a source of the meaning that gives life its worth and individuals the feeling that they are actualizing, or fulfilling, themselves.

These dual aspects of commitment beyond self may be illustrated in the following account by a colleague of mine, a professor of counseling psychology, of an incident in which she was called on to help some friends of a friend:

I volunteered to help a family in crisis introduced to me by a friend—two parents who were lawyers and their 16-year-old daughter, who finished junior high school with such poor grades that she wasn't accepted to any academic high school in her area. The family was in deep distress, and my friend thought I might be of help. I went to meet the father and daughter, despite being seriously ill at the time, because I felt they were in great need and didn't know where to turn.

From the girl's negativistic and theatrically evasive behavior toward her father and from his irate and exasperated demeanor, the intense tension in their relationship was obvious. She faced the wall, deliberately avoiding eye contact with us, and ignored my overtures. But finally, she reluctantly agreed to speak with me alone, without her father. In halting, intermittent conversation, I began the challenging work of breaking down the young woman's resistance. Our meeting warmed gradually and lasted for more than an hour. The father, peeking in and re-exiting, looked astonished at his daughter's mood and cooperative air. At this point, I felt a pleasing sense of satisfaction with myself and my ability to render a change in this disturbed girl's functioning. I said to myself, "What a good thing I made the effort to come today." When the father finally did join us, the extent to which his daughter had opened up and to which I had gained an understanding of the complex problems at hand became apparent. I felt a deep sense of achievement and inner strength. Then, after some further guided communication and clarification, the girl turned to look at her father and their eyes met for the first time. My heart beat faster as I realized that something wonderful was happening between them. I felt uplifted and excited to see the way they looked at one another and spoke together, intensely, tenderly. It was an extraordinary feeling to witness their encounter—one of true exaltation. I forgot all about myself, about my role as a catalyst, as I sat there watching the two of them reconnecting with one another.

My colleague's motives, as she tells them, were disinterested: to help a family in distress "because they were in great need and didn't know where to turn." She went, although she was ill, and with no expectation of reward, including self-reward. Her friendship with the person who introduced her to the family and asked her to help them played a role in her readiness to put herself out, but her focus was on the family's need and not any quid pro quo.

At the same time, she clearly enjoyed the "challenge" of trying to get through to the troubled girl, and even more her success in doing so. She was invigorated by the improvement in the girl's mood and rewarded for her investment of time and energy with an unashamedly augmented sense of satisfaction, self-worth, professional competence, and inner vitality. At the same time, as she watched the softening of the relationship between father and daughter and savored the healing process that had begun, she was suddenly lifted out of herself to become selflessly absorbed in their reconnection with one another.

This experience would probably qualify as a peak experience, in the humanists' sense of the term. It brings great joy, and it raises the individual to an elevated plane where she is so absorbed in the experience that she forgets about herself.

For all their differences from Frankl, the humanist psychologists who put forth self-actualization and peak experiences as features of the "optimal" or "healthy" personality were equally adamant that the ability to give to others is no less essential. Following Frankl's lead, Maslow

(1971) placed increasing emphasis on what he called the "B"—or "being"— values, which include the traditional moral values of truth and justice along with aesthetic values such as beauty and completeness. As Maslow presented them, the B-values were at the top of his hierarchy of needs, attended to only when our biological needs and our needs for love and security are met. Where Maslow differs from Frankl is that, whereas Frankl argued that ideals exist outside the self (i.e., in religion and traditional morality) and thus require one to transcend the self, Maslow emphasized the internalization of ideals, which also obliterates the traditional dichotomies between selfish and unselfish:

> The B-values transcend many of the dichotomies, such as selfishness and unselfishness, flesh and spirit, religious and secular. If you are doing the work that you love and are devoted to the value that you hold highest, you are being as selfish as possible, and yet are also unselfish and altruistic. If you have introjected truth as a value so that it is as much a part of you as your blood, then if a lie is told anywhere in the world it hurts you to find out about it. The boundaries of yourself in that sense now extend far beyond your personal sphere of interests to include the entire world. If an injustice is being committed against a person in Bulgaria or China, it is also being committed against you. Though you may never meet the person involved, you can feel his betrayal as your own. (p. 187)

Frankl preferred to maintain the dichotomies and criticized Maslow for obliterating them. But it seems to me that the difference between Frankl's point, that human beings must transcend themselves in order to live by ideals and to act and feel for others, and Maslow's point, that we must expand the boundaries of the self to include others, is philosophical (maybe even semantic) rather than practical. In both formulations, giving to others and benefiting the self are interrelated; neither sees self-benefit as a major motive in dedication to others, and both see self-benefit as an outcome of such dedication. Jourard and Landsman's (1980) assertions that self-actualization is "a by-product of active commitment . . . to causes outside the self" and that "without some such mission in life, a person is likely to experience boredom and a sense of stultification" (p. 5) sound like Frankl as much as Maslow.

The difficulty in motivational differentiation, as I see it, stems from the very fact that every act in which a person transcends the self gives meaning to that person's life and makes the world seem a better place. Except in the extreme and nonrepresentative case of profound self-sacrifice, I propose that dedicating oneself to another does not come at the expense of dedicating oneself to the self. To the contrary, the giving person becomes enriched, strengthened, and elevated from the experience. In contrast to the paradigm that polarizes prosocial behavior as motivated either by egoistic or altruistic motives, a more relevant perspective emphasizes the connectedness between commitment beyond self and the sense of meaning in human existence.

MEASURING COMMITMENT

As described above, commitment beyond self refers to the willingness to give of oneself to others, whether directly to friends, family, or other individuals or indirectly through causes that one considers important or worthy. As distinct from altruism, it extends beyond isolated acts of kindness or helpfulness, constituting a pledge, to be realized over time, to use one's resources to actualize an inner vision of a better world and to produce the future that one regards as most valuable and good (Jourard, 1972).

The Life Aspirations Questionnaire

Commitment beyond self was measured by what was termed the Life Aspirations Questionnaire (LAQ), which, like the Positive Experience Questionnaire, is an open-ended instrument that poses a single question: "What is the best thing you would like to do in your life or with your life?" This question sought to offer an unobstructed framework for adolescents' free, unguided, and sincere responses about their life goals and dreams. Unlike the many measures of altruism and helping behavior, this instrument examines intentions rather than behavior. It avoids the artificiality, hairsplitting, and problems of interpretation in laboratory studies of altruism and helping behavior, as well as their extrapolations from brief, one-time, and pre-specified behaviors, which may reflect a variety of motives and constraints (Eagly & Crowley, 1986).

The purpose of the measure was to examine young people's inwardly felt tendencies toward actual commitment and to determine whether adolescents in fact had the desire to give of themselves. Its underlying assumption was that the wish for commitment beyond self is inherent in human nature and would thus emerge even when not elicited specifically. The measure was thus intentionally indirect, vague, and nondirective, so as to encourage the respondents to look into themselves and to relate their fantasies, longings, and ambitions, however self-centered, hedonistic, or materialistic—from which one could then discern any commitment beyond self that they possessed.

The title, Life Aspirations Questionnaire, written large on the top of each form, was phrased to foster the respondents' tendency to relate important deeper yearnings rather than fleeting, short-term desires. Yet, the responses were not scored to assess life aspirations; responses to the LAQ were scored exclusively on the basis of the expression of commitment beyond self. The participants could express selfish, even hedonistic, desires such as, "I'd like to have an exciting, thrilling life always. A party every night. So I'll never be bored," or "To do whatever is in my head and whatever I want to at any given moment." Or conversely, they could reveal a partial or full desire to commit themselves to a specific purpose in society or to be of help to others, such as, "The best thing I would like to do in my life would be to use my music ability to its fullest. I would like to try and help people appreciate music and teach them music, since I feel this area is my best," or "To be in the army. To defend my country in its hour of need, to volunteer for different organizations that help others and people in need."

Because so much of the literature stereotypes teenagers as confused, conflicted, and selfish, it was important to avoid all suggestion or prompting, in order to establish that any expressed willingness to look beyond their own selves to the needs of others was uncoached and totally natural. It was hoped that anonymous self-appraisal without intervention of any kind—without pressure, guidance, or the need to please the researcher—would bring out the adolescents' unfeigned desires, authentic yearnings for the future, and sincere aspirations.

The term *life aspirations* as used in this work differs from the term *level of aspiration,* which is described throughout the psychological literature. The latter term was coined by Lewin (Lewin, Dembo, Festinger, & Sears, 1944) and referred to the experience of success and failure. He claimed that the experience of success and failure is not a consequence of real achievement but rather, a ratio between real achievement and the expectations of the individual. Aspirations have been widely studied as they relate to adolescents' educational, occupational, and social status goals associated with success (Barber & Eccles, 1992; Breen & Quaglia, 1991; Gibson & Lanz, 1991; Marjoribanks, 1991, 1994; Marsh, 1991; Overmier, 1990; Quaglia & Perry, 1995). These studies have indicated that individuals with varying levels of aspirations were differentiated by diverse personality characteristics (Hernandez, 1995; Teevan & Smith, 1975). Life aspirations in terms of education, vocation, and quality of life have also been a focus of interest for professionals investigating disadvantaged, disabled, and at-risk youth (e.g., Alvarez, 1991; Barber & Eccles, 1992; de Oliveira, Baizerman, & Pellet, 1992; Hernandez, 1995; Overmier, 1990; Szivos, 1990).

By contrast, our usage of the general terminology life aspirations was much narrower. It was specifically intended to unearth the desire for commitment beyond self. The participants' answers to our LAQ were expected to reveal how they anticipated the future and how they described those circumstances under which they saw themselves attaining personal wishes, aspirations, and desires.

Scoring

The LAQ responses were scored on a 4-point scale, ranging from no commitment to anyone or anything beyond the self, to evidence of a high degree of commitment to other human beings and society at large.

The classification based on the four levels of the LAQ scale is illustrated with a few examples that the adolescent participants offered:

Level 1:   Hedonistic or selfish:

To live well, with no commitments

To get me a job and a nice car and be wealthy, a party every night and keep cool.

To live in the jungle on my own without favors from anyone, not to be dependent on others except myself or things like nature and its law. I am not scared of death but I am scared of getting old and weak. In the jungle I'll die when I won't be able to take care of myself. This is the best way I want to live my life.

The above examples from the adolescent respondents to the LAQ illustrate simple hedonistic life aspirations, where the young people are completely self-involved, exhibiting egocentric concern for their own pleasure, satisfaction, fame, or materialistic gain. It should be noted that no reference whatsoever is made by these adolescents to anyone or anything other than themselves. By contrast, life aspirations that include plans for studying or establishing a career at least express inherent readiness to invest efforts and to undertake some activity; therefore, academic or occupational articulations are rated as achieving at least the second level of aspirations.

Level 2:   Selfish, but includes reference to other people or causes:

> My aspiration is to be a gym teacher, to get married and to bring up children. To fly to Germany and see my uncle's house.

> To get married to a man I'm crazy about and of course that he'll love me too, and we'll have an honest relationship.

> I would like to go to college, then play major league ball, then go hunting a lot this coming winter.

This second level of life aspirations is achieved when young people include in their aspirations some reference to other human beings or activities. However, the essence of these responses remains selfish, geared toward personal gain from any endeavors or relationships formed. Both career and family goals (regardless of the occupation or family lifestyle chosen) are evaluated as Level 2 unless they contain explicit mention of the desire to enhance the welfare of others. Interestingly, a great number of adolescent aspirations that were classified as attaining the second level on the LAQ did, in fact, include both the wish to fulfill a career and the longing to establish a happy family or a significant relationship. On the other hand, these responses excluded any reference to a willingness to contribute oneself to others or to a cause.

Level 3:   Includes elements of a desire for commitment beyond self, or a global wish:

To do something worthwhile that would give me satisfaction and so I won't feel my life's a waste. I'd like to help, to volunteer, but also to have a good time, not to have a boring life.

To improve my country with regard to its criminals and thieves, so there will be as few of them as possible, and that there won't be fighting between one person and another, and that the country will be one where each and every person will be like a brother to the other.

To start a family that's happy in every area, where everyone will feel good and free with themselves inside the family, and to give joy to everyone around me.

Level 3 involves clear indication of some desire to be of help to others, to contribute of oneself, or to be devoted to a cause outside oneself. Not all of the life aspirations expressed by a youngster must necessarily be of a prosocial orientation in order to qualify for the third level (or fourth, for that matter); other more self-oriented life goals may also be interjected. It is the extent to which prosocial goals dominate that differentiates Level 3 from 4. To achieve the highest level of commitment beyond self, issues other than the desire to give of oneself to others should be significantly less emphasized.

The global wish expressed at Level 3 indicates a measure of interest and concern regarding people outside the self or causes for the greater good of society, but such wishful statements do not yet reflect an intention or plan to personally commit the self to achieving these goals. It can still be understood from their descriptions that powerful others— those "in high places"—are expected to execute the actions necessary to bring about the changes desired by the adolescent. Only at the fourth level of life aspirations does the young person articulate personal plans and concrete means through which he or she intends to aid, contribute, and become committed to others.

Level 4:   Fully expressing a desire for transpersonal commitment:

This is my goal: To make someone happy, people who are lonely. To make them feel like they have someone.

I want to invent something useful maybe in medicine. To improve hospital conditions and equipment so that people will see the hospital as a place for healing not as an inquisition.

I think I would like one day to teach music. Because I feel that music makes life a little more beautiful. Everyone has the right to experience music and how it feels.

Anything that would help rehabilitate boys and girls from drugs and to raise awareness about the seriousness of this. To prevent people and especially young people from trying even the easy drugs.

The young people whose aspirations coincide with Level 4 share a specific wish to contribute something of themselves, whether through career choices or emotional interactions, along with an abounding desire to confer those self-related resources onto their fellow human beings. The readiness of these adolescents to give of themselves to others is central to their depiction of their life goals, and their responses encompass a distinctive account of their intentions for commitment beyond self.

The overall validity of the LAQ was evaluated by determining whether these verbal expressions of readiness for transpersonal commitment reflected an inclination to actually act on behalf of other people or purposes. Among other studies, Israeli adolescents in Grades 10 through 11 who had done volunteer work for at least a year were compared with those who had not (Magen & Aharoni, 1991). Findings showed that the youngsters who had actually volunteered scored significantly higher on the LAQ than their nonvolunteering peers, demonstrating the validity of the verbally expressed responses to our open-ended question.

4

Adolescence—Greenhouse for Humanistic Values

What a cunning mixture of sentiment, pity, tenderness, irony surrounds adolescence, what knowing watchfulness! Young birds on their first flight are hardly so hovered around.

George Bernanon, *The Diary of a Country Priest* (1936)

Like most counselors and educators, I have been directly confronted with the stark contrasts in adolescent personality and behavior. Teenagers are blatantly concerned with themselves, their personalities, and satisfying their own needs. They also experience constant tension between contradictory desires: the wish to be alone, to look inward into themselves, and, at the same time, to be in the presence of others, to be surrounded by people and friends. Adolescents are very eager to have others notice, pay attention, and show interest in them; at the same time, they ask not to be disturbed, to have privacy and be left alone. Adolescents are inordinately absorbed with themselves: their rapidly developing bodies, their suddenly heightened and fluctuating emotions, their new thoughts, and their newly awakened awareness of their appearance. They look at the world anew, as if examining it for the first time, and, by assessing their strengths and weaknesses, they measure themselves against it. Their needs for independence and for the freedom to make their own decisions seem to conflict with their strong need for guidance, relationship, and, not infrequently, dependence. Sadness changes as if by magic into gladness, melancholy into exuberance. Self-imposed demands to give of themselves to other people and to worthy causes mingles with highly selfish behavior.

The coexistence of these polarities is actually very important in adolescence. It is through the wide and seemingly rampant swings from one pole to another that adolescents discover who they are. Yet, for the better part of the twentieth century, professionals have taken these fluctuations as evidence that adolescence is a time of "storm and stress." Professionals' view of adolescence has changed little from Hall's 1904 view of this period as a time of exceptional turbulence. Bringing to bear much of the same psychobiological approach on which Freud based the better part of his theories, Hall emphasized the *adolescent turmoil* (his coinage)—the extremes of mood swings and behaviors—brought about by the process of physical and emotional maturation (Coleman & Hendry, 1990; Rapoport & Lomsky-Feder, 1988; Ziv, 1984).

For Anna Freud (1958), too, adolescence is a period of "upheaval" between the calm of childhood and the calm of adulthood. In her view, the upheaval is the external manifestation of the adolescents' efforts to cope with their intensified drives and to transfer their libido from the prepubescent love objects—the mother and father—to a love object outside the family. Upheaval at this age is normal in her view, and psychic equilibrium even a sign that something is amiss: that the young person's drives are too weak or the defenses against them too strong. In a similar vein, Blos (1967) and later Rabichow and Sklansky (1980) continued to view adolescence as a time of inevitable, and perhaps even essential, inner disruption as the personality reorganizes itself for adulthood while the biological changes of puberty make it especially vulnerable. From a somewhat different perspective, Erik Erikson (1963, 1967, 1968) linked the process of identity formation, during which the adolescent is confronted with pressing questions—Who am I? What do I feel? What do I believe? What do I like? dislike? Where do my talents lie? Where do I belong in the world? What will I do with my life?—to what he called the "crisis" of youth. As Erikson saw it, all young people have an *identity crisis*. It is a period of confusion before they make critical life choices. Such a crisis is normative. In the course of it, adolescents feel ill at ease in their bodies, lack a sense of inner continuity and of knowing where they are going, and lack too a sense of inner assuredness of the confirmation of those who matter to them.

Beginning in the 1980s, however, psychologists began to question the harsh inevitability of adolescent crisis and the depiction of adolescence as a time of solely turbulent processes (Offer, Ostrov, Howard, & Atkinson, 1988; Shulman, Seiffage-Kremke, & Samet, 1987; Smilansky, 1991; Youniss & Smollar, 1985). Note was taken of the fact that, from Hall (1904) on, the storm and stress model was based on clinical populations and, to correct the distortion, attention was turned to studying ordinary teenagers in their day-to-day interactions with their families, friends, and people at school. This trend coincided with psychologists' increased interest in human development throughout the life span, which led to experimental investigation of all life stages and provided more information on adolescence.

Several school- and community-based empirical studies, some of them cross-cultural research on normative populations, have provided an alternative picture of the teen years. These studies have demonstrated that many normal adolescents experience stable or relatively uninterrupted growth and are capable of incorporating their new affective, cognitive, biological, and social experiences into their basic personality structure with fairly little disruption (e.g., Gibson-Cline, Dikaiou, Haritos-Fatouras, Shafrir, & Ondis, 1996; Offer, Ostrov, & Howard, 1981; Offer et al., 1988; Rutter, Graham, Chadwick, & Yule, 1976). The vast majority of adolescents in these studies reported feeling generally relaxed and in control, exhibiting no more than mildly unpredictable or rebellious behavior. They were described as facing the acquisition of adult roles with confidence, demonstrating good coping skills, affirming the value of work, and forming positive relationships with peers while maintaining good relations with their parents. There is recognition that, despite adolescents' unique vulnerability to stress, they are capable of coping with the challenges they face actively and productively and of seeking solutions that use the resources available to them (Gibson-Cline et al., 1996).

Others suggested that the process of identity formation need not be tumultuous. Flum (1993, 1994) proposed a style of identity formation that entails neither crisis, on the one hand, nor a premature foreclosure of identity or identity confusion, on the other. Flum called it an *evolutive* style of identity formation, in which those who undergo it emphasize their individuality against the backdrop of strong positive connections with their parents and peers and cope with identity issues in a gradual, sequential, and manageable fashion. There is also recognition that the cultural, familial, social, and economic contexts in which adolescents grow up affect how they experience this period, the distress they feel, and their tendency to act it out (Silbereisen & Todt, 1994). To be sure, a notable minority of essentially normal adolescents in countries all over the world do portray themselves as depressed, anxious, emotionally empty, or confused. Moreover, the incidence of behavioral and psycho-logical difficulties has been shown to increase during adolescence, especially in girls (cf. Rutter & Garmezy, 1983).

These conflicts can perhaps be seen most clearly in adolescents' relations with their parents. In their pursuit of independence and uniqueness, young people may seem disrespectful, angry, and estranged from their families. Friction or conflict and adolescents' ambivalence and rebelliousness toward parents are commonly cited (Jurich, Schumm, & Bollman, 1987; Marcia, 1993; Sprinthall & Collins, 1988). Clinical evidence and empirical observations continue to report a sense of alienation, breaches in understanding, and frustrated communication between parents and their adolescent children (Conger & Petersen, 1984; Patterson & McCubbin, 1987; Smetana, 1988).

Anne Frank's (1952) expressive diary, written in her Holocaust hiding place, dramatizes something of this alienation and rebellion:

> They mustn't know my despair. I can't let them see the wounds which they have caused. I couldn't bear their sympathy and their kind-hearted jokes, it would only make me want to scream all the more. If I talk, everyone thinks I am showing off; when I am silent they think I am ridiculous; rude if I answer, sly if I get a good idea, lazy if I am tired, selfish if I am eating a mouthful more than I should. (Entry for January 30, 1943)

Yet, at the same time, research findings over the years have sug-gested that most parents have a good relationship with their adolescent

children (Newman, 1989; Pardeck & Pardeck, 1990; Steinberg, 1990).
Cross-cultural data have shown that teenagers continue to feel love and
admiration for their parents and to expect parental approval and pride,
even as they develop positive relations with their friends (Offer et al.,
1988). These youngsters reported accepting and esteeming their parents
and were confident that their feelings were reciprocated.

A series of empirical studies exploring Israeli teenagers' and parents'
perceptions of what makes a good parent (Magen, 1994) have explored
these conflicting expectations. For all their striving for independence,
adolescents, much like younger children, expect their parents to set
limits, provide guidance, and serve as models. In their own words,
"good" parents "steer their children through life," "teach manners,"
"keep their children from getting into trouble," "get angry when they
should," and "behave in a way that sets an example for their children."
On the other hand, they clearly emphasize the supreme importance of
parents' allowing autonomy and privacy. A good parent, in their words,
"doesn't butt in too much," "lets his child be independent," "knows
when to leave me alone," and "understands that his kids have things of
their own."

As distinct from the younger children who were interviewed, the 14-
and 15-year-olds were not eager to spend time with their parents and
did not associate good parenting with giving gifts or money. Their
responses indicated the great need they felt, which was not at all evident
in the young children, for their parents to respect and trust them, to
always be ready to listen to what they had to say, and to try to understand
their own different interests and desires. A good parent "trusts his child,"
"shares important decisions with her children," and "respects his child's
needs," they stated. But like younger children, they continued to value
their parents' expressions of love and warmth. As they put it, a good
parent "demonstrates his affection," "shows her love," and "is warm and
sentimental."

Similarly conflicting expectations have been found by other researchers as well (Lecoroy, 1989; Smilansky, 1991). They reflect the
duality inherent in the individuation process (Blos, 1979; Callan &
Noller, 1986; Sebald, 1986). In their strivings for autonomy, adolescents develop personal lives outside the family and formulate new
expectations of their parents (Steinberg, 1990). They no longer view
parental authority as absolute and emphasize their own decision-making

abilities (Eccles et al., 1991; Montemayor, 1983; Youniss & Smollar, 1985). Yet, they continue to want emotional intimacy with their parents and parental approval. These conflicting needs may confuse parents and sometimes foster the misconception that their adolescent children no longer want their input.

The literature on normal adolescents confirms the need to reconceptualize adolescence, and to recognize not only its particular problems but also its richness, variety, and vitality.

VALUE OF POSITIVE EXPERIENCE
IN ADOLESCENCE

The importance of meaningful positive experience in adolescence is suggested in two books. One is by Violato and Travis (1995), *Advances in Adolescent Psychology*; the other by Csikszentmihalyi (1984), *Being Adolescent*.

Violato and Travis (1995) have developed a theory of adolescence based on the idea that adolescents are particularly sensitive to lacunae— to the gaps, ruptures, incompleteness, and insufficiencies in their lives and the world around them. Although all people's lives have a great deal that is missing, adults are often too busy to notice. Adolescents are more aware of the hiatuses and more troubled by them because of the "particular mix of inexperience, biological readiness, marginal status, managed experience, and cultural confusion" (p. 52) that accompanies the adolescent condition. In their in-between status, their lives are suddenly depleted of unacceptable childish contents but have not yet been replenished by adult prerogatives:

> Adolescents, like all humans, have a life in the world as well as a private, inner life. That is, they are political beings and can feel powerless. As social beings, they can be lonely. As economic beings in a pecuniary society, they can suffer a shortage of money. As family beings, they might feel unconnected. As sexual beings, they may suffer from unfulfilled desire. Any one or more of these *lacunae* can dominate the centre of an adolescent's experience at a given time. (Violato & Travis, 1995, p. 60)

Violato and Travis are not the first or only investigators to have pointed to the gaps in the adolescent's life. As early as 1939, for example,

Lewin observed that adolescents, who do not have full membership in either the world of childhood or the world of adulthood, belong to a marginal "no-man's land" between them.

What Violato and Travis (1995) have added is the idea that adolescents' acute sensitivity to what is missing can drive them to strive to fill the gap by searching for, creating, or restoring harmony or completeness. In particular, the authors have claimed, adolescents suffer from the sense of a shortage of beauty, of truth, and of goodness. The authors' remedy is greater focus on these traditional values in education, through the restoration of traditional, serious cultural contents and through more stringent demands for excellence, which will give adolescents worthy goals to strive for. It is my view that experiences of joy that raise those who undergo them out of themselves may also help meet the adolescent's needs for completeness, harmony, and perfection.

Csikszentmihalyi (1984), whose work predates that of Violato and Travis, has also dealt, although from a rather different perspective, with adolescents' needs and efforts to improve upon the unsatisfactory humdrum of their daily experience. As noted in Chapter 1, Csikszentmihalyi is one of the only scholars who has focused his attention specifically on adolescents' happiness.

Among the various research approaches that Csikszentmihalyi used for his investigations, one was quite simply the question, "What are the things in your life you enjoy doing most?" followed up with a probe into why. Out of the embarrassment of riches he received in response—51 activities in all, most of them leisure activities, half active, half passive, with no mention of sex, only one of drugs, and TV mentioned only in conjunction with other activities—he developed his notion of flow, which I described earlier. More accurately, he applied to adolescents the theory of flow that he had first formulated to describe happiness in adults (Csikszentmihalyi, 1975).

What Csikszentmihalyi's thinking has in common with Violato and Travis's (1995) is the idea that there is something in the adolescent condition that leads at least some teenagers to seek meaningful, enriching, and joyful experiences, which meet a natural need and which foster their growth and development. Violato and Travis saw it as the need for completeness and harmony, which, in their view, adolescents seek more than adults. Csikszentmihalyi implied the need for psychic order in both adolescents and adults, but he also implied that the greater variability and disorder in adolescents' day-to-day lives, their comparative inexperience, and their abounding energy all propel their search for it. Conversely, he suggested that the absence of such experiences is detrimental. In a subsequent study of a group of Italian students in the last 2 years of high school, he and his colleagues gathered evidence that suggested that the lack of flow experiences, where challenge and skills are balanced, results in apathy and may constitute a risk of psychological regression and disorganization (Massimini, Csikszentmihalyi, & Carli, 1987).

IS HAPPINESS POSSIBLE IN ADOLESCENCE? _____

Csikszentmihalyi's (1984) work clearly showed that happiness, in the sense of the optimal experience in which flow inheres, is not an illusory quest in adolescence. It also showed that the activities that issued in flow were not essentially hedonistic. Although most of them were leisure activities, such as sports and the arts, and interpersonal interactions with a friend or friends, the ones that gave them greatest enjoyment were those that demanded rigor and took them beyond themselves. His findings go a long way toward dispelling long-held assumptions that adolescents are incapable of happiness and at best can experience only hedonistic pleasure.

Certainly, the prevalence of such assumptions helps explain the dearth of studies of happiness in adolescence compared to the wealth of studies on adolescent storm and stress. Yet, because those assumptions are so entrenched in both professional and popular views, they warrant some additional discussion.

It is not that elation, ebullience, joy, and other manifestations and varieties of happiness have not been noted. They have. But they were invariably noted in connection with adolescent mood swings; the highs are mistrusted as symptoms of volatility. Nor do these moods fit into the definition of happiness as satisfaction, which drove much of the research in the last few decades.

Csikszentmihalyi (1984) convincingly argued that adolescents' rapid and sharp mood swings are not a sign of pathology but a response to the variability of their daily activities. Although adolescents' mood swings are more rapid and extreme than adults', they are no less predictable. Adolescents are generally exposed to more events in the ordinary course of their lives than are adults and respond to the varied exposure with due changes in mood. His findings show that adolescents with the most dramatic mood swings reported being as happy and as much in control as their steadier counterparts and showed similar levels of adjustment (Larson, Csikszentmihalyi, & Graef, 1980). Similarly, surveys of representative samples of people of all ages in many nations have shown that no time of life is significantly happier or unhappier than others (Inglehart, 1990; Latten, 1989; Myers & Diener, 1995; Stock et al., 1983).

Building on Csikszentmihalyi's work, Waterman (1990) defined happiness in terms of *personal expressiveness*. The self-motivated, intensely involving activities in which the individual experiences flow are activities that are personally expressive. By personal expression, Waterman means not just any expression of the self or of any aspect of the self, but the expression of one's potential excellences. The activities that are experienced as personally expressive are those in which individuals advance their highest potential and convert their aptitudes into skills. Because it allows for process, this concept of happiness, which, borrowing from Aristotle, Waterman also termed *eudaimonia,* makes happiness attainable by children and adolescents. Children experience eudaimonia as they develop the many skills of childhood. Adolescents experience it as they become aware that their goals are not necessarily those of their parents and develop the capacity to chose their own life purposes. Activities that promote those purposes are personally expressive in adolescence. Thus, Waterman clearly linked the capacity for happiness in the teen years with the developing sense of identity as adolescents look inside themselves and discover where their abilities and talents lie and what their life purposes are.

Yet, Waterman (1990) too ultimately deemed happiness in the earlier years of life to be inferior to that of adults. Children's eudaimonia does not embrace any mature sense of life's purpose or at least any felt ability to achieve it: "Thus, having come to recognize the possibility of a far richer experience of *eudaimonia* than was possible during childhood, adolescents feel thwarted by their inability to know that experience in any sustained way" (p. 62).

EGOCENTRISM AND COMMITMENT
IN ADOLESCENCE

"It is normal for an adolescent . . . to be more idealistic, . . . generous and unselfish than he will ever be again, but also the opposite: self-centered, egoistic, calculating." So Anna Freud (1958, p. 275) phrased the commonly noted polarity in adolescent behavior of egocentrism and caring. Yet, although both poles have received considerable professional attention, it is perhaps the self-absorption that most strikes the untrained eye, and sometimes the trained eye as well.

Egoism is so accepted as an integral part of adolescent behavior that scholars have sought its sources as if it were a bacillus of some sort. O'Conner and Nikolic (1990) linked adolescents' self-concern—their feelings of specialness, invulnerability, and being targets of magnified attention—to the self-consciousness of their identity formation. More specifically, these authors found that the more aware young people were of the process, either because they were actively probing and exploring their identity or because they had completed their explorations and ostensibly found it, the more egocentric they tended to be. From a cognitive perspective, Elkind (1967) attributed adolescent egoism to the lack of consolidation of formal operational thought, which, he claimed, leads teenagers to project their own concerns onto others. Although his theory has not been substantiated either empirically or conceptually (Lapsley & Murphy, 1985; Riley, Adams, & Nielson, 1984), the salience of egoism in our thinking about adolescence makes it necessary to address the question of how we can expect these self-absorbed youngsters to show any revelation of commitment beyond self.

In fact, there is equal developmental evidence that, at the same time as adolescents are egocentric, their awareness and sensibilities are turning outward toward the world. According to Jung (1959, 1961), during the "psychic revolution" of adolescence, young people begin to open up to the collective realm. Adolescents define for themselves the values they consider meaningful and explore the goals that they regard as worthy to strive for. They become aware of abstractions such as the good, the beautiful, and the real. They discover the outermost perimeters of their world and see that human life teems with problems and adversity. Every generation of teenagers uncovers anew the areas where society is lacking, even as they come to recognize their own limitations and flaws.

The process of identity formation, despite its associations both with adolescent turmoil and adolescent egoism, can also be seen as the basis for commitment beyond self. As Erikson (1963, 1967, 1968) described it, the successful formation of a viable and coherent sense of personal identity enables individuals to commit themselves to a partner, to an occupation, and to goals and values that are consistent with societal norms and expectations, yet in harmony with their own unique sense of individuality. The need for fidelity, according to Erikson, is among the major needs of this period. It is a need that may result in young people's blindly following gurus, demagogues, or totalitarian leaders with easy answers to complex problems. But in young persons who are able to look within without fear or censorship and to assess the values they encounter without preconception, the same need for fidelity may also serve as the basis for their readiness to rise beyond their immediate concerns and to commit themselves to moral causes.

Similarly, adolescents' increased cognitive ability can be seen as driving not just an exaggerated self-reflection, but an increased interest in the world as well. Piaget (1967) showed that by early adolescence, children are liberated from intellectual egocentricity and can differentiate between the self and the world. Adolescents' thinking process is thus decentered, and they are able to reason about the world and the self using formal operations. A newly acquired capacity for logic, orderly analysis, and reflection enables them to give greater meaning and cohesiveness to their experience (Offer et al., 1988).

Kohlberg (1981; Kohlberg & Gilligan, 1971) argued that adolescents' cognitive development may form the basis for their moral development. At the same time as he observed that the adolescent's discovery of the self is associated with adolescent egotism and hedonism, he emphasized the adolescent's increasing capacity for moral judgment. Whereas children's moral thinking focuses purely on reward, punishment, and the exchange of favors, preadolescents become concerned with maintaining, supporting, and justifying the social order, embodied in the rules of their family, group, or nation. They become interested in acting in a socially approved manner and doing their duty. Then, in adolescence, as they develop the capacity for complex perspective-taking and for abstract reasoning, they evolve a philosophic view of values and society. They can form an autonomous, reflective perspective on societal values and construct universal moral principles.

Kohlberg's argument is that adolescents have the cognitive capacity for advanced moral reasoning; however, he explicitly noted that this capacity is not always developed. Gilligan (1982) modified his theory somewhat, emphasizing gender differences. In a large accumulation of studies, Eisenberg (e.g., 1986, 1991; Eisenberg et al., 1995) borrowed many of his and Gilligan's concepts as well as Batson's ideas about empathy (discussed in Chapter 3) and tested their application to various types of helping situations involving children of different ages. In a detailed longitudinal study of the moral reasoning of youths in their early and mid-teens (ages 13-14 and 15-16, respectively), Eisenberg (1991) empirically confirmed much of what the theorists had expected.

Eisenberg (1991) found that the tendency noted among elementary school children to reason on the basis of expected self-benefits and losses—in other words, hedonistic reasoning—declines during adolescence. Among other things, mid-teens use less direct reciprocity reasoning; that is, they think less about what they have to gain or lose from the person they help or do not help. They also use less reasoning that is oriented toward obtaining approval or acceptance and less reasoning based on stereotypes of a good or bad person.

At the same time, the other-oriented reasoning—or self-reflective empathic orientation—that emerges in late childhood (age 11-12) increases in use. Eisenberg (1991) thus found that adolescents base their thinking more on sympathetic concern and caring for others and will give more weight to the good feelings that they may gain from making someone else feel good.

Finally, Eisenberg (1991) showed that some forms of abstract, value-oriented moral reasoning first emerge at this age. These include reasoning based on an internalized sense of responsibility, duty, or need to uphold laws or accepted norms and values. The personal thus gives way to the social. Although these forms of abstract moral reasoning emerged somewhat earlier in girls, boys caught up within 2 years.

Of particular relevance to our studies, Eisenberg (1991) also found that higher levels of moral reasoning—both other-oriented and value-oriented thinking—were related to actual helping behavior as well as to empathy, sympathy, and perspective-taking. Conversely, in other studies, she found that prosocial behaviors correlated negatively with hedonistic priorities (Eisenberg, 1986; Eisenberg et al., 1987) and that the association between prosocial moral reasoning and behavior increases with age (Eisenberg et al., 1995; Kohlberg & Candee, 1984).

Along similar lines, others (e.g., Ziv, 1984) have shown that the value adolescents attribute to helping others increases in linear fashion from the seventh to twelfth grades. Call, Mortimer, and Shanahan (1995) suggested that adolescents' heightened awareness of others' needs may have important implications for their willingness to demonstrate helpfulness.

These studies should not be glibly interpreted to mean that adolescents are inevitably compassionate, committed moral beings or that all the self-centered thinking of childhood suddenly evaporates. Indeed, Eisenberg also found that after its sudden drop in late childhood and early adolescence, hedonistic reasoning increases among 15- and 16-year-old boys (Eisenberg, Miller, Shell, McNalley, & Shea, 1991), and then again in late adolescence and early adulthood in response to dilemmas in which the cost of helping is deemed too high (Eisenberg et al., 1995).

Findings also show that moral reasoning begins very early and develops as childhood progresses. Four and five-year-olds who were asked to explain why they had shown kindness to someone (Eisenberg-Berg & Neal, 1979) often replied in terms of friendship, the "needs" of the other person, or a simple wish to help or to share. We're way beyond the crude reciprocity that Kohlberg posited. By the age of 5, children apparently comprehend that to be a "good helper," they must know what the other person needs (Borke, 1971; Ford, 1979). In elementary school, children begin to offer more other-oriented reasons and fewer hedonistic reasons to explain prosocial behavior (Eisenberg, McCreath, & Ahn, 1988). They become concerned with approval, enhancement of inter-personal relationships, the desire to behave "well," and direct reciprocity. Moreover, the use by adolescents of internalized emotional responses (e.g., guilt), self-reflective sympathy, and perspective-taking to explain moral decisions already starts in late elementary school (Eisenberg et al., 1995).

But the findings do show that adolescents become less self-centered, more independent, and more thoughtful in their thinking about morality; that the cognitive basis of empathy and sympathy becomes stronger in these years; and that the self-centered tit-for-tat reasoning of childhood gives way to an emergent concern with society, rights, equality, and justice. To the child's question—What will this act do for me as an individual?—the adolescent has a greater tendency to add: What will the impact of my actions be on the society of which I am a part?

STUDYING ADOLESCENT HAPPINESS
AND COMMITMENT BEYOND SELF _____

Adolescence is, on several grounds, a fascinating and significant time to consider positive human tendencies, but the modesty of the literature on the positive aspects of adolescents' lives, as well as our lack of knowledge of the positive, obstructs our attempts to help teenagers channel their distress into constructive outlets and prevents us from realizing the full impact of our role as educators. Our studies specifically focused on both adolescents' capacity for intense happiness and their ability to reach out to give to others. The ability to transcend basic need fulfillment was thus our principle concern. Within the evolving self of the adolescent, the task of developing positive social values and behaviors is especially relevant. The adolescent develops an increased capacity for empathy, moral judgment, responsibility, and social involvement and interaction, all of which can enhance positive social behavior. We aimed to determine the nature of the relationship between young people's experiences of exhilaration and jubilation and their view of the world as a place to which they wish to become connected by trying to make it a better place.

Relying on the actual voices of many adolescents, I strove to extract the universals in positive adolescent experience; at the same time, I selected a particular sociocultural climate in which to identify these universals. Israel is an especially resonant chamber for such an experiment. As it continues to struggle for survival, this society demands high personal commitment from its members but at the same time places a strong emphasis on the value of human life and individual achievement and fulfillment.

Part II

Research Findings

5

Methodology

Thus far, we've emphasized the essentially qualitative nature of our research; namely, the open-endedness of the PEQ and LAQ, rather than the categorical rankings of more precise and structured test designs. Of course, there's always a debate raging between proponents of both styles as to the place of qualitative and quantitative analyses in the social sciences. However, we are not taking sides here. Indeed, Lewy (1988) may have articulated the best basis for a synthesis, terming it "From Disdain to Détante:"

> For decades the two paradigms of research, the qualitative and the quantitative ones, have represented conflicting views, and the gulf between them has constantly deepened. This is so despite the fact that for more than a quarter of century Zetterberg (1965) advanced the hypothesis that quan-

titative and qualitative approaches have distinct roles in the advancement of disciplinary knowledge and that both of them are essential. Qualitative field work can help to illuminate the theoretical and measurement issues in new areas of study, while quantitative methods are appropriate for testing the hypothesis derived from rigorous field methods. (p. 97)

We have likewise found considerable use for more strictly quantitative methodology as a complement to the PEQ and LAQ. Along with open-ended questions that allowed for the expression of the diverse content appearing in the adolescents' responses, we also devised scales to assess the intensity of the experiences and the degree of commitment that was revealed.

The inclusion of additional structured diagnostic instruments—the High School Personality Questionnaire (HSPQ) and Sense of Coherence Scale (SCS) (described below)—add new dimensions, broadening the scope of interpretation for the findings. Thus, in developing this research orientation, I hoped to exploit the advantages of self-reported qualitative raw material—in the form of individual teenagers' actual narratives of personal events, thoughts, feelings, and hopes in their lives—while maintaining the empirical power to conduct comparative quantitative analyses through statistical manipulations (such as multiple regression and discriminant analysis) in order to enhance our understanding of the issues at hand.

The findings presented in the following pages are based on a large number of studies carried out between 1980 and 1993 on adolescents' positive experiences—exploring moments of joy and happiness in their lives—and on their commitment beyond self, by which I mean their desire to be devoted to causes that go beyond selfish gratifications. These studies investigated numerous adolescent samples, and their results have in part been published in the literature. Representative studies from the research series will be discussed here in Part II of the book. Figure 5.1 presents a schematic overview of a decade of research on the relationship between a desire for prosocial commitments and the experience of happiness and joy in adolescents from different cultural backgrounds.

The first and most far-ranging study in the series was a cross-cultural comparison of 1,094 Christian Americans with Jewish and Moslem-Arab Israeli adolescents ages 14 to 16, which sought to ascertain the universality and specificity of the two dimensions, namely, positive experiences and commitment beyond self (Magen, 1983a,

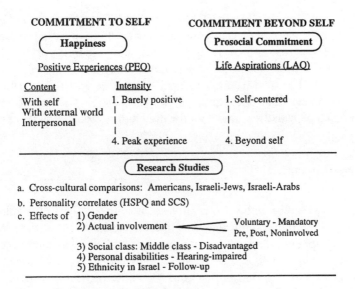

Figure 5.1. Research methodology: Adolescents' quest for happiness as related to their commitment beyond self.

1983b, 1985). American adolescents represented modern Western culture; Israeli Arabs, traditional Eastern culture; and Israeli Jews, a mixture of traditional Eastern and modern Western cultures. The students from all three samples attended junior high and high schools in urban and rural areas and had various academic and socioeconomic backgrounds. Although the schools attended by both Israeli groups were located in various parts of the country, none were in mixed Arab-Jewish neighborhoods. The Jewish youngsters were tested in all-Jewish schools and the Arab youngsters in all-Arab schools. Follow-up cross-cultural studies of Israeli Jews and Arabs were also conducted.

Other research studies were conducted among Israeli Jewish adolescents, representing a range of populations, in a natural progression where each study attempted to address questions raised by a prior study. Several studies attempted to identify characteristics of those young people who were involved in activities geared toward the benefit of society or causes outside the self (e.g., Magen & Aharoni, 1991). Other studies compared youths of different socioeconomic status and at different stages of involvement in actual work aimed toward improving the lives of other people. One study (Magen, Birenbaum, & Ilovich, 1992) investigated underprivileged youngsters who lived in disadvantaged neighborhoods, as defined by the local city municipalities on the basis of standard criteria (see the International Committee, 1984). Several studies looked at hearing-impaired adolescents (e.g., Magen, 1990a). All in all, over 2,500 teenage boys and girls ranging in age from 14 through 16 provided the raw data for the studies reported in this book.

INSTRUMENTS

In all of the studies with various adolescent samples, the PEQ explored adolescent happiness through positive experiences (Magen, 1983a, 1985); the phenomenon of commitment beyond self was measured by the LAQ (Magen, 1983b). Two additional instruments were used in the research studies reported in this book. The intensity and nature of the positive experience and the extent of commitment beyond self were examined in relation to the adolescents' personalities, using the HSPQ (Cattell & Cattell, 1975); their sense of coherence was measured by SCS (Antonovsky, 1987). Appropriate procedures for translation and back-translation between English, Hebrew, and Arabic were observed to ensure uniformity of meaning for each instrument (cf. Zak, 1979b).

Details on the PEQ, including criteria for rating its two dimensions —intensity levels and content categories—were provided in Chapter 2. The full description of the LAQ measuring commitment beyond self was presented in Chapter 3. Here I will describe the HSPQ and SCS scales used in our research and provide details on the research procedures for administering and rating the PEQ and LAQ.

The High School Personality Questionnaire

The HSPQ was used to assess adolescents' personality attributes in relation to their positive experiences and commitment beyond self. The HSPQ (Cattell & Cattell, 1975) is an objective test designed for assessing the personalities of 12- to 18-year-olds. The respondents were asked to answer 142 questions about their preferences, behaviors, attitudes, and so on by selecting one of three possible responses to each. These responses were then analyzed so as to rate the participants on each of Cattell and Cattell's (1975) 14 independent personality factors. Each factor was on a continuum of 1 to 10, with one set of personality traits at one end and its contrasting set at the other. Each respondent was thus placed somewhere along the continuum for each factor.

The 14 personality factors, which cover relatively independent aspects of personality, have been confirmed and validated in various experiments in the United States (Cattell, 1969, 1973) and have been shown to exist in other cultures as well (Cattell & Cattell, 1975; Cattell, Eber, & Tatsuoka, 1970). A cross-cultural check on the 16 personality factors (adult version) conducted in Israel (Zak, 1979a, 1979b) showed the questionnaire to be transferable across cultures and languages. For the present study, a cross-cultural check, adding the Arab population scales, was carried out. The factor patterns found in the combined sample of Israeli participants resembled those found in earlier Israeli studies (Zak, 1979a, 1979b).

As in the case of the positive experiences and life aspirations that were recounted, every effort was made to prevent built-in value judgment bias. No implication of superiority or inferiority was attached to any of the 14 personality factors.

The Sense of Coherence Scale

Sense of coherence has been conceptualized as a global orientation indicating the extent to which a person has an enduring, dynamic confidence that his or her internal and external environments are predictable and that there is a high probability that life situations will work out as well as can be expected (Antonovsky, 1979, 1987). The SCS was used in our studies to expand our understanding of the factors that foster healthy development. The SCS (Antonovsky, 1979, 1987) includes 29 items on a 7-point Likert-type scale comprising three components: (a) *Comprehensibility*—a person's insight into his or her achievements and difficulties; (b) *Manageability*—the extent to which the environment is perceived as predicted and structured, and the extent to which the inner and outer resources at the person's disposal seem adequate to meet environmental demands; and (c) *Meaningfulness*—the extent to which life appears emotionally sensible and worthy of energy investment.

The total score for the three aspects of the SCS reflects the individual's generalized orientation of confidence and optimism. This scale was employed in our study (Magen et al., 1992), where the Cronbach alpha coefficient of internal consistency for the total score was 0.81.

RESEARCH PROCEDURE

In all the studies, the questionnaires were administered by graduate students in counseling programs or licensed school counselors whose cultural backgrounds matched those of the participants and who had received detailed instructions from the author on data collection procedures. The adolescent participants were gathered in groups of no more than 20 in their own schools for two consecutive class periods. To ensure anonymity, they were asked only to indicate gender, age, and school on their questionnaires.

Prior to administration of the questionnaires, a general introduction was given to the students regarding the aim and special character of our research, with reference to our interest in exploring the adolescent world and gaining a better understanding of the positive aspects of their lives.

In administering the PEQ, additional verbal instructions were offered. Before replying to the PEQ, the participants were told that they were to describe in it their most wonderful experiences:

> Take a few moments to think of your best experience, the one which made you feel that life was wonderful. Describe your feeling as fully as you can. You may include any details, however intimate or personal. You don't have to sign your name or otherwise identify yourself.

The administration of the LAQ was not accompanied by specific verbal instructions; moreover, any queries or requests for clarification of its aim by the adolescents were simply answered with, "Try to write down the best thing you would like to do with your life," or "The idea is to write the best thing you would like to do with your life or in your life." This nonspecific reply was intended to maintain the nondirective stance established by the LAQ in order to elicit a free and genuine expression.

In all studies, the PEQ and LAQ instruments were administered in a different sequence for randomly but equally divided members of the group (i.e., PEQ first for half the sample and LAQ first for the other half), to eliminate order effects of the instruments. No differences were found in the level of LAQ or in the intensity or content of the PEQ with respect to the sequence of administration. When additional secondary instruments were also administered, a similar procedure was used to counterbalance the sequence, again demonstrating no order effects for any of the studies.

Rater Training and Rating
for the PEQ and LAQ

As principal investigator, I trained and supervised all the training sessions and rating teams but did not evaluate any responses. Training and reliability testing were conducted separately for the LAQ and for the two subscales (intensity and content) of the PEQ. The trainees were given definitions and examples for each dimension (i.e., the four intensity ratings and three content domains of the PEQ and the four aspiration levels of the LAQ), as well as related reading material (e.g., Maslow, 1971, for intensity; Jourard & Landsman, 1980, for content).

Emphasis in training was placed on avoiding moral or social judgment of the responses. For example, the personal experience can be joyous, can make the adolescent feel connected with others and the world, can infuse him or her with a sense of meaning, yet this does not mean that the experience, if judged in a larger context, is necessarily one that is socially positive. In addition, the raters underwent training exercises specifically designed to teach them to apply the indices for the classification schemes without assigning credit on the basis of verbal ability or writing style.

After familiarization and discussion of the material in the training groups, the raters practiced the rating procedures until they felt sufficiently confident for reliability testing. Ratings of the PEQ were performed in two stages: All the descriptions were rated on the intensity of the most remembered positive experiences; then the categorization by content domain commenced.

The reliability of the ratings was estimated repeatedly with new samples until a high interrater reliability coefficient was obtained. For the various studies using the LAQ scale, high Pearson product moment coefficients as estimates of reliability were achieved, ranging from .87

to .95. For the intensity of positive experiences, those coefficients ranged between .75 and .88 in the various studies. For content category of positive experiences, an interrater reliability level of 90% was established by Fox's (1969) procedure for computing reliability of content analysis.

Rating in the Cross-Cultural Study

Training the judges for the large cross-cultural study was especially challenging. On the one hand, it was felt that reliable ratings could be obtained only if the adolescents' responses were evaluated by raters from their own culture, who would understand the cultural nuances of their responses. On the other hand, to enable comparison, it was necessary to ensure that the assessments in all the cultures would be made according to the same criteria.

Twelve raters, four from each of the three cultural groups, were selected to rate the PEQ and LAQ responses. All the raters had counseling degrees. To ensure consistency across cultures, training was carried out in three culturally overlapping training groups of five raters each: four Israeli Jewish raters and one Israeli Arab rater; four Israeli Arab raters and one Israeli Jewish rater; and four U.S. Christian raters and one Israeli Arab rater.

After interrater reliability was established on both dimensions, six culturally homogeneous rating teams of two raters each were formed to evaluate the responses of the participants belonging to their respective cultures. Interrater discrepancies were resolved by a third rater belonging to the same cultural group.

6

What Makes Adolescents Happy

O body swayed to music, O brightening glance,
How can we know the dancer from the dance?

William Butler Yeats,
Among School Children (1928)

What makes adolescents happy? What kind of experiences make them feel good about themselves and the world? What makes them feel that life is wonderful? In this chapter, we listen for an answer in the adolescents' own voices. The overriding wisdom in letting these adolescent voices speak for themselves was clear from our initial studies in which adolescents were asked to "just talk about beautiful events or moments of great joy." Once encouraged to recall past positive experience, to observe the beautiful elements of their lives, and to remember one time when the world seemed good, adolescents in many cases opened up in surprising ways to reveal feelings and thoughts that they had perhaps never acknowledged to themselves and certainly not to others. Answering such a question was extremely difficult for many of them at first, yet, they responded to our suggestion and in so doing achieved a level of awareness and openness.

In keeping with the research methodology, the following discussion is organized along the three ways of *being-in-the world* derived from Heidegger and used in Landsman's (1967) factor analysis of responses to a research questionnaire of a large adult sample: experiences with the self, experiences with the external world, and experiences with others. Beyond and across these categories, however, we also observe a variety of recurrent themes that add to our understanding of what moves adolescents to feel good and what makes them feel happy.

In an attempt to go beyond statistical compilations and quantitative reports, this chapter presents a qualitative perspective on the contents that pervade young people's positive life experiences. Our examples thus provide a rich view, not only of the different kinds of experiences in which adolescents find their happiness, but of the multiple sources and multifaceted quality of those experiences.

EXPERIENCES WITH THE SELF

Joy derived from encounters with the self can be evoked by such diverse events as recognizing an important self-realization, achieving a hard-won accomplishment, listening to or playing music, or having a religious experience. Whatever its source, the joy in such encounters lies in feeling oneself fully alive, or in looking into oneself and becoming aware of attributes and strengths and wishes of which one had not until then been fully aware.

The joy of self-discovery can be seen in the description of this young woman from the United States:

I felt a bond grow between us that at the moment nothing could break. We sat there for 2 hours or more discussing beliefs and attitudes about teenagers, finding that many of our views were the same. For those 2 hours, I was closer to myself, my friends, and the world than I think I have ever been. I was extremely happy.

(American girl)

An American youngster recalled the day he decided to "be me":

The day I decided to be me is the best experience in my life. I used to go along with the gang, so to speak. I would do things that weren't me. I just did them because my friends did. Some things that we did were really bad and I regretted every minute of it. But one day the light of the world came shining through, and I realized I had a soul and a life just like my friends, and I had to live it my way. I talked to this one special lady, she was one of my teachers, and she told me I should be independent and not depend on my friends. I got out and found new friends, who had good names and not bad ones. Today I think I am a very mature boy. That day I found myself I started a brand new life and ever since then I've enjoyed living and most of all I have enjoyed myself.

(American boy)

These descriptions recall Maslow's (1971) observation that one of the behaviors that leads to self-actualization is listening to the "impulse voices"—that is, to the authentic self, without poses, without concern for what others think—and taking full responsibility for what one does and who one is. Deep happiness can reside in such authenticity.

Quite a number of the adolescents wrote that their happiest moment was when they felt a sense of accomplishment, the feeling that I made it, I achieved something, I did something, I overcame obstacles, I exceeded myself. Such feelings may be brought on by a good grade or a first prize, by praise or recognition for talent or good work. These externals are not the core of the experience, but only the triggers. The heart of the experience is the person's feeling of having done something that matters.

This feeling can occur in any area of the adolescent's life where there is a challenge to grow and develop. Accomplishments in school or sports were frequent themes. Here the adolescent feels the gratification of attaining new skills and competencies. Other repeated themes included overcoming a hardship, helping someone in need, and assuming responsibility for oneself and others. Perhaps, the motif of accomplishment was so common because it coincides by nature with the thrust toward growth and development that characterizes adolescence.

The following examples show adolescents deriving great happiness from the discovery of abilities they hadn't previously known they possessed. Whether the ability is academic, physical, or the fortitude and strength of character to kick a habit or overcome a serious illness, its

discovery makes the adolescent feel strong, satisfied, worthy, and good
about himself or herself and the world as a whole.

> The most best experience I had in my life was when I stopped smoking marijuana. I
> felt good. I know why. I am never going to start back. . . . Everything is really good
> here, even though sometimes things don't go right. But I know that is going to happen
> sometimes.
>
> (American boy)

> I didn't believe that I could pass. The closer we got to the difficult part, the more my
> fears and doubts increased. And how great was my satisfaction and feeling that life
> was wonderful when I succeeded in passing, with great effort, something I never
> believed I could achieve. When I sat on the bench, tired but satisfied, I had a very,
> very good feeling, and life to me was wonderful.
>
> (Israeli Jewish girl)

> I have leukemia in my legs and I had to have surgery 9 or 10 times and after the next
> to the last one, I was told I would never walk alone again. And I didn't for 3 years, but
> once again, I went in for another operation and after another year, I could walk again
> and I haven't had any trouble hardly at all since the last operation.
>
> (American boy)

In these experiences with the self, the adolescents learned of their
capacities for persistence and endurance. In one way or another, these
are also experiences of mastery, in which the adolescents learned that
their efforts and actions have an impact and that they can shape their
own lives. They are fortifying experiences, evidence of both the adolescents' increasing maturity and an impetus to further growth. The boy
who kicked his marijuana habit was certain that he would be able to
overcome other difficulties in life, and this was part of the happiness that
he felt in his accomplishment. The boy who, after repeated operations,
was able to walk against the odds could derive deep satisfaction from
knowing that he can "walk" into adulthood with pride and confidence.

Indeed, one recurring experience of our adolescents with the self is
precisely that experience of taking on adult responsibilities and assuming
an adult role, as this statement by a young American illustrates:

> When I got my first job working in a restaurant making two dollars an hour. It made
> me feel good to buy my own school clothes and buy stuff for my four brothers and
> sisters without getting money from my parents.
>
> (American boy)

Working and earning money gave this adolescent the independence and ability to take care of others, which made him feel like a worthwhile human being. Yet, the pleasure of independence attained by earning one's money and doing what one wants with it is also cited as a pleasure in its own right:

> Working and buying the things I want, like a car, and fixing it up like I want with my money and if it tears up I get it fixed, not my father.
>
> (American boy)

Although the joy of accomplishment is essentially independent of other people's observations or judgments, it is not always, and perhaps not usually, an entirely solitary experience. The encouragement and reinforcement of friends, teachers, and family not only provide an incentive for the accomplishment but are also part of the pleasure.

The Jewish girl who derived so much pleasure from passing a test she didn't think she would pass has an Arab counterpart who recounted a similar experience, only with his friends added to the picture:

> It was during the math exam. I was scared, knowing that I could fail. The fear followed me even after I turned in the paper. But when the results came, my friends came running to tell me that I passed. This moment was the most important in my life.
>
> (Israeli Arab boy)

The American boy who felt such gratification in taking on the responsibilities of working and earning money resembles the following Arab youngster, who told of the deep pleasure he felt in helping his father on his fishing boat:

> Our family is supported by fishing. My father has a fishing boat. Last summer, some misunderstanding caused a quarrel in the family and separated my brothers from my family. They stopped working and helping at sea. My father is an old man and can't manage with a fishing boat by himself. So I had to help, and indeed during 2 months of summer vacation I used to go out with him before sunrise and to help him with his work. It was pleasurable and satisfying in spite of all the problems we had. I wasn't used to the kind of work, so it was hard. But I felt I had meaning in my life, value, as I was doing and accomplishing things that have value and benefit. I felt proud, I felt real joy, I felt that life is beautiful and happy.
>
> (Israeli Arab boy)

For the two girls quoted below, one Arab, the other Jewish, the sense of accomplishment in their academic performance was made all the sweeter by the praise and recognition they received from peers and teachers and other adults:

> Once I had to take part in a competition about our city. . . . As the time approached, my fear became stronger. I never had to stand in front of such an audience before, with so many people, as I did then. When the competition started, I felt my heart beating very fast. When my turn came I got terribly frightened and excited, but my friend encouraged me and calmed me down, and when I was asked the questions, I thought very fast, and gave clear, correct answers. Everyone clapped hands. I felt gay and happy. All my fears disappeared. I felt that I was ready to take part in many other competitions, to help to promote the reputation of our school.
>
> (Israeli Arab girl)

> I had to give a lecture in literature in front of the district inspector. I was standing in front of the class trembling. The time flew without my realizing it. But what was unforgettable were the last moments of the lesson, when the eyes of all the pupils, the teacher, and the inspector fastened on me with such admiration that I just melted with joy. I'll never forget the moment when they all came up to me and praised me and said "you were great." The inspector said, "you have a future," and indeed, life seemed wonderful and the future promising.
>
> (Israeli Jewish girl)

In both of these examples, the source of the adolescents' happiness was their successful performance, but the stimulus to make the required effort was no doubt implanted by those who challenged them, fostered their expectations of success, and rewarded their success with praise and recognition.

The happiness derived from accomplishment, whether in schoolwork or athletics, a performance before others or a solitary activity, partakes of the flow depicted by Csikszentmihalyi (1984). Our samples particularly illustrate how, as Csikszentmihalyi describes it,

> In flow, one is carried away by the interaction between the self and the activity: the climber and the rock, the painter and the canvas, the surgeon and the operation. To the extent that one feels immersed in the activity, the distinction between *I* and *it* becomes irrelevant. (p. 250)

But activity is only one source of happiness with self. Among the adolescents' reports were descriptions of religious experiences that require a receptive rather than active stance. Religious experiences are naturally rare, and they were rare in our sample as well. In the following description, the rarity of the experience underscores its elevating and transforming quality.

> It was June. . . . Summer had just begun. Our church youth group had been planning a special trip to a place called Lake Junaluska, North Carolina. We were spending a week at this beautiful Methodist retreat camp, high in the mountains. On the last night at the camp, which was a Thursday, all the many different churches from around the U.S. participated in a talent show. It was a lot of fun. But the highlight of the night and the week was the communion service held after. That was the night I found God, and I had never been more happy in all my life. I still have that feeling, and it has changed my life greatly, and I now look at life in a more meaningful way.
>
> (American girl)

Some adolescents are brought into joyful contact with themselves through music, as was this girl who felt the special connection with her grandmother through her piano playing and enjoyed a strong sense of accomplishment:

> Ever since I was a little girl, I wanted to learn to play the piano. My grandmother teaches piano, and in the summer she would teach me short songs. This made me want to play the piano even more. When I was at the end of the fifth grade my parents, with my grandmother's help, got the family a piano and I started taking piano lessons. Last February, I entered a music festival. You play two songs and the judges rate you according to how well you play. I got the highest rating you could get. I was very happy, and it was one of the best moments in my life.
>
> (American girl)

While other art forms did not appear at all among our respondents, musical experiences recurred. For the next boy, playing at a piano recital in memory of his late teacher brought him a sense of the teacher's enduring presence and lifted him out of the numbness of grief into a renewed sense of feeling and life:

> One experience that gave me a good feeling was when I did my piano recital. The recital was in honor of my piano teacher, who had just passed away. When I found out that he had died, I lost all enthusiasm to play my piano. Then, about 2 weeks later, a lady called and asked me to play in honor of him with 12 other selected pupils. At first, I didn't want to, but when I got up on the stage and started playing, all that he had told me came back and I played the best I had ever done. I was very proud to have

been one of his pupils, and I felt that I had done a very good deed. After that day, I
have felt his presence near me, and I will keep him in my heart always.

(American boy)

These are not solipsistic, self-absorbed experiences. Quite to the
contrary, the authentic, enlightening, and happy meeting with the self
seems to bring the adolescent into closer connection with the people and
world around and to provide a foundation for going beyond the self. His
ability to work and earn money not only empowered the young American, there was also a natural awareness that this power could lead
eventually to bettering the lives of others. The Arab girl who derived
pleasure from doing well in a school competition wanted to continue to
contribute to her school by representing it in other competitions. The
Arab boy who was so proud of his difficult work on his father's fishing
boat found gladness and meaning by doing a job that had to be done and
by helping his family. Their becoming aware of their powers and capacities in their experiences with the self seems to have given them a sense
of belonging to a larger world and encouragement to develop those
capacities yet further. The religious experience recounted by the American girl is perhaps prototypical of an experience anchored in the self that
brings one beyond the self.

EXPERIENCES WITH THE
EXTERNAL WORLD

Gradual exposure to a broader world is inevitable in adolescence for, as
the adolescent grows, so do the dimensions of the world. The experiences with the world in which adolescents find happiness are varied and
far-ranging.

Perhaps the simplest of these are experiences with objects (or animals) that can be had and held, as illustrated in the following statements:

When I was very little I wanted a horse. So my parents and I moved from Key Largo
to Citra and I did get a horse, as a matter of fact, I got five. That was the most wonderful
thing that ever happened to me.

(American girl)

One time I had a real good experience on my birthday. I had thought that I wasn't going to get anything but a few little gadgets until at the last moment I saw my bike. It made me happy. I almost cried.

(Israeli Jewish boy)

Yet, the material possession is not necessarily the only important aspect of the experience. In many instances, the physical object is charged with meaning for the adolescents, and the happiness it evokes derives from that. For example, the objects this Arab boy won at the fair were given away, proving a connectedness between belongings and personal ties:

I went to the fair. I won a big dog, a pillow, a smaller dog, and a tiny dog. I gave the pillow to my oldest sister, the biggest dog to my youngest sister, and the tiny dog to my grandma, and I kept the small dog.

(Israeli Arab boy)

Similarly, the money this American boy got from his mother could be used to buy things for her at the shops in the amusement park:

The best thing that ever happened to me is when we went to Six Guns. I had a lot of fun. My mother gave me $10 to buy something. We had free rides and we took our lunch. We met a lot of people from different places. We rode on the train to get into Six Guns, and at one o'clock, we got back on the train and went out to our buses. They had lots of stores where you buy different pretty things for your mother.

(American boy)

Fairs and amusement parks are prototypical fun experiences for young people. Yet, interestingly, neither the Arab nor American boy mentioned the fun aspect as the source of the pleasure he found in his visit. Both derived pleasure from the physical objects they could take away with them and bring back to someone else. Only the American boy also derived pleasure from the new experiences—riding the train, meeting new people —that the outing opened up for him.

As adolescents go forth into the world, their horizons are indeed expanded, and this too seems to be a source of pleasure. The excitement of getting to know the world seems to be behind the pleasure of moving from city to small town, or from town to city, which was cited by a number of the adolescents. Here is an example from a girl in the United States:

> The best experience that ever happened to me was when I moved from Orlando to Keystone. It was really a change because Orlando's a big city and Keystone is a little town.
>
> (American girl)

More palpable is the pleasure in the glimpse of underwater life that the following American boy gave as his best moment:

> I went to Key West—it was really exciting because we went out in the ocean really far in a boat, and we went down to the coral reefs and saw many different kinds of fish and what they do under water.
>
> (American boy)

As adolescents develop, they look at the world anew. In the process of their identity formation, they "reformulate" the world, taking repeated looks at what they have seen before, reexamining it and reconnecting to it in new ways. They are better able to "see" the world and to appreciate its beauty than children are, and often they are consciously looking for beauty. The beauty can be man-made, as was the beauty of the decorated Christmas tree that this American girl describes:

> I always feel especially joyful around Christmas time. Last year, we found a perfect Christmas tree, and it was really beautiful, when decorated. In fact, someone asked me if it was real or not. We have a sort of window inside our house. On Christmas eve, as I was going to bed, I glanced through the window and saw the colored lights of the tree gleaming distortedly through the glass. It made me feel so exhilarated.
>
> (American girl)

More often, it was the beauty of nature that moved the adolescents, as this Arab boy reveals:

> What most affects me are the seasons of the year. Especially in our country, we are blessed with beautiful views. I especially love autumn, a season that makes me feel life is wonderful. When a person feels sad or depressed, all he has to do is go out his door and look at the beautiful flowers and trees and forget his sorrow. This brings peace to life.
>
> (Israeli Arab boy)

The beauty that evokes happiness could be close at hand, just outside the door or window, as in the latter examples. Or it could be somewhat farther afield, reached by an excursion, as the beauty of the sea in the next example:

> I get the feeling that . . . life is wonderful every time I go to the ocean (I go a lot). I love it there and I feel wonderful with the warm sun on me and the cool water all around me. When the wind blows I feel as if I could dance along with it. It is a beautiful place, where nature is at its best. The blue sky, the hot sun, the cool water, the nice breeze, the fresh salty smell. Nature is just all around me and life is great. When I look out to sea and see how the water goes on, I begin to realize how big the world is.
>
> (American boy)

It can be a familiar beauty that revives the spirit and brings a sense of peace, connectedness, and abiding wonder at the world's grandeur, as in the examples above. Or it can be a new and unfamiliar beauty that moves the adolescent to feelings of awe and exhilaration:

> The first time I saw the mountains I was about 10. I had never seen them and I was excited. When I first saw them, I was filled with awe. . . . Later we hiked up. . . . Everywhere around us were beautiful flowers and little bugs . . . wild flowers towering above our heads. . . . All around you could see mountains . . . blue and rugged. To me this was something that made my life beautiful.
>
> (American girl)

For some adolescents, the pleasure of beauty is intertwined with the pleasure of traveling and seeing new vistas, as in the American boy's visit to Montana cited in Chapter 2 (see p. 20).

> We traveled to the United States and Canada during summer vacation, and for a month and a half, I was the happiest I could ever feel. I visited the big cities like New York, Los Angeles, Boston, etc., that were until then, and still are, objects of my admiration. It was the most wonderful thing in the world . . . the realization of my dreams . . . I felt I was "on top of the world."
>
> (Israeli Jewish girl)

Unlike the experiences with objects, the experiences with beauty— especially nature—are untainted by possessiveness or acquisitiveness. The happiness they evoke also seems to be deeper and more intense than the happiness triggered by things or travel. Each meaningful encounter with nature or the physical world around them further increases adolescents' ability to "see" what is in their field of vision, and to appreciate and enjoy what they see.

Just as many of the adolescents' joyful experiences with the self bring them into closer connection with others and the world, a joyful encounter with nature can bring adolescents into closer communion with themselves and with others.

Like nature, music was also a potent source of joy with the external world for some of the adolescents, although cited less often. Like the religious experience recounted above, this young American was lifted out of himself during a pipe organ recital:

> The time that most sticks out in my life that made me feel "good" about life and myself is the time I listened to my first pipe organ recital. My father and I had gone to our neighborhood church to listen to their organ. We walked into the church, sat down, and waited. I wondered what it would sound like. Would it be loud, soft, or just a regular tone? We waited and then he started with loud chords, and then my mind started to wander with the heavenly tones and great pedal sounds and pupil whisps. I thought about how lucky I was to be alive, well, and happy. I really felt good. That feeling stays with me and comes back to me sometimes when I feel low. But that was really the "first" time I realized how good life was.
>
> (American boy)

In experiences with the external world, adolescents make a sensuous connection to the physical aspects of the world—not with a materialistic or selfish possessiveness, but rather with a sense of keen emotional attachment to the meaning behind or within the episode. They transcend because they immerse themselves, even temporarily, in a "piece" of the outer world.

EXPERIENCES WITH OTHERS _____

Of the three ways of being in the world, the "with other" was the most frequently described source of happiness, cited by about half the adolescents. Experiences within this category also yielded the most intense happiness. Both frequency and intensity support the importance of the human bond in adolescent development, no less than at other stages of the life cycle. Experiences with others that brought happiness were also variegated, encompassing warm and meaningful encounters with parents and relatives, close friends and age mates, and even strangers. They include being trusted by one's parents or profiting from their guidance:

> The best experience I ever had was when I was given my first hunting rifle from my parents. It let me know they trusted me enough to own a machine capable of killing. I received more pleasure knowing they believed in me and trusted me than I did owning the gun.
>
> (American boy)

> Once I did something wrong that was pretty bad and my parents found out. I thought I was dead, and my Dad said he wanted to see me so I went in there, and he started talking to me. He didn't yell, he didn't hit me, he just reasoned with me and talked with me until I knew I did something wrong. After it happened, I was kind of glad he caught me because he helped straighten me out.
>
> (American boy)

The parental trust and paternal reasoning made these American boys feel valued and respected by the person whom they valued and respected. Being loved is similarly a source of great happiness for adolescents:

> Before my Bar Mitzvah party I felt—or rather, I didn't feel that I was loved, or that anyone really liked me. But after I got there, to the party, I felt so great, such a good feeling that I could have jumped and yelled for joy. I also found myself becoming more confident and a lot more open, and I got to know myself much better, until I felt really happy.
>
> (Israeli Jewish boy)

> On my birthday, I went for an afternoon walk with a friend. When I got back home, there was a full house of friends. All my family fell on me with kisses. And the rest sang Happy Birthday. My feeling was very good. I felt that I'm loved, and that they wanted to make me happy on my birthday. I got goose pimples all over, and I felt myself blushing and could hardly speak. I felt that life is wonderful, despite all the difficulties (with a boyfriend, lots of schoolwork, argument with girlfriends). I felt that all in all, life has a lot of meaning and that you have to take the positive from life and not to get upset about everything.
>
> (Israeli Jewish girl)

Whether the love comes from family or friends, it is a source of meaning and self-confidence and a springboard to greater self-knowledge and openness to the world. At such moments, adolescents might easily revert to self-absorption and bask in the confirmation of their self-importance. Yet, most of the adolescents who reported experiences with others went beyond the joy of receiving to the joy of giving. Some derived their greatest happiness from the sharing and mutual understanding of close friendship:

> The moment I found a friend that could understand me, and I was able to tell her everything that was happening in my life, and she would tell me about her life, I felt wonderful when I found her. The one who would understand me and I would understand her. Everything seems so good, so simple and easy, when you have someone beside you.
>
> (Israeli Jewish girl)

Others found it in their first sexual love. Giving and getting are one, being with another and being one's true self can come together, and the explosion of physical feeling reinforces the miracle of finding a soulmate:

> We fell in love like they say "at first sight." After a few dates, we held hands—a wonderful feeling. Later, he hugged me—it was an even more wonderful feeling. We enjoyed being together. After a few months, we started kissing, first on the cheek and later on the lips. That was the best feeling I've ever had in my whole life. I felt my heart would jump right out because I was so happy. And from so much happiness and joy, I started to cry. My boyfriend comforted me, and I blushed, and I wanted to do it again and again as much as possible.
>
> (Israeli Jewish girl)

Yet others found their greatest happiness in helping people where there is no obvious reciprocity. The happiness or well-being of the person they help is its own reward, as this Arab boy tells:

> When I can help people and do things for people. I like to see the happiness on people's faces. You're happy if other people are happy.
>
> (Israeli Arab boy)

For the following American, helping someone in need was so gratifying and the memory it left so positive that she didn't mention, or apparently even think about, the risks involved:

> One day I was in my yard and I saw a little boy in the street. Then I saw a car coming around the curve in the road so I ran out there and picked the kid up and got him out of the way. I don't know if I saved his life or not, but I felt good that I did something about it.
>
> (American girl)

In getting and giving, adolescents' lives are intertwined with those of other people. Some adolescents emphasize the joy of this interconnection as they recount the happiness they derive from being part of a community. Thus, a number of the young people in these studies located their happiest moments in visits to relatives or in reunions with them after long separations. This American boy tells of the pleasure of family dinners, with their sense of belonging, familiarity, and fondness:

> When my family get together to eat dinner, and I mean my brothers and sisters, I have one of my best times because we have so much fun. Everybody is feeling good, and we joke a lot as we eat. The atmosphere is light and happy. Sometimes I eat more than I want just so I can continue to be together. My brother and I are usually like cat and dog, always fighting, but at dinners like these (which are few and far between), we don't fight or if we do, it's a friendly fight. It is at times like these that I feel best about life, the world, and myself.
>
> (American boy)

Others find happiness in the warmth, fellow feeling, and sense of community that the encounter with age mates enables. The following accounts by a Jewish girl and an Arab girl are remarkably similar in this respect:

> I remember the pleasant experience I had during a long hike with my classmates. We walked, were together, and I felt real well-being. And I hoped this would go on for a long time. We joked, told stories, and really, as they say, "were enjoying life." We were good friends, close to each other. There were no quarrels, only laughter and pleasure. I felt that life could be wonderful.
>
> (Israeli Jewish girl)

The most impressive event for me was when we went to youth camp and spent 3 days and nights there. All us boys and girls were gay and happy. Preparing our food by ourselves, eating together, playing ball and other games. We enjoyed being together, spending our time with love and full of joy. I wished I could stay there for a whole month. Being with pupils, boys and girls from my school and others, and acting like siblings and even more. We all felt satisfaction in anything we did together.

(Israeli Arab girl)

Adolescents' sense of community can extend beyond their known world of family, friends, and neighbors to the larger society of the nation, as the Arab and Jewish boys quoted here testified:

On Land Day, when all the Arab villages went on strike, workers didn't work and all the young people were crowded in the streets, pupils refusing to go to their classes. At that time, our brothers in Lebanon were struggling for their land. On that day, coming back from school, I had a strange and special feeling. I was happy to see all the young people together as if they were one strong body nothing could separate but death. My joy was so strong, I never felt happier in all my life. I had such a wonderful feeling because I took part in the pupils' strike.

(Israeli Arab boy)

That day, I felt life was really wonderful. It was the morning when I heard that our hostages were released by our Army. That day, I visited my aunt, and my father called and told us the great message. I had such a hard feeling to describe. The knowledge that you have someone to rely on and someone to trust in our country, which is always surrounded by anger, made me feel so good, so safe, such a wonderful feeling.

(Israeli Jewish boy)

The above descriptions show that the experiences in which adolescents find happiness or joy need not stem from unusual, out of the ordinary events. For the most part, they are intertwined with the adolescents' daily lives. Listening to the adolescents' voices, one hears too that the most intense experiences of joy have a highly integrated quality in which each of the three ways of being enhances the other. For example, in the religious experience cited above, the American girl's connection with the beautiful mountain setting and her sense of connectedness with the other young people at the retreat come across strongly as part and parcel of her finding God. The young pianist's good feeling at the piano recital in memory of his late piano teacher encompasses the pride of playing well, of being one of his selected pupils, and of doing a good deed; the sense it brought him of the teacher's enduring presence; and the recovery of his lost enthusiasm for an activity that he loves. The American boy's joy at hearing his first pipe organ recital is certainly enhanced by the presence of his father, which he mentions.

The following account of the joy of an early morning by an Israeli girl brings together her deep pleasure in being in the world with a strong sense of connection to her self and her home and pet:

One experience that gives me a very good feeling is when I sometimes get up very early and go outside by myself before anyone else is up. This gives me a very good feeling about being alive. I feel like I have the whole world and I can do what I want with the day and live it all for what it brings. I am alone but I feel far from lonely. Usually my dog is roaming around, and a few people might be up or going to work. But when I go out early, just myself, I can really look and breathe and hear. It makes me feel very good and alive. That life is worth all you can give it and the moments like these can be remembered forever.

(Israeli Jewish girl)

The experience of happiness can give adolescents a mature sense of proportion, as it did for the girl (p. 22) whose joy in learning she was loved taught her to take the positive from life and not to get upset about every- thing. Far from opening up a narcissistic floodgate, as Maslow's detractors have averred, the pursuit of happiness can take adolescents, so typically absorbed in themselves, out of themselves:

My worries were suddenly unimportant and everything seemed to be in a different proportion. . . . School was not terrible. The trees were blooming and the birds were chirping.

(Israeli Jewish boy)

7

The Universality and Specificity of Adolescent Happiness

Different men seek after happiness in different ways and by different means, and so make for themselves different modes of life and forms of government.

Aristotle, *Politics* (fourth century B.C.)

A recurrent question in studies of happiness is how universal is it. That is, how much do people in different cultures, of different genders, and with different life situations and personalities resemble or diverge from one another in how happy they feel and in what makes them happy? Applied to adolescents, these questions relate to the broader issue of how universal the course of adolescent development is and, conversely, to what extent and in what ways it is affected by the local context in which it occurs.

Studies of happiness in adults from different cultures yield rather complex and not always consistent pictures. The fundamental assumption is that culture affects the formation of the self and hence the way that individuals feel, think, and behave (e.g., Chang, 1996; Triandis, 1989). The general consensus among investigators likewise seems to be that national differences exist in levels of happiness (Diener, Suh, Smith, & Shao, 1995; Inglehart, 1990; Veenhoven, 1995). Diener and Diener (1995) go so far as to show that different factors predict subjective well-being in traditional and modern cultures, and they suggest that these predictors of happiness in different cultures have not been adequately studied. On the other hand, Chang (1996) found a more complicated pattern in his comparative study of Asian Americans and white Americans: The former are more pessimistic than the latter, but not less optimistic. At the other end of the spectrum, Csikszentmihalyi (1990) claims that the flow experience, which he sees as the ultimate expression of happiness, is universal in people of all cultures, including adolescents, but he has not examined this claim empirically. Conversely, Allen Ivey (Ivey, Ivey, & Simek-Morgan, 1993) has stressed that the individual's unique ethnic background and cultural and historical forces impinge on his or her worldview, resulting in very different belief systems and ways of organizing and constructing experiences.

It is evident that these various findings are not unequivocal. However, with one exception, they were obtained in adult populations and do not pertain to the young people who concern us here.

Anthropological and cross-cultural studies of adolescence (e.g., Coleman & Hendry, 1990; Offer et al., 1988) have attempted to discover the degree to which adolescent development is universal or, conversely, is influenced by the unique conditions of different cultures. Some studies found that adolescents in modern Western societies differ from those in traditional ones in their identity acquisition and self-concept, attitudes toward parents and family, and social desirability responses, as well as in their peer cultures and sex role identification (Adams, 1973; Gibson-Cline, 1996; Havinghurst, 1965).

INQUIRIES ACROSS THREE CULTURES: AMERICAN CHRISTIANS, ISRAELI JEWS, AND ISRAELI ARABS

Universality of happiness was explored in a comparison of American Christian, Israeli Jewish, and Israeli Arab youths, all of them 14 to 16 years old. The American adolescents were drawn from urban and rural areas in northern Florida, representing modern Western culture. Israeli Arabs and Israeli Jews represented two distinct cultures; the Arabs, about 15% of the Israeli population at that time, maintained their separate identity through distinct residential environments, language, child-rearing practices, and schooling. However, Israeli Arabs may no longer represent the pure traditional Arabic culture, which might still be found in Arabic countries. If American adolescents represent modern Western culture and Israeli Arab adolescents traditional Eastern culture, Israeli Jewish youngsters represent a blend of traditional Eastern and modern Western cultures because Israel is an immigrant society; its Jewish population is divided fairly equally between those whose parents or grandparents hail from Europe or the United States and live a fairly westernized lifestyle and those whose families came from Asia or North Africa and have retained many elements of the traditional cultures of those countries.

Arab and Jewish adolescents in Israel too have been found to differ in numerous ways. Arab high school students, for example, showed higher vocational aspirations than their Jewish counterparts, a less structured personality makeup, and fewer intrapsychic conflicts (Giora, Esformes, & Barak, 1972). In a large-scale study of Israeli Arab Moslems, Arab Christians, Druse, and Jews of different ethnic origins, perceptions of family dynamics have been shown to differ, where Israeli Arab Moslem youngsters reported the lowest level of family adaptability and Israeli Jewish youngsters of Western background showed the lowest sense of family cohesion (Florian, Mikulincer, & Weller, 1993). Similarly, among Arab youths, the extent to which they felt closeness with their parents was related to the number of rules restricting their conduct, whereas among their Jewish counterparts, no such relationship between closeness and excessiveness of rules was found (Mikulincer, Weller, & Florian, 1993).

These variables, related to the traditionality and communal orientation of the Arab family unit, assuredly affect the adolescent's identity development. In addition, the Israeli cultural differences (modernity for the Jewish population and traditionality or transition into modernity for the Arab population) and sociopolitical differences (being a dominating majority versus being a dominated minority) have been traced in terms of their effect on adolescents' orientation toward the future, including career, family, and collective issues (Mar'i, 1982; Seginer, 1988). Thus, cultural differences were also found in adolescents' development of ego identity; Arab youths were found to be higher than their Jewish peers on commitment and purposefulness, solidity, continuity, and genuineness, but they were lower on social recognition, physical identity, and meaningfulness-alienation (Tzuriel, 1992).

In light of these known cultural differences, we sought to explore both the specificity and the universality of adolescents' positive experiences in the three cultures (Magen, 1983a, 1985). In particular, we wished to determine whether, beyond the differences that could be expected, there were also commonalities in the adolescents' positive experiences.

In fact, the findings demonstrated commonalties over and above cultural differences. Differences were found in both the intensity and content of the positive experiences, but several more relevant points of similarity were evident. The majority of adolescents in all three groups recounted positive experiences in one of the upper two levels of intensity—inspiring and transforming (12% at Level 4) or meaningful and joyful (43% at Level 3)—whereas fewer recounted merely pleasurable and satisfying (38% at Level 2) or barely positive (7% at Level 1) experiences.

On the other hand, Israeli Arabs recounted somewhat less intense positive experiences than the American and Jewish adolescents (mean intensity 2.40, 2.68, and 2.76, respectively), $F(2, 1087) = 18.74, p < .001$. It is difficult to know the extent to which these differences reflect cultural or social factors. There might be cultural differences in the acceptability of feeling and expressing positive emotions, such as have been found, for example, between the United States and Pacific Rim countries (Diener et al., 1995). It has been maintained that people in collectivist cultures generally report lower subjective well-being than people in individualistic ones. The cross-cultural differences between Israeli Arabs and Jews have similarly been interpreted in terms of differing degrees of collectivist-communal versus individualist-contractual cultural orientation in Israeli society (Weller, Florian, & Mikulincer, 1995).

Alternatively, the happiness of the Arab youths might be dampened by their living as a minority in Israel, where they feel discriminated against, and/or by their relatively lower standard of living as measured by indicators such as income and housing. Perhaps these Arabs living within the state of Israel were negatively affected by historical-political factors, like their Palestinian Arab counterparts living on the West Bank

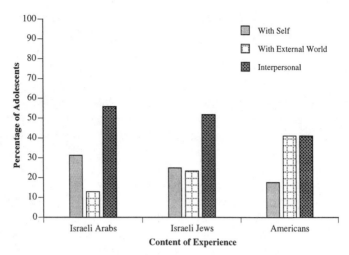

Figure 7.1. The frequency distribution of the three positive experience categories in each of the cultures ($N = 1,094$).

and in refugee camps in Lebanon (Punamaki, 1988). The study of Palestinian children's coping has suggested the powerful impact of traumatic ethnic conflict on children's psychological development. Veenhoven (1995) observed that standard of living correlates with people's life satisfaction, and Verkuyten (1989) found the same for minority status in Holland. Both these objective links to happiness have, however, been disputed (Myers, 1993).

Cross-cultural commonalities were, in any event, impressively predominant. In all three cultures, the rank intensity of the three experiential domains was similar. In all three, interpersonal experiences were the most intense ($M = 2.71$, $SD = 0.74$ for the total sample), experiences with the self were less intense ($M = 2.61$, $SD = 0.84$), and experiences with the external world were the least intense ($M = 2.44$, $SD = 0.73$). This ranking held true in all three cultures.

In addition, experiences with others were the most frequently recorded source of happiness for both the Israeli groups, cited in about half the accounts (see Figure 7.1). Among the Americans, the frequency of the interpersonal experience was virtually identical to that of experiences with the external world.

As can be seen, the cultural groups differed in the relative frequency of the other two areas of experience contributing to their happiness—

with external world and with self, χ^2 (4) = 81.09, p < .001. The American adolescents stood out. Compared to Arabs and Jews, a higher proportion of American youth found their happiest moment in experiences with the external world, whereas experiences with the self were substantially less frequent than among the other adolescents. This content distribution may reflect the powerful image of wide open spaces in American mythology, the yearning for nature in the most urban and technological of the three cultures, the relative grandeur and distance of America's natural setting when compared to Israel's, or the greater consumerism and relative lack of introspection of American culture.

The Arab youths were at the other end of the spectrum. Only a small proportion of them described positive experiences with the external world, whereas a comparatively large percentage described positive experiences with the self. These data may reflect the lesser importance of material possessions in their culture. It might also reflect cultural expectations that children, especially girls, stay close to home and under their family's protection.

The Israeli Jews were in the middle, although somewhat closer to the Arabs than to the Americans. It seems that the more traditional the culture, the more its adolescents find happiness in interpersonal experiences and experiences with the self, and the less in experiences with the external world. The wide applicability of any such conclusion would have to be checked, however, by looking at the sources of joy of youths in yet other cultures, both traditional and modern.

THE INTERPERSONAL EXPERIENCE WITHIN CULTURES

Another perspective for examining the similarities and differences in adolescent happiness across cultures is to look at certain specifics in their descriptions. A cursory overview of our examples indicates many resemblances in the descriptions from the different cultures. Passing a difficult test, excelling in a competitive activity, the warmth of a class trip, playing the piano, working at a job, bringing a gift to a family member, visiting relatives, feeling loved or appreciated—these and other experiences were cited as happy or joyous by adolescents from more than one of the cultures. True, no Arab adolescents described joyful moments

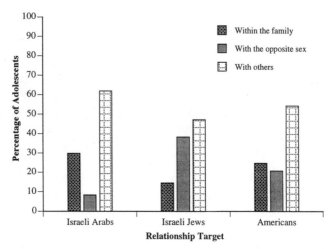

Figure 7.2. Relationship targets of interpersonal experiences in the three cultures (*N* = 1,094).

with music, no American described the thrill of a school trip, and the only religious experiences that were related came from Americans. Yet, the numerous overlappings are striking.

The one partial exception I found was in the interpersonal experience category. In reading and rereading the descriptions, I was struck by what looked like certain distinct cultural characteristics in these experiences that I did not find so much in the other two categories. Because the interpersonal experience was also the most widespread source of happiness, I decided to carry out a more methodical content analysis and comparison.

The interpersonal experience could be analyzed along two dimensions: with whom it occurred, the *target*; and the *nature of the encounter.*

Interpersonal Targets

Three main targets of interpersonal experience were found: family members, members of the opposite sex, and "others," who included classmates, friends, acquaintances, and people met incidentally. As can be seen in Figure 7.2, whereas "others" was the most frequently reported target in all three groups, the groups differed sharply in their reports of the other two targets, $\chi^2(4) = 47.24, p < .001$. The Jewish adolescents were the most prone to find happiness in an experience with the opposite sex and the least prone to find it in an experience with their families. The Arab youths, in contrast, reported the lowest percentage of experiences with the opposite sex—proportionally less than a quarter of the number of such experiences reported by their Jewish counterparts, and less than a third of those reported by the Americans—and the highest percentage of experiences with their families. The American adolescents were closer to the Arab youths in the frequency of their positive experiences with family and closer to the Jewish youths in the frequency of their positive experiences with the opposite sex.

These distributions suggest that, although relationships with others provide the greatest source of happiness for adolescents in all three cultures, they are also the experiences that are most affected by cultural norms. This is consistent with Triandis's (1989) finding that social behavior differs in traditional and modern societies. We may see in the differing frequencies the relative acceptance of emerging adolescent sexuality in Israeli Jewish culture and the great emphasis that the Israeli educational system places on peer relations and peer modeling, on the one hand, and the strong prohibition of contact between the sexes that is still a strong tenet of Arab cultural values, on the other. The devotion to family among Israeli Arab adolescents has been described in the literature, where their closer dependence on and concern for their family of origin and other relatives have been highlighted, in comparison to those of their Jewish counterparts (Seginer, 1988).

Further insight is gained if we look more closely at the adolescents' descriptions. Those Americans who described experiences with family members tended to tell of intimate exchanges with their parents and siblings: of their parents' trust, their father's guidance; of warm gatherings, such as at meals, when the nuclear family is together; and of enjoyable summer visits to aunts and uncles. The Arab youths tended to tell of more intense experiences with the extended family. There is nothing in either of the other two cultures quite like this Arab boy's joy in his reunion with a long absent uncle:

One day some friends came over to tell me that my uncle from Jordan came. First, I didn't believe it, but then they swore to it, and I ran home and saw my uncle kissing all the members of the family. I fell on him and kissed him. I was thrilled and happy because we hadn't seen him in 17 years. I felt such a good feeling, and I hoped for more visits. I hope that every year, some relative will come to us, and our families will be united.

(Israeli Arab boy)

The Jewish adolescents who described happiness in their families tended to focus on special occasions, such as a family picnic or bar mitzvah:

The most beautiful experience I ever had was my brother's bar mitzvah, where we danced and went wild, were happy, ate and drank, and the entire evening was really beautiful and also enjoyable, and I would have wanted it to go on for more than one day. And when my brother gave his torah reading, then a huge chill passed through me. I was all excited, because this prayer named my grandfather and grandmother and my mother's late mother. I was very moved when he said the prayer.

(Israeli Jewish girl)

The experiences with the opposite sex are tinged with sweetness, gentleness, and excitement. They can be nearly platonic, with the physical feelings well-submerged or kept in check:

This was when I loved a boy and he loved me. I had a wonderful feeling, I was light-hearted, happy, and everything was rosy. I forgot all my problems and sorrows. Everything seemed so good and ideal to me.

(Israeli Jewish girl)

The few Arab adolescents who told of happiness in encounters with the opposite sex (only 3 of the 400 sampled) all told of love without physical expression. This description by an Arab girl of her happiest moment gives a good idea of why:

An experience that caused me to feel that life can be wonderful was last year. I realized that our neighbor's son (he's my age) kept looking at me from their house. I decided never to look back, so I wouldn't feel ashamed. But is he in love? Would our parents permit it? I'm very careful to hide the secret. I know and am aware that we're still young, but this is the most wonderful and happiest experience in my life.

(Israeli Arab girl)

Some of the descriptions by Israeli Jewish and American youngsters tell of the first tentative and almost disguised touch. Yet, in more than a few of the Israeli and American descriptions, the sexual feeling is conveyed in its full power, and the adolescent's joy rises out of his or her first connection on both the physical and emotional planes:

My first love was when I was 14. I had a girlfriend my age. One evening we walked, embraced on the seashore, and suddenly I felt such a wonderful feeling of inspiration, a stream of love, if it can be called that. We were sitting on a bench and I felt a very strong feeling I wanted to express in some way. I didn't want to embrace her with force as it would hurt her. I didn't know what to do with myself. I felt like hitting the bench to let out my emotions, which were "like boiling water," "like boiling milk." Finally, I touched her face and talked to her, trying to put into words some of my feelings, I can hardly remember what. It was very exciting. I could barely find a way to express all the feelings and emotions I felt.

(Israeli Jewish boy)

When I was going with a girl by the name of Karen, we were in love and had a lot of fun together. I loved her very much. I went with her for 2 years, and we really loved each other very much. One time, we were swimming at the lake, and she went under water and pulled my feet out from under me. We started kissing, and we lay there in each other's arms. I told her how much I loved her, and she told me how much she loved me. That was the best experience I ever had. I felt how wonderful is life. I have never been in love since then. I still love her very much.

(American boy)

No such physical encounters were described by any of the Arab youths. The feelings of love for a girl related by this Arab boy are nonetheless intense as any:

It happened one day. I got ready to go to school and wanted to pack my school bag. A girl passed our house. And she looked at me. She looked at me as though I were an angel in paradise. I looked at her, and stopped still, and I wondered and marveled. That's how we met—she and me, me and her. There was a wedding in the village, and she was there. I looked at her for many minutes. When the wedding was over and everyone went home, I stood next to the wall on the street and waited. Suddenly, one of her relatives, a friend of mine, came and stood at my side. We started to talk. She passed near us, stopped, and called my friend, and asked my name and who I am. I

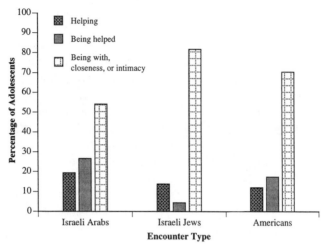

Figure 7.3. Type of interpersonal encounters in the three cultures (N = 1,094).

trembled all over and could hardly stand on my two feet. I used my brain, since otherwise I would have fallen to the floor. I couldn't stand it any longer and went home. That's how I knew that it was the most wonderful and happiest day of my life.

(Israeli Arab boy)

Nature of Interpersonal Encounter

There was an analogous pattern of similarities and differences in the nature of the interpersonal encounter that led to the adolescents' happiness from culture to culture. The adolescent's joy could stem from helping, being helped, or being close to or with any of the three relationship targets (see Figure 7.3).

In all three cultures, relationships marked by closeness, intimacy, or being with were the most likely to yield happiness, although they were cited more often by the Jewish and American youths than by the Arab adolescents, possibly because this category includes encounters with the opposite sex, χ^2 (4) = 37.90, $p < .01$. Being with people who care about them and for whom they care makes adolescents feel good, as revealed by this American youngster:

I don't really know what to say about this, but the only thing I can think of is that when I can get together with my friends and have a good time. . . . It really makes me feel good. I think life is wonderful. Because you have people who surround you and who love you and you just feel good about it.

(American girl)

The joy in relationships marked by closeness or being with was exemplified earlier by the numerous descriptions in the previous chapter, including the Jewish girl's finding a friend, the Arab and Jewish girls' school trips, and the piano recital that gave an American boy an enduring sense of his deceased teacher's presence.

Yet, though the highest proportion of adolescents in all three cultures described relationships characterized by closeness or being with as their happiest moments, the groups differed considerably in the frequency with which they cited both helping and being helped. Here, too, the Jewish and Arab youths were the furthest apart, with about half the Arab adolescents but only a fifth or so of the Jewish ones describing encounters of helping or being helped.

The major difference seems to stem from the reluctance of the Jewish youths to receive help, or their discomfort when they do get it. In both the Arab and American samples, a somewhat larger number of youths enjoyed being helped more than helping. The differential pattern may reflect the importance of mutual support in traditional Arab culture, on the one hand, and the view of needing help as a sign of weakness in Israeli Jewish culture, on the other. This possibility is very much borne out by the fact that three times as many Jewish youths found joy in helping as in being helped.

At an individual level, there are youths in all three cultures who nonetheless derive their greatest joy from reaching out and helping others with their problems:

The experience that gave me a very good outlook on life and made it seem worthwhile was when I was able to help a friend through some emotional difficulties he was having. Knowing that I had helped someone in trouble gave me a great feeling that is still with me today.

(American boy)

One of my best experiences was probably the day that our youth movement went on a field trip. Four of us were sent to deliver meals to elderly people who couldn't fix their own. The old people were so grateful and sweet to us and it made me feel really good. I guess because I helped someone and it was like a good deed.

(Israeli Jewish girl)

Once when I was sitting and reading important books, my dearest friend came over, crying, her face red. It hurt me to see her like that, and I sat with her and she told me a secret I would never have guessed. I was very sorry and started to cry, because I remembered the words of my dear mother, who was keeping me from continuing my high school studies, and I really like to study. Afterward, I took my friend to her house and I told her mother her secret. And we were able to solve her problem quickly and easily. We were so happy, and our hearts started to beat fast and tears of joy fell. I think that was the greatest and most joyous event that I have had, because my problem and my dearest friend's problem were solved.

(Israeli Arab girl)

Needless to say, the nature of the help given may reflect the culture of the helper. It seems less likely that an American or Israeli Jewish adolescent would have found occasion to help a friend overcome her mother's opposition to continuing high school. The following example, in which an Arab girl tells of the joy of being able to help her family by doing routine household chores similarly highlights the cultural context:

When I was 12, my 17-year-old sister got engaged. I used to sit and study or read at home and didn't do the things that most girls my age did—I mean helping my mother with the chores. After my sister finished twelfth grade, she married, and so the house was filled with joy and happiness. Her wedding day was a very joyous day for me. First of all, because of my sister's good fortune and her joy in life, and second, because I started to take on responsibility and to help in the house. I am very happy when I am working energetically helping my family, and I also learn willingly and take on responsibility even while I am still young (15).

(Israeli Arab girl)

It is difficult to imagine a girl from a modern society so happy to be able to help her mother with the housework. This girl's joy in helping her family—as opposed to a friend or stranger—is once again suggestive of the interdependence of family members in traditional Arab society and of the socialization of children to promote their family's welfare.

There are also youths in the three cultures who see in the help they get from others expressions of warmth and caring that make them happy. I cite Jewish and Arab examples:

> The experiences which affect me most are connected with encouraging words and comments that I get from my parents and teachers. I can recall one when my teacher asked me over to show me my final grades, and while talking, he gave me good advice to study and encouraged me a lot. This was very encouraging and till this day I love life and school.
>
> (Israeli Arab boy)

> I fell on the stairs and was badly hurt. On this day, I felt that everyone really loves me and cares for me. I was very pleased. It assured me that all the people around me chose to stay with me because of love and not because they had to.
>
> (Israeli Jewish girl)

The political conflict is also reflected in the account of the following Arab boy's encounter, where the Israeli enemy reinforces the pleasure of group solidarity and provides the opportunity for adolescent daring and bravado:

> On March 30, Land Day, we gathered together and the soldiers came with ammunition. We got up immediately and burnt tires in the middle of the road and resisted the soldiers and threw stones at them. They started to throw smoke bombs and tear gas. Suddenly, one of these fell in our midst, and half my clothes were scorched. But I wasn't deterred, and I stayed in the front line and kept throwing stones. But another tear gas bomb fell nearby, and my clothes and my skin were singed, but I didn't pay attention and kept resisting until we succeeded in getting the soldiers out of our village. This was a wonderful experience.
>
> (Israeli Arab boy)

In sum, it seems that, besides the cross-cultural differences in the adolescents' positive experiences, there were also commonalities. The analyses showed variations in the intensity of the happiness of the three groups, in the propensity of adolescents of the different cultures to find happiness in experiences with the world or experiences with the self, and in the particular nature of the experiences with others that brought them happiness. On the other hand, we found that the majority of the adolescents of all three cultures found happiness in experiences with others and that, in all three groups, such happiness was the most intense, whereas the happiness stemming from experiences with the world was the least intense.

The salience of the interpersonal experience is consistent with the widespread professional emphasis on the importance of interpersonal relations in human development (Buber, 1961). Although this study did not investigate the high-functioning individual per se, the finding that meaningful experiences with others contribute so much to making adolescents feel good about themselves and the world seems to go along with Adler's (1917) conviction that social interest (*Gemeinschaftsgefuhl*) is the major factor in the development of the healthy personality, that people who have such social interest will cope in the most appropriate and desirable way with the tasks of life, and that these individuals will know how to both give and take. It also seems to be consistent with Kubovy's (1977) demonstration that positive interpersonal experiences with teachers play a crucial role in the attitudes, behaviors, and academic achievement of school children as well as with Fuerst's (1967) report that most turning-point experiences are experienced in relation to others.

8

Gender, Personality, and Disability: Patterns in Achieving Happiness Across Cultures

The great end of all human industry is the attainment of happiness.
For this were arts invented, sciences cultivated, laws ordained, and
societies modeled. Even the lonely savage, who lies exposed to the
inclemency of the elements and the fury of wild beasts, forgets not,
for a moment, this grand object of his being.

David Hume, *The Stoic* (1742)

This chapter will take another look at our research in order to
address the universality issue across culture, gender, personality,
and life situation, including an examination of adolescents with hearing
impairments, considered as a distinct culture.

GENDER AND CULTURE

Research studies on the differential capacity of males and females to
achieve happiness have produced mixed results. Myers and Diener

(1995) cited a number of studies showing that males and females express similar levels of life satisfaction but that females—who exhibit more intense sadness than do males—may also have a slightly greater capacity for joy. Tolor (1978), however, found no significant difference in the scores of his male and female participants on a joy of life scale, whereas Verkuyten (1986, 1989) found that Dutch women and female Dutch adolescents scored lower for both hedonic affect and life satisfaction than their male counterparts. Offer et al.'s (1988) cross-cultural research found that, among adolescents, boys reported a greater degree of happiness than did girls. Males have also been found to emphasize active, physical, instrumental, and immediate qualities, whereas females emphasize symbolic and interpersonal features (Kamptner, 1991).

Analyzing our own cross-cultural data from American Christian and Israel Jewish and Arab adolescents (Magen, 1983a), it appears that, although both the intensity and source of the youngsters' positive experiences are affected by their cultural origin, the pattern of gender differences is fairly consistent across cultures. The happiness of girls and boys was found to differ in both its intensity and content. In all three cultures, girls clearly showed more intense positive experiences than boys. The effect of gender was significant: Females: $M = 2.31$, Males: $M = 2.01$, $F(1, 1087) = 17.71$, $p < .001$, but the gender/culture interaction was not. American girls described the most intense positive experiences, Arab boys the least.

In addition, as can be seen in Figure 8.1, in all three cultures, a higher proportion of girls than boys found their greatest happiness in encounters with others, whereas a higher proportion of boys than girls found their greatest happiness in an experience with the external world; Arabs: $\chi^2(2) = 9.65, p < .001$; Jews: $\chi^2(2) = 1.85, p > .05$; Americans: $\chi^2(2) = 27.75, p < .001$. Although in the Israeli Jewish sample, differences did not reach statistical significance, the trend was similar.

This difference is consistent with earlier findings to the effect that girls tend to be more interested and involved in interpersonal and family matters than boys (Eagly & Crowley, 1986); with findings that girls and boys differ in social orientation (Carlson, 1965); with Kamptner's (1991) findings that girls focus more on the interpersonal whereas boys focus on the instrumental; and with an earlier study by myself (Magen, 1972) that showed that American and Jewish Israeli girls described their most positive experiences as being with others, whereas the boys in those cultures described them as being with the external world.

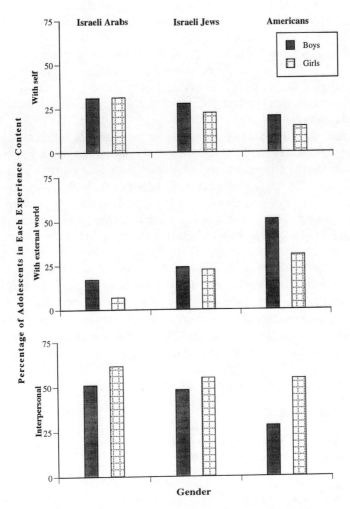

Figure 8.1. Frequency of male and female respondents by nature of the positive experience within each culture (*N* = 1,094).

In some matters, gender differences were apparently linked to cultural ones. Arab girls reported a relative scarcity of positive experiences with the external world, not only in comparison with Arab boys, but also in comparison with the girls in the other two cultures. This may reflect the restrictions Arab culture still places on girls' freedom and exposure. Along somewhat different lines, a particularly small percentage of American boys cited an experience with others as their source of joy whereas a particularly large percentage cited an experience with the external world. This may say something about differential sociocultural influences on males in the United States regarding the role of interpersonal relations in their lives and the importance of nature and material possessions.

There were also variations in the pattern of gender differences from culture to culture. Of the three groups, the Jewish girls and boys were the most similar to one another in how they found their happiness in the world, as well as in the intensity of their happy moments. The greatest gender differences, surprisingly, were found among the Americans, despite the greater emphasis in American legislation and recent culture on gender equality. The expectation that the greatest gender differences would be found in the Arab group, where gender roles are still the clearest, was not borne out. Perhaps, American adolescents, as they test out new roles and behaviors and define self-identity, are reacting against political, academic, and media efforts to blur gender differences. Thus, they may adhere more closely to almost traditional gender roles, at least in their private worlds, than do their contemporaries in conservative but less pressured and sexually frightening milieux. We may conjecture that a culture that does not raise the flag of equality and even "sameness" between the sexes evokes less of a counterreaction.

PERSONAL CHARACTERISTICS
AND POSITIVE EXPERIENCES

The supposition of humanist psychologists that joyous experiences mark the high-functioning personality or otherwise elevated human being begs the question: What kind of people tend to have such experiences? What, if any, personality traits do they share that distinguish them from people who report less intense positive experiences?

Other questions that may link positive experience and personality also suggest themselves at this point in the discussion. Is the way of being in the world in which a particular adolescent finds his or her most joyous moment random and incidental, or is it connected with aspects of his or her personality? Or, to put it another way: Can adolescents who, for example, find their greatest joy in being with others be expected to have different personality traits from those who find theirs in an experience with the self or with the external world? And will those latter two groups, in turn, differ from one another?

Both these sets of questions relate to yet a third, the question of cultural variability. Will adolescents with similar personality traits find their happiness in the same way of being in the world regardless of the variations in their cultures? Such questions really boil down to the issue of how intrinsic the most positive moment an adolescent experiences is to his or her personality; that is, to what extent, if any, do the intensity and content of the most positive experience stem from and reflect something in the personality makeup of the adolescent who reports it?

Researchers studying peak experiences have sought to relate both their content and intensity to measurable personality traits (Cottle, Pleck, & Kakar, 1968; Ebersole, 1972; M. Landsman, 1995; Margoshes & Litt, 1966; McClain & Andrews, 1969; Paffard, 1970). So have researchers studying happiness (e.g., Costa & McCrae, 1980; Emmons & Diener, 1985; Pavot, Diener, & Fujita, 1990). Tolor (1978) investigated some attitudinal and temperamental correlates. As already noted, however, none of the studies were carried out on adolescents, and few explored the issue across cultures.

Our present study explored the personality correlates of the intensity and content domain of adolescents' positive experiences in the three cultures by using the HSPQ described in Chapter 5 (Magen, 1985).

Intensity of Positive Experience and Personality Traits

A multiple regression (see Table 8.1), in which culture was controlled, was conducted to determine the relationship between the intensity of the positive experience and the 14 personality factors—or, to put it simply, to see what personality features were related to the reports of highly positive experiences.

In all three cultures, the more intense the positive experience, the more the person who reported it tended to be humble and accommodating (E), tender-minded and sensitive (I), resourceful and self-sufficient (Q_2), conscientious and morally aware (G), and scholastically intelligent (B).

Table 8.1 Regression Models Testing Effects of Personality Factors on Intensity of Positive Experience, Controlling for Cultural Factors ($N = 1,094$)

Indpendent Variable	High Meaning	Low Meaning	Simple r	Partial Beta Coefficient	R^2
Culture	(as a two-vector dummy)		.18	−.206**	.032
Culture			.14	.043	.035
HSPQ E	Dominant	Obedient, submissive	−.15	−.131**	.067
HSPQ B	Bright	Dull	.16	−.139**	.089
HSPQ I	Tender-minded	Tough-minded	.14	.110**	.098
HSPQ G	Moralistic	Expedient	.05	.095**	.103
HSPQ C	Stable	Easily upset	.10	.072	.106
HSPQ F	Enthusiastic	Sober, serious	.04	.054	.108
HSPQ Q_2	Self-sufficient	Socially, group dependent	−.03	.067*	.111
HSPQ H	Adventurous	Shy, timid	.03	.051	.113
HSPQ Q_4	Tense	Relaxed	.04	.036	.114
HSPQ J	Reflective	Zestful	−.03	−.029	.115
HSPQ O	Insecure	Self-assured	.01	−.033	.115
HSPQ D	Impatient	Deliberate	.03	.025	.116
HSPQ A	Warm-hearted	Reserved	.03	−.020	.116
HSPQ Q_3	Controlled	Uncontrolled	−.04	−.012	.116

SOURCE: Magen (1985). Copyright © 1985 by the American Psychological Association. Reprinted by permission.
NOTE: HSPQ = High School Personality Questionnaire. Overall $F = 8.8$, $p < .001$, $R^2 = .116$.
*$p < .05$. **$p < .01$.

The prominence of intelligence, which taps verbal ability, might raise the suspicion that the intensity perceived by the raters stemmed from the teenager's descriptive powers rather than from the remembered experience itself. The large size of the sample and the fact that intensity was treated as a continuous measure made it possible to control for intelligence in the multiple regression analysis. Even after this was done, the other four personality factors remained operative as highly differentiating traits.

The personality test used in this study was not designed to determine whether or not those who took it were high-functioning people. The traits of those who reported intense positive experiences do nonetheless seem to point to the image of the high-functioning person advanced by humanist psychologists. The humility and sensitivity of the young people who related more intense positive experiences suggest a greater harmony with the world and openness to experience than that shown by their more aggressive and tough-minded peers, whose positive experiences are less intense. In their conscientiousness and moral awareness, they seem to have a certain moral consciousness. Their resourcefulness and self-sufficiency (as opposed to group dependence on the other end of the continuum) may likewise point to the autonomy and independent thinking of the high-functioning person.

The association between intense positive experiencing and distinct personality traits bolsters findings by M. Landsman (1995) on individuals who can be identified as "beautiful and noble persons." According to his findings, these individuals, like those in our high-intensity group, described rich and intense positive experiences and, moreover, were differentiated from their peers who were not so identified by numerous personal features, including their sociability, love for their parents and peers, and high level of subjective well-being.

Personality and Ways of Being in the World

A discriminant analysis (see Table 8.2) was conducted to examine the relationship between the three content categories of the positive experiences and these personality factors—again, simply to see what personality pattern was related to the report of each domain of positive experience.

The three ways of being in the world in which the adolescents located their best moments were each associated with somewhat different personality traits.

Adolescents whose happiest remembered moment was anchored in an experience with the self (see y_2) tended to be more intelligent scholastically (B) and more self-disciplined (Q_3) than the other two groups, as well as more impatient (D) and more reflective (J) than those who found their happiness with others, and calmer (C) than those who found it in an experience with the external world. Although, surprisingly, these youngsters were not uniquely resourceful and self-sufficient, their

Table 8.2   Standardized Coefficients of the Two Functions of Discriminant
Analysis Among the Three Content Categories of Experience

| | Personality Factor | | | |
Letter	High meaning	Low meaning	First Function: y_1	Second Function: y_2
A	Warm-hearted	Reserved	−.21	−.11
B	More intelligent	Less intelligent	−.17	.39
C	Calm	Easily Upset	−.07	.49
D	Impatient	Deliberate	.20	.42
E	Aggressive	Humble	.40	.09
F	Enthusiastic	Sober	−.05	−.24
G	Moralistic	Expedient	−.18	.17
H	Adventurous	Timid	.12	−.18
I	Sensitive	Tough-minded	−.35	−.16
J	Reflective	Zestful	.25	.38
O	Insecure	Self-assured	−.29	.09
Q_2	Resourceful	Group dependent	−.06	−.00
Q_3	Self-disciplined	Lax	−.42	.31
Q_4	Tense	Relaxed	−.19	.26

NOTE: Loads exceeding .3 are italicized.

traits suggest that they are individuals with considerable capacity to perform effectively. These findings lend support to those of Privette and Landsman (1983) and Puttick (1964) that well-being and high-level performance are associated with self-awareness.

Teenagers who found their happiness in an interpersonal experience (see y_1) tended to be more humble (E) and sensitive (I), more warm-hearted (A), more deliberate (D), and more zestful (J) than those in the other two groups, as well as more self-disciplined (Q_3) than those who reported their best experience with the external world. The latter, who reported their best moment in an experience of admiring nature and beauty, as well as those who gained great joy from materialistic pleasures, tended to be more tough-minded and realistic (I) and more assertive (E) than the others, and less scholastically intelligent (B). Inductively, those who located their positive experiences with others and those who located them in the external world tended to be at opposite ends of the continuum in three personality factors that were characteristic to them (E, I, and Q_3): The humility, sensitivity, and self-discipline of the former contrasts sharply with the latter's assertiveness, tough-mindedness, and laxity (in the sense of following their own urges and being careless of social rules).

These findings suggest that the contents of the remembered positive experiences are not random but rather indicate the adolescent's overall orientation to the world. As we noted in an earlier chapter, the most intense experiences generally included more than one way of being in the world, but here we see that, as dominant content categories, each was associated to a significant degree with rather different, and in general, mutually exclusive personality traits. Moreover, the personality traits associated with each of the three ways of being in the world were much the same whether the adolescent was an Israeli Arab, an Israeli Jew, or an American Christian.

The assumption of the humanist psychologists that positive experiences affect personality development leads to the proposition that the behavior patterns reinforced by positive experiences become entrenched as personality traits. Conversely, however, adolescents may have their most positive memories in the personality domain in which they already feel most competent—or least incompetent. Intuitively, the two propositions should not be mutually exclusive, and personality and positive experiences may each help shape the other.

This study did not address the issue of causality. Our only access to the adolescents' memories was via their reporting, as elicited by a given question at a given time under given circumstances. The selection and quality of a memory and the mode of its reporting may be affected by a wide range of factors. The relevance of the present findings is thus confined to the contributory effect of certain personality traits on the participant's report.

In the previous chapter, we saw that culture played a role in both the intensity and domain of the positive experiences that the adolescents reported. In concrete terms, the findings showed that a random Israeli Arab teenager, for example, was not only more likely to report a positive experience with others or with the self, and less likely to report one with the external world, than a teenager from either of the other two groups, but also more likely to have an experience of less intensity than an age peer from another culture whose happiness was anchored in the same way of being in the world.

Throughout our studies, we found that both culture and personality play a role in the content and intensity of teenagers' positive experience. Yet, our findings suggest that personality is, finally, the much stronger determinant, representing the more forceful part of the equation. The implications are naturally very significant, because it suggests strong shared modes of experience across cultural lines, between boys and girls of different and often conflicting backgrounds. That being the case, it raises hopeful possibilities about the capacity of people to share harmoniously in the bounty of being human despite those conflicts. In concrete terms, a teenager from an Arab village in the Galilee was likely to be closer in personality to a teenager from Tel Aviv or Florida who reported a best moment in a similar domain and/or with similar intensity, than to a teenager from his or her own village who found happiness in an experience in a different domain and felt it with a different intensity. Our findings about shared qualities among high-functioning individuals from diverse cultures should evoke the awareness of politicians, educators, and even young people chancing upon one another in the street.

LISTENING FOR HAPPINESS: THE CULTURE
OF HEARING-IMPAIRED ADOLESCENTS _____

Objective conditions have been widely investigated in connection with happiness, especially from a cross-cultural perspective, yielding ambiguous results. Research has often indicated that life circumstances seem to exert only a modicum of influence on one's global sense of well-being. Even the onset of disability has been shown to have only a temporary emotional impact on well-being. Following a period of adaptation, the person with disabilities usually reports a near-normal level of general life satisfaction (Diener, 1994). Veenhoven (1991), who criticized the methodology of these research studies on people with spinal cord injuries, congenital physical malformations, and so on nonetheless stressed the importance of the relatively small differences in happiness between people with handicaps and the control groups. These ambiguous findings seem to imply the need for further research on disabilities and the capacity for achieving happiness in different subcultures.

Educators, researchers, and linguists working with people who have hearing impairments are increasingly likely to regard them as a cultural minority group rather than as individuals with an audiological disability (Parasnis, 1996). *Deaf culture* has long been a term used to describe the group experience of this community, but recently, the sociocultural depiction has become more refined. Hearing-impaired people have more often been considered recently to belong to a *bicultural minority* group, whose experiences frequently overlap with the experiences of the hearing majority culture, but at other times may best resemble the hearing-impaired minority culture. A view of the hearing-impaired child as a bicultural-bilingual minority child shifts the focus of research away from examining deficits and toward examining differences. A deeper understanding of the unique life experiences of hearing-impaired people must thus take into account not only the linguistic but also the cultural diversity of their experience.

Deaf culture has been defined as a way of life that is transmitted through social interactions and the language of the deaf community (Parasnis, 1996). The hearing and hearing-impaired cultures differ in terms of their socialization processes, language, interactions, semantics, world of associations, and a range of other aspects, even the physical distance and use of physical touch sensed as comfortable during communication (Weisel, 1995).

As much as adolescence is universally acknowledged as a critical developmental period where one questions and assesses values, aspirations, relationships, and responsibility (Conger & Petersen, 1984; Erikson, 1968; Waterman, 1982), this same period for hearing-impaired youngsters may be especially tense and stressful, presenting formidable challenges to self-realization and social maturity (Bullis & Reiman, 1989; Feinstein & Lytle, 1987; Vernon & Andrews, 1990). The centrality of the adolescent developmental stage for hearing-impaired persons has been emphasized by the disproportionately high percentage of adolescent behavior problems and emotional disturbances described among this population (Kusche, Garfield, & Greenberg, 1983; Meadow & Trybus, 1979).

Whereas hearing-impaired students studying in special educational settings with hearing-impaired peers demonstrated positive feelings about their social experience at school (Mertens, 1989), much research has shown that adolescents with hearing impairments who are mainstreamed into the regular school system often report social isolation, peer rejection, loneliness, and little opportunity for friendships with their hearing peers (Holcomb, 1996). These difficulties in social integration and peer acceptance stem from the need for more verbal, casual, and spontaneous interactions with hearing youngsters outside the classroom environment (Foster, 1988).

Despite their greater need for support and closeness compared to their hearing peers, hearing-impaired adolescents often face a more pronounced isolation, which, in turn, impedes social and emotional maturity (Mertens, 1989). Yet, they must provide for themselves and others, work at important positions, develop independence, and cope with normal life stresses—all with a deficiency that can impede, thwart, slow down, and sometimes nearly eliminate the opportunity to find happiness and self-fulfillment.

Although most of our studies were conducted with normally hearing adolescent populations, it was determined that a similar study should be conducted to investigate the nature and intensity of the positive experiences of hearing-impaired adolescents in order to help design interventions to overcome inherent developmental impediments for this population as well (Magen, 1990a). (Life aspirations and the tendency among these adolescents for transpersonal commitments were also investigated. These findings will be discussed separately in Chapter 9.)

Attention was directed at recapturing and creating instances of joy and fulfillment, rather than moments of fear and trauma, in order to achieve a better understanding of those factors that have enriched and empowered the lives of hearing-impaired adolescents. The main research question asked was: Would reported positive experiences of hearing-impaired adolescents differ from those reported by hearing adolescents in content and intensity? (The other research questions, revolving around correlations between the positive experiences and the desire for transpersonal commitment, will be discussed in the next two chapters.)

Forty-two hearing-impaired (HI) and 79 hearing eighth-, ninth-, and tenth-graders in urban and rural Israeli Jewish junior high schools of similar socioeconomic level participated in this study. Of the HI adolescents, 15 students had severe hearing loss (above 90 dB) and studied in special schools, and 27 had less severe hearing loss and were mainstreamed into regular schools. Fifty percent of the 42 HI students used sign language as their only means of communication. No differences were found between groups of hearing-impaired adolescents compared according to degree of hearing loss, type of educational setting, or use of sign language. The frequency distribution of Landsman's (1969) three content categories (with self, with external world, interpersonal) among both samples revealed that the most frequently reported experience for both hearing and HI adolescents was still the interpersonal experience. Interestingly, despite this low level of significant difference between the two groups as to content of experience, a higher frequency of interpersonal experience was found among the HI (66.7%) than the hearing (45.3%) youngsters. The joy and excitement gleaned from encounters with other human beings was unmistakably evident in the HI teenagers' responses to our questionnaire, regardless of the linguistic difficulties they may have demonstrated in trying to convey these experiences:

> I feeling very happy, I was went to the club all day, I went to the club, and I saw a handsome boy and I know him and I met him and to get to know him. I wanted to be his girlfriend. I was so happy that he said to me today meet and go for a walk if you want. I answered yes I do. And he takes me and I was awfully excited. My face was red.

Among the group of HI adolescents, no significant differences were found in the frequency of the positive interpersonal experiences they reported having with other HI young people, as compared to experiences shared with hearing peers. One adolescent described her joyous experiences with a range of other people in her mainstreamed elementary school:

> I went to B. School from third grade till sixth grade. I had a wonderful experience because I had a teacher who taught us for 5 years. . . . My class and I sometimes called her by mistake: Mom. I had hearing friends . . . really cute and rowdy and fun for me to be with. I had one cute little blond boy. He liked me from fourth grade to sixth and I liked him too. It was fun because he was hearing and I hard of hearing and that the big difference between us. Till now . . . I remember him about the past and I'll remember my whole life and never forget him. . . . That was a wonderful experience the best for me.

Although the rank order of the three category frequencies was similar in both groups, there was a paucity of experiences with self in the HI sample. The following excerpt is one from two rare illustrations of HI teenage girls:

> This year I had an experience. On Purim I got dressed up as an artist and it was my idea. There was a costume ball at school and they picked me and I won the prize, an interesting book. The next day was the Purim holiday, and they invited all the [neighborhood] residents to the square . . . for a costume parade. . . . I ran to the stage and pushed my way between all the people . . . the judges gave me a note that I was going up to Phase B. I was so excited and happy in my heart . . . When it was my turn my heart raced. The host said the cute artist whose name is L. in front of everybody. I enjoyed it so much. And then came the prizes and I won fourth prize. . . . Everyone was happy and I felt such an experience. . . . I was so excited and I sang "Wonder of Wonder, Miracles of Miracles," what a wonderful day of surprises.

Experiences of HI youngsters with the external world resembled those of hearing youngsters in content matter. For example, one HI youngster depicted the experience of scuba diving:

> A good experience that happens to me last time, a day the summer vacation and my father borrowed the scuba gear about from my cousin—oxygen tank, for a short while, I dived with it into the water—the Mediterranean. I spent a few long minutes under the water and the bubbles raised up to the sky—and I felt it was the first time I stayed under water for a long time, and I looked up my father and brother swam above me to protect me from danger and this simple experience made me have a pleasant wet feeling around me and I looked at a group of tailed fish swimming lazily in the water and some other stationary objects resting on the bottom. I felt it was fun to see the underwater world like I walked the first time on the bottom.

A very frequent motif exhibited by the HI youngsters consisted of travel, often where the remembered positive event was related to experiences with the external world, as in the following example where a teenage girl portrayed her experience abroad:

> The most wonderful experience I ever had in my life was a trip overseas. And what my eyes saw was a different wonderful world, different from here in Israel, and I felt pure and clean and dreamy and blinded by the beauty of another land that was a green

expanse of grass full of the scent of spring. The fragrance makes me excited and chills went down my body, and I felt like running and skipping and rolling on the green grass. And then I saw the clean beautiful houses with their red roofs and walls as white as milk. And it warmed my heart and I thought the people who live here must enjoy it and don't want to leave this place. . . . I felt I was in a different world that was rosy and good, in short I had a good feeling that is hard to describe.

In sum, the findings of this study revealed positive experiences reported by HI adolescents that were similar in intensity to those of hearing adolescents. These adolescents, notwithstanding their disability, were apparently able to recall moments full of meaning and happiness, moments when they felt that the world was good and life wonderful. In spite of the linguistic deficits that commonly pervaded their descriptions of experiences, the HI group managed to convey to the raters their feelings of joy and happiness, enabling almost total interrater agreement.

Intensity and frequency of interpersonal experiences were highest for the HI group in the current study, as was the case for the nonimpaired. Young people with severe obstacles to free communication thus cannot be assumed to prefer solitary experiences over those involving encounters with others. Quite to the contrary, the results indicated that positive experiences with self were very rare among HI adolescents (7.1%).

Although the sense of "being alone with oneself" may actually prevail among HI adolescents because it is a condition thrust upon them by their disability, it is not a situation that necessarily forms a basis for happiness and satisfaction. Instead, adolescents will elect to counter and offset this imposition by reaching more deeply into their natural social selves. Intuitively, perhaps, they sense and gradually bring into their lives those experiences with other human beings that create and culminate in highly intense happy and meaningful experiences. For HI people, such experiences involve moments of contact and communication with individuals—encounters of love and trust with others. The quality of the interconnections established by those with hearing impairments deserves further inquiry. In a current study, for example, I am conducting a comparative investigation of HI children whose parents are or are not hearing impaired themselves.

These results strongly underscore the need to develop sociocultural models to amplify our understanding of this minority group. Recently, tremendous interest has been expressed in empowering the HI community through recognition and respect for its language and culture, as well as our understanding of issues and experiences these people have within the context of cultural and linguistic diversity (Parasnis, 1996). I hope our findings may contribute to such efforts to enhance the self-identity and group identity of this community's members and to further develop the sensitivity of parents, educators, and professionals.

9

Commitment as a Concomitant of the Search Beyond Self

A man of humanity is one who, in seeking to establish himself, finds a foothold for others and who desiring attainment for himself, helps others to attain.

Confucius (sixth century B.C.)

Our assessment of young people's life aspirations was purposeful; we were looking for evidence of their desire for commitment beyond themselves. But our studies attempted no intervention of any kind; the purpose was to see if research participants would reveal in their life aspirations a wish to give of themselves to others—when not asked directly. Our development of the nondirective, open-ended LAQ sought to offer an unobstructed framework for adolescents' free, unguided, and sincere responses about their life goals and dreams.

The research progressed through several phases, at times paralleling our study of happiness and at times pursuing a separate course. The investigation of the phenomenon of commitment beyond self in adolescence developed during our process of research. It was a new issue, but one that could be neatly related to our previous studies of how adolescents experience happiness, including use of the LAQ, which measures responses along a four-level scale from extremely selfish to extremely other-directed (see Chapter 3).

Phase A: In our initial explorations, we posed the question: What proportion of teenage youngsters, in the throes of adolescent self-questioning, will express a tendency for commitment transcending selfish personal needs? We first investigated the extent to which a substantial group of adolescents ages 14 to 16 (from our large cross-cultural sample of Israeli Jews, Israeli Arabs, and Americans) verbally expressed their willingness to dedicate themselves to others or to goals and purposes in society at large. We anticipated genuine responses from these adolescents in all three cultures, as they were not asked to disclose their identities and were unaware of the research aim; that is, the question posed to them alluded to their life aspirations, not explicitly referring to their capacity for commitment beyond self.

These evaluations were based on adolescents' responses to the LAQ rather than on any activities they may or may not have undertaken in reality. We were nonetheless able to assume that an expressed commitment to a cause, even when still unrealized, is an important element in a person's identity formation and a first step toward actual involvement. Commitment makes action possible (Jourard, 1971b) even if there are goals that the human being approaches but never practically attains. "It is certainly best to make these goals conscious even though they cannot be attained because this consciousness gives direction to the motivational vectors" (Maslow, 1963, p. 130).

Phase B: Despite our assumptions about the efficacy of stated intentions, there were still concerns about our methodology, and whether the written responses to this probe did in fact indicate the youngsters' true readiness for transpersonal commitment. Did the verbal response to our questionnaire genuinely reflect a willingness to become involved, or was it only granting lip service to prosocial goals that the individual knew he or she should strive toward but really had no true interest in pursuing? It would not be surprising to obtain a correlation between an intent to help and actual prosocial behavior, but previous research has not always been conclusive (Ajzen & Fishbein, 1977; Eisenberg, Fabes, et al., 1989). To determine how closely stated prosocial intentions and wishes were linked with an actual commitment to the welfare of others, we continued our investigation by comparing statements and declarations between adolescents who had and who had not *actually* been involved in prosocial endeavors. In this way, the validity of the LAQ scale was demonstrated. This and subsequent explorations did indeed reveal a significant relationship between word and deed, as we will show. In addition, seeking connections between prosocial life aspirations and personality attributes was consistently our goal as we compared volunteers and nonvolunteers in this phase and, later, as we differentiated between beginning and experienced volunteers.

Phase C: We found earlier that the person actually involved in activities aimed toward helping others or furthering external causes expresses a stronger willingness for transpersonal commitment on the written test instrument in comparison to other individuals who are not actively involved. The challenge also arose of determining whether the written responses reflected a predisposition in these youngsters to actually pursue such activities in reality. In other words, do these connections between activity and verbal expression stem from the actual volunteer involvement, where the adolescent is exposed to the experience of contributing to others and of being involved in prosocial causes, thus fostering his or her ability to express prosocial desires? Or is there such a phenomenon as a predisposition toward prosocial behavior, as evidenced by higher levels of related personal attributes even before youngsters participate?

For answers, we devised a study contrasting three groups of adolescents: students who were not involved in prosocial activity, students who had been involved in such endeavors for a whole year, and students who had merely committed themselves to the prospect of volunteering but had not yet begun their activity. This methodology allowed us to look at the possibility of both predisposition toward prosocial action among some adolescents and the idea that actual involvement in prosocial activity itself stimulated change in the young person.

Phase D: The prior research as well as other studies were conducted in disadvantaged neighborhoods. Against a backdrop of impoverishment, we sought to assess just how potent and universal the willingness to transcend could be, despite conditions normally thought to discourage any possible interest in self-fulfillment via service to others.

Phase E: We next examined whether social and political changes over time affect adolescents' readiness to contribute of themselves to communal causes or the personal welfare of others. To achieve this objective, after striking social and political developments in Israel and the Middle East region, we approached Israeli Jewish and Arab adolescents again in 1988, 8 years after our initial cross-cultural exploration.

Phase F: In the final phase of commitment research to be reported in this volume, we spotlighted adolescents with hearing impairments. Our aim was to probe the phenomenon of commitment in young people who can be distinguished as a cultural minority, with specific interpersonal implications stemming from their deficit.

The following descriptions give a fuller view of each of these six phases.

PHASE A: CROSS-CULTURAL EXAMINATION OF AMERICANS AND ISRAELI ARABS AND JEWS _____

Seeking to establish the specificity and universality of social commitment, our cross-cultural study comparing Israeli Jews, Israeli Moslem-Arabs, and Christian Americans used the LAQ instrument to investigate the presence and degree of adolescents' verbal expression of their commitment beyond self (Magen, 1983a, 1983b). Our findings revealed that the breakdown of LAQ responses among the four levels of commitment appeared to be similar in all three cultures. Of the 1,094 total, 13% fully reached the highest apex of commitment beyond self registered by our study, and a further 20% of the total sample included in their life aspirations wishes that were not self-focused but rather expressed some desire to contribute to the welfare of others. On the other hand, over one third (36%) of the adolescents across cultures expressed merely

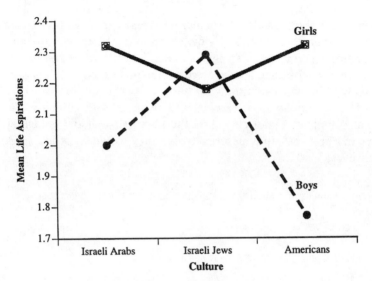

Figure 9.1. Means of male and female adolescents' responses to the Life Aspirations Questionnaire in three cultures (*N* = 1,094).

hedonistic and selfish aspirations for their lives. Almost another third (31% of the total sample) strove only for selfish goals, albeit ones that included some reference to other people or causes.

Although the culture effect was not significant in the results—using a 2 × 3 analysis of variance, $F(2, 1087) = 1.85, p > .05$—a significant gender effect was obtained, $F(1, 1087) = 23.25, p < .001$. It was found that females overall expressed a higher desire for commitment than did males (see Figure 9.1). However, the Israeli Jewish sample demonstrated a different pattern of gender differences in contrast to the other two cultural groups. The gender-culture interaction was significant: $F(2, 1087) = 5.17, p < .001$. The Israeli Jewish males expressed a stronger disposition to give of themselves than did their female peers.

American and Arab females' stronger desire for commitment beyond self, compared to males, substantiated gender-role expectations in our society that girls and women are more oriented toward nurturing and responsibility and show more interpersonal behaviors and expressive tendencies (Bosworth, 1995; Eagly & Crowley, 1986; Feiring, 1996; Kolaric & Galambos, 1995; Urberg, 1995). However, the reversed pattern in the Jewish Israeli sample by no means undermines our conclusions about gender, particularly because it is so readily explicable. Young Israeli Jews, particularly males, are brought up with the ideal of defending a country that struggles to defend its borders and to protect its people; Jewish men are expected to donate years of military service, forfeiting personal aspirations for the good of the nation.

The sociopolitical dimension underlying gender variations in the Israeli sample is supported by how the 14- to 16-year-old Israeli Jewish boys in our 1980 study described what they would most like to do in their lives:

To get drafted into the army and contribute as much as I can to this country.

To save lives.

To contribute to my family and my country.

I hope that our nation will be united, the whole Jewish nation. And that all the religious and nonreligious will live side by side. I hope for international peace and brotherhood between all of the countries in the world, for cooperation and mutual acceptance among them. Because only in this way will life be good.

The relationship between personality characteristics and life aspirations beyond cultural differences was also analyzed. The 14 personality factors of Cattell and Cattell's (1975) HSPQ were submitted to a multiple regression analysis in order to investigate the effect of each factor within the entire system (Magen, 1983b). Culture was computed as a dummy variable, and cultural differences were controlled by forcing it into the equation. As shown in Table 9.1, the entire system was found to be significant ($p < .001$), yet, it nonetheless emerged that cultural differences did not affect life aspirations scores. By contrast, personality factors were found to exert significant effects on the life aspirations score, accounting for 7.7% of the variance. Although the explained variance was relatively small, the findings suggested a relationship between a desire for commitment beyond self as expressed in life aspirations and several personality characteristics (see Table 9.1). These included sensitivity and tender-mindedness (I); lack of dominance and aggression or competitiveness (−E); and high intelligence (B). The low proportion of the explained variance, although significant, does not allow for any further generalizable conclusions.

Table 9.1 Regression Models Testing Effects of Personality Factors on Life Aspirations, Controlling for Cultural Factors ($N = 1,094$)

Independent Variable	*Personality Factors*		Simple r	Partial Beta Coefficient	R^2
	High Meaning	*Low Meaning*			
Culture	(as a two-vector dummy)		.05	−.360	.002
Culture			.01	−.020	.003
HSPQ I	Tender-minded	Tough-minded	−.19	.112**	.042
HSPQ E	Dominant	Obedient, humble	−.19	.126**	.056
HSPQ B	Bright	Dull	.09	.074*	.061
HSPQ Q_4	Tense	Relaxed	−.04	−.054	.065
HSPQ G	Moralistic	Expedient	.11	.055	.067
HSPQ C	Stable	Easily upset	−.03	−.072	.069
HSPQ D	Impatient	Deliberate	−.07	−.043	.072
HSPQ Q_3	Controlled	Uncontrolled	.07	.039	.073
HSPQ A	Warm-hearted	Reserved	.09	.048	.074
HSPQ H	Adventurous	Shy, timid	−.02	−.043	.075
HSPQ J	Reflective	Zestful	−.05	−.023	.076
HSPQ F	Enthusiastic	Sober, serious	−.05	−.017	.076
HSPQ Q_2	Self-sufficient	Socially dependent	−.05	.012	.077
HSPQ O	Insecure	Self-assured	−.02	−.004	.077

NOTE: HSPQ = High School Personality Questionnaire. Overall $F = 5.5$, $p < .001$, $R^2 = .077$.
*$p < .05$. **$p < .01$.

The self-centered aspirations in response to the open-ended question for the total sample in the cross-cultural study reflect a strong need for material security, with fame and fortune as part of the winnings. Such aspirations usually signal the acquisition of something concrete and measurable. The following excerpts typify the selfish responses (Level 1) offered by about 36% of the cross-cultural sample:

To travel abroad and stop school.

(Israeli Arab boy)

To go gamble in a casino. I think I've found a system for roulette and then I could make a ton of money and hang out all day.

(American boy)

I want to have a really healthy inheritance fall in my lap from somewhere. Then I could do all of the things I've wanted to do—buy a Ferrari, a fancy house, and all that. Afterward, a little trip around the world.

(Israeli Jewish girl)

The common trend among adolescents who expressed only Level 1 aspirations for their lives centers around a fantasy of absolute freedom from obligation or work of any kind; a life of utter leisure and repose; or of new excitements stimulated by travel or by eminent success and celebrity. No mention of other human existence is made; no allusion is made to a sense of caring for others. The life aspirations among an additional 31% of the adolescents from the three cultures retained a substantial degree of self-centeredness. Yet, these youngsters did begin to evidence some burgeoning capacity for interpersonal relationships along with life goals that encompass some socially meaningful pursuits (Level 2):

Finish school and get me a good job and a nice car and be wealthy and have a roommate, maybe two or three roommates, party every night and keep cool. Get married when I'm about 24 or 25, wait about a year, and then have a kid and wait about two more years and have another kid. And be rich all my life.

(American girl)

Get married, have children, get a good job and live in a good neighborhood and live next to my best friend.

(Israeli Arab boy)

First of all, to have a family with five kids, to live in a small house with my husband (like in all dreams). I want to be a lawyer or psychologist, but to make an effort that my work will not disturb family life. Most important is not to have a routine life, to try and enjoy life to the end, just to take everything easy and to live.

(Israeli Jewish girl)

Several interesting components filter through these responses, especially the focus on long-lasting wealth, an ideal mate, an enviable professional career, and a happy, undisturbed family life, which would eliminate worries and concerns. Although these adolescents recognize the importance of being involved with others, their need for such involvement only rises to the level of how much benefit they can derive.

By contrast, life aspirations in which commitment beyond self was present (Level 3—20% and Level 4—13%) were revealed in these following selections from the cross-cultural study. Many of them dealt with giant global concerns, reflecting the poignant and innocently stated dreams of the young in the face of inexplicable and frustrating realities:

> In my lifetime, I would like to save many lives, stop all wars. Stop the pain and suffering of all life. Cure all disease and let there be peace on earth.
>
> (American boy)

> The best thing I would like to do in my life is to help someone in a way that he would be happy as a result and I'll feel good and happy when watching his happiness.
>
> (Israeli Jewish boy)

These examples typify an abstract wishing without consideration of the logistics necessary for realizing these dreams. To "cure all disease" and to "let there be peace on earth," as the American adolescent vowed in his aspirations, are goals that have eluded the human race for centuries. Yet, even in order to pursue more realistic global aspirations, the means must be methodically guided and pursued throughout adolescence into adulthood and must be surrounded by generally successful role models and outcomes.

Many adolescent respondents did suggest specific routes that would lead them to achieve a happiness not unlike their more self-centered contemporaries. Yet their responses suggested a fulfillment found along avenues devoted to greater causes:

> One of my greatest aspirations in life is to come to know many people in different countries and various ways of life. I mean to do some investigations on that. Because when human beings do recognize others' wishes, desires, they start to understand each other, and this is one of the foundations for peace among nations in the world.
>
> (Israeli Jewish boy)

> My aspiration in life is to be an oceanographer, to organize a research team that aims to find new sources for food that are deep in the ocean. In my opinion, finding new sources for food supplement is a crucial problem for mankind in the whole world and especially in poor countries.
>
> (American boy)

Be a truck driver and be able to haul fruits, vegetables, meat to all parts of the country. That's one way I will know people will get food and clothing and other needs.

(American boy)

The aspiration of the American boy above is particularly interesting, as it contrasts with the statements of adolescents who aspire to obtain an interesting or prestigious job with the purpose of affording a richer lifestyle and security for one's own family. A truck driver fulfills a humble but imperative role in the functioning of society and the disbursement of human essentials, without which even those self-absorbed respondents would be at a loss. At the same time, some adolescents' professional aspirations expressed commitment beyond self:

I hope to be a lawyer in order to defend innocent people, because many times innocent people go to jail for nothing, as I can see on TV.

(Israeli Arab girl)

The best thing I would like to do is to be a journalist. As I am an Arab girl, I wish to give expression to opinions of my people in every aspect, and so I would be able to express my own ideas and I like this job.

(Israeli Arab girl)

My life aspiration is to study medicine. I pray to Allah to help me to realize my wish. I would like to help sick people and especially babies.

(Israeli Arab boy)

I would like to become a nurse and be stationed in a foreign country and help with disease and other things people need help with. It's true people in the United States need help, but there are more people in other countries that need help more than the Americans, and I am going to try my best to become a nurse.

(American girl)

As has been noted earlier (pp. 73-74), the experiences need not all be positive, but rather responses to even sorrowful experiences can also offer a reliable context in which adolescents hone their perceptions and increase their sensitivities to deeper issues and feelings. One such respondent was the teenager with leukemia who was told after a series of operations that he would never walk again, and who drew from his experience of illness to discover purpose in his life:

I know the emotional and physical strain people go through, and I would really like to help people like me because I can walk again. After 4 years in a wheelchair, I know what it's like. I just got out of a wheelchair. . . . I would like to explain how I was saved to people who aren't yet saved or never will be.

(American boy)

Our cross-cultural research uncovered many of the ingredients that, merged together, embody these young people's expectations, aspirations, even dreams. We discovered that, beyond the cultural differences between these three distinctive groups, universal patterns emerged in their expressions of a desire to become involved in prosocial enterprises. Yet, these impressive cross-cultural findings reflected only adolescents' verbal expressions, accentuating the need to validate the LAQ responses via actual behavior.

PHASE B: WHEN ACTIONS SPEAK LOUDER THAN WORDS

As described in Chapter 5, to assess the overall validity of the LAQ, it was felt important to determine how much *action* would follow the verbally expressed *desire* to commit, that is, word versus deed to implement prosocial commitment. Sometimes people's tendency to thematize experience or reason about important events and feelings takes center stage (i.e., according to Piaget, 1972); at other times, people's willful actions, strivings, or conations are the focus of interest (Santrock, 1993). *Conation* has been defined as a capacity for striving, for spirit in performance or action (Violato & Travis, 1995).

The limitation of the previous study—using a commitment index based on verbal statements rather than actual behavioral data— prompted a validation of the LAQ instrument through the study of 260 Israeli Jewish adolescents who had or had not actually been involved in at least 1 year of volunteer activity (hereafter referred to as *involved* and *noninvolved* groups) (Magen & Aharoni, 1991). The involved group consisted of 134 students (42 males and 92 females) who were involved at the time of the research in activities that contribute to the welfare of others according to our criteria. The involved students were eligible if they were volunteers in youth movements (e.g., the B'nai B'rith Youth to Youth program, neighborhood Scouts clubs) or in other programs, such as holding Big Brother/Big Sister positions, working with the handicapped or elderly, and so on. Students involved in school-supervised programs (e.g., psychology and education) were not included in the study. The noninvolved control group consisted of 126 students (66 males and 60 females) studying in parallel classes in the same schools as the involved group and who were matched on age, socioeconomic, and academic achievement criteria.

A two-way analysis of variance (ANOVA) was performed to examine the differences in level of prosocial commitment expressed by involved and noninvolved male and female adolescents, with involvement and gender as the independent variables and level of commitment beyond self as the dependent variable. A higher level of commitment was demonstrated among the involved than the noninvolved adolescent groups: Involved, $M = 2.60$, Noninvolved, $M = 1.84$; $F(1, 256) = 57.14$, $p < .001$. A significant main effect was also found for gender: Males, $M = 2.12$, Females, $M = 2.32$; $F(1, 256) = 5.60$, $p < .05$. Eta square revealed that involvement accounted for 19% of the variance, whereas the gender variable explained only 1% of the variance. The interaction between involvement and gender was not significant, demonstrating similar patterns of commitment among both genders.

Thus, the involved group of adolescents was found to score significantly higher on the LAQ than did their noninvolved peers, establishing the validity of the youngsters' verbally expressed responses to the open-ended questionnaire. Students who were actually involved in prosocial activity revealed less egocentric life aspirations and a greater desire to contribute of themselves to others and to society, rather than to gratify their immediate personal needs. The link discovered between actual helping behavior and a higher level of verbalized life aspirations thus served to further validate the LAQ measure and to highlight the relationship between word and deed in adolescents' prosocial commitment. Youngsters who were already involved in a stable helping relationship, whether through a community service program targeting the poor or elderly or through a volunteer job with neighborhood children or in a local hospital, had a stronger ability to vocalize their willingness to commit themselves to others beyond selfish needs or gains.

PHASE C: INACTIVE AND ACTIVE
VOLUNTEERISM VERSUS CONTROLS _____

A later phase of study focused on identifying those sources that would account for the emergence of these consistent connections between actual prosocial involvement and an expressed desire to commit oneself to causes beyond self. Some of our questions were designed to show if these connections stemmed from the actual volunteer activity whereby the adolescent is exposed to the experience of contributing to others and of being involved in prosocial causes, or if those teenagers who sought out volunteer activities were somehow predisposed toward prosocial behavior. Such a predisposition would be evidenced by higher levels of specific personal attributes among those who decided to become active volunteers, even before actual participation.

We (Magen et al., 1992) compared 137 Israeli Jewish adolescents ages 14 to 16 divided into three groups: (a) 57 *experienced volunteers,* who had actively participated in continuous volunteer activities for at least a 12- to 14-month period; (b) 38 *beginning volunteers,* who had volunteered to participate and had registered in volunteer settings but had not yet begun their activities; and (c) 42 *noninvolved* youth, who reported no past or current involvement or plans for future volunteer activities. This study employed a cross-sectional design, in which the three groups were tested simultaneously in order to control for possible effects of external events. The three groups were compared on relevant demographic variables, and no significant differences were found between the three groups regarding: adolescents' level of academic achievement, socioeconomic status, country of origin, parental occupation and educational level, number of siblings, or rank birth order.

However, significant differences were found between the groups regarding gender. As described earlier, the gender role differences depicted in the literature indicate that girls and women in our society show a stronger orientation toward nurturing and responsibility and exhibit more interpersonal behaviors and expressive tendencies (Bosworth, 1995; Eagly & Crowley, 1986; Feiring, 1996; Kolaric & Galambos, 1995; Urberg, 1995). In line with these gender expectations, the percentages of females among the experienced volunteers, beginning volunteers, and noninvolved were 77.2%, 67.3%, and 28.6%, respectively.

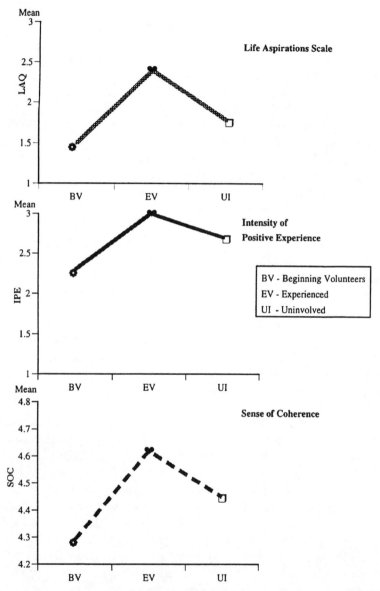

Figure 9.2. Comparison of the three adolescent groups on life aspirations (LAQ), intensity of positive experience (IPE), and sense of coherence (SOC) ($N = 137$).

SOURCE: Magen (1996). Reprinted with kind permission from Kluwer Academic Publishers.

Based on these distributions, the effect of the gender variable was controlled in further analyses comparing the three groups on the dependent variables.

We found that adolescents who had been involved in prosocial activity for a year or more tended to express a higher yearning for a commitment to humankind. As can be seen in Figure 9.2, they obtained higher scores than their two nonvolunteer peer groups on the LAQ measure. The ANOVA results indicated a stronger verbal expression of the desire to contribute to others, $F(2, 130) = 7.37, p < .001$. Several young volunteers explained the "best thing they would like to do with their lives":

> To contribute to others. Lots of things in this country bother me, like traffic accidents and the treatment of the elderly, but the solution is not to run away but rather to try and change things.

> To help people who are needy, who have financial and social problems, and so on.

> To help people understand the human mind, with the goal of helping them with their problems and giving advice to guide them.

> The thing I'd most like to do is to help someone so that he will be happy because of that, and I'll feel good and happy when I see him happy

A similar intergroup pattern emerged from the ANOVA conducted for the intensity of these adolescents' reported positive experiences (see Figure 9.2); experienced volunteers clearly demonstrated the ability to more fully experience moments of gladness and exuberance, $F(2, 130) = 5.32, p < .01$. Our study investigated an additional variable: the sense of coherence (SOC), which denotes a sense of comprehensibility, manageability, and meaningfulness in one's inner self and external environment. As can be seen in the figure, the adolescents who had experienced a full year of helping those less fortunate revealed (using ANOVA) a more enduring, dynamic confidence that both their inner world and their outer environment were comprehensible, manageable, and meaningful in comparison to the other two groups, $F(2, 130) = 2.77, p < .05$.

The fact that beginning volunteers did not exceed the noninvolved on the measures studied does not substantiate the view that adolescents predisposed to becoming involved in activities for the sake of others would be differentiated from their peers. Quite to the contrary, actual involvement over some period of time, rather than stated intent or even a genuine intention to get involved, appeared to be the crucial variable. Interestingly, young people who had only registered for volunteer activities had lower coherence scores and experience intensity than did completely noninvolved adolescents. It's possible that, as they anticipated the volunteer activity, those youngsters who merely registered were undergoing a period of self-questioning, insecurity, and lack of clarity regarding their true needs, values, and motives.

These findings thus highlight the critical importance of doing, not merely saying. It appears that, beyond personality variables that affect prosocial commitment, young people's actual continuous involvement in such activities generates a multifaceted impact. Being able to provide significant help to others in need fostered the adolescents' sense of personal identity, meaning in life, coherence, and a personal ability to experience life with more confidence and joy.

PHASE D: THE CULTURE OF POVERTY—
FURTHER OBSERVATIONS ON VOLUNTEERISM _____

The Magen et al. (1992) study was conducted with disadvantaged adolescents who had been found in previous research to score very low on intensity of positive experiences as well as on verbally expressed prosocial commitment (Yahel & Ilovich, 1985). Severe apathy, group discontent, resignation to their present situation, a sense of alienation from social norms, and a tendency to complete less schooling reflect their risk of maladaptive socioemotional and academic development (Alterman, Carmon, & Hill, 1982; Blass, 1982; Danziger & Danziger, 1995; Felner et al., 1995; Frankenstein, 1979; Olson, Roese, Meen, & Robertson, 1995; Yaar-Yuchtman, 1983). Youngsters growing up in an environment of socioeconomic hardship reveal a poor sense of self-esteem, evidencing a lower perceived academic and social self-competence even when they are gifted academically (Van-Tassel-Baska, Olszewski-Kubilius, & Kulieke, 1994).

In light of the low scores found among disadvantaged youth on the three measures studied (commitment beyond self as well as positive experiences and sense of coherence), and in view of the body of empirical findings linking volunteer activity with healthy personal attributes among adolescents from established neighborhoods, we investigated whether involved adolescents from impoverished Jewish neighborhoods in Israel would also score higher than their noninvolved counterparts on these three measures (Magen et al., 1992).

Indeed, as reported above, the study demonstrated that when three groups of adolescents from underprivileged neighborhoods were compared, the group that had been involved in a year or more of volunteer activity in various community or individual projects expressed a stronger wish to improve the lot of humankind. The group likewise revealed a capacity to more fully and intensely experience life's moments of joy and expressed a more robust sense of coherence in their lives, sensing their inner and outer worlds to be more comprehensible, manageable, and meaningful. These research findings suggest that involvement in other-oriented activities among disadvantaged youth may thus exert an impact on their perceptions of their own potential as people within society; it can elicit greater meaning and satisfaction from life events and interpersonal interactions and may increase their sense of control and self-directiveness.

The developmental perspective encompasses several factors characteristic of the adolescent period, including developments in cognitive, moral, and social role-taking abilities. These developments accompany the adolescent's attempts at identity delineation, which incorporate a search for inner morality, values, and personal meaning and are concurrent with the struggle for autonomy and control over one's destiny (Bar-Tal, 1982; Ziv, 1984). These findings suggest that this age group may offer excellent potential for exploiting the affirmative impact of volunteer involvement on impoverished youth. However, the relation between age and personal coherence, and between age and the ability to experience positive events at their fullest, requires future empirical scrutiny to effectively identify at what age interventions might be optimally effective.

The lack of substantiation in this research (described above) for the notion that people predisposed to becoming involved in activities devoted to the welfare of others would possess more healthy personality attributes actually bodes well for the potential inherent in interventions with impoverished youth. One may in lieu of such substantiation speculate that being involved in repeated, daily experiences of applying oneself to another's welfare constitutes an effective formula for rendering significant changes in self-perceptions and attitudes about meaning in life. Certainly, the predominance of females among those who volunteered also calls for further research and implies the sagacity of planning interventions that attract males to prosocial activity, thus optimizing the untapped capacity of young underprivileged males for other-oriented involvement.

The following excerpts from the teenagers' own aspirations justify optimism for such empowerment of deprived adolescents:

> I want to use my life to the fullest and not just to move forward in life and to try to be the best but also to enjoy life itself. I want to finish school, to change my personality a little, to open up and think about others more and not just about myself, I want to work at a job that I'll enjoy. I want to be a better person and to contribute to my surroundings too.

> The best thing I'd like to do with my life is: To perform some kind of change in the world or in the immediate environment or to invent some innovative thing that will be talked about for a long time and also will help the environment and affect the future.

> I want to join an organization or some kind of institution for retarded children or children with deformities. And to help the institution care for the sick children.

> The thing I'd want to happen is for the whole world to unite, to worry about the ecology, that we could discover new planets, other living creatures, to progress in science and simply that the whole world would take care of more important problems than wars and idealistic skirmishes. The way the world looks now couldn't be worse, therefore some kind of change has to come, and I think that with the help of my opinions I can change a lot of things.

PHASE E: ISRAELI SOCIAL AND POLITICAL EFFECTS ON COMMITMENT

Adolescents are not only considerably influenced by those in their immediate environment (family, peers, school), but representatives of a more distant circle (community, city, country, political party, religious affiliation, etc.) will decisively affect their sense of self in relation to the

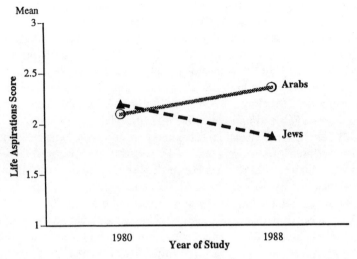

Figure 9.3. Commitment beyond self of adolescent Jews and Arabs in Israel: 1980 ($N = 1,094$) and 1988 ($N = 353$).
SOURCE: Magen (1996). Reprinted with kind permission from Kluwer Academic Publishers.

world. To assess which social and political factors relate to young people's readiness for prosocial involvement, we reexamined a cross-section of Israeli society. Eight years after the first cross-cultural study was carried out (1980, as reported in Magen 1983a, 1983b), we returned to two Israeli populations—Jews and Moslem-Arabs. A similar adolescent sample ages 14 to 16 was derived (Israeli Jews: $N = 188$; Arabs: $N = 165$) (Magen, 1990b) using the same procedure in the same neighborhoods as the earlier study. Whereas the first study (Magen, 1983a, 1983b, 1985) demonstrated no significant differences between these groups, the follow-up (Magen, 1990b) showed that Arab adolescents verbalized a significantly higher desire for prosocial commitment compared to both their 1980 peers and the 1988 Jewish sample (see Figure 9.3). By contrast, the 1988 Jewish youth were less oriented to prosocial activities than their 1980 peers.

The varying results of this follow-up study certainly seem to reflect social and nationalistic processes occurring in Israeli society. The sparks of Arab nationalistic fervor were lit during the interim years by political events, particularly the *intifada* uprising of Palestinians—especially youth—against Israeli retention of the West Bank and protests of the sluggish pace of the peace process. Conceivably, the arousal of such a sense of nationalistic solidarity and social unity boosted young people's motivation to become connected positively with their social group and national values. The condition of Israeli Arabs as a cultural and sociopolitical minority may have been conducive to greater ethnocentrism or sociocentrism (Seginer, 1988), and it highlights the intensity and uniqueness of Palestinian collective identity (Nakleh, 1975).

By contrast, the Israeli Jewish society was undergoing a reevaluation of its national convictions and was palpably uncomfortable with a political situation that did not conform with the humanistic values and beliefs that had permeated the education and upbringing of Israelis since the country's establishment. Perhaps, the inner conflicts with which the Israeli Jewish adults were struggling had trickled down into the ranks of the young people, precipitating disillusionment and prompting a decline in their interest and willingness to contribute of themselves to their own society.

These findings were felt to seriously implicate the social and moral changes occurring in Israeli society. As a result, another follow-up study was conducted. A subgroup of Jewish adolescents ($N = 85$) who had voluntarily participated in prosocial activities was examined (Magen, 1990b). These young people had higher prosocial commitment scores than their noninvolved peers (Jewish or Moslem-Arab) and also reported more intense experiences of joy and happiness. These findings reinforced the point that, even amid national malaise, adolescents involved in endeavors beyond themselves are significantly differentiated from noninvolved peers in their power to commit to humanistic goals and values.

PHASE F: ATTUNED FOR COMMITMENT:
LIFE ASPIRATIONS AMONG ADOLESCENTS
WITH AND WITHOUT HEARING IMPAIRMENTS _____

There are naturally any number of adolescent subgroups where the same issues explored among adolescents differentiated by age and ethnic background would likely also yield equally trenchant results. One such subgroup, hearing-impaired adolescents, once again proved intriguing.

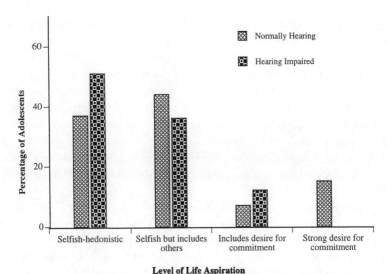

Figure 9.4. Percentage of respondents for the four levels of life aspirations among normally hearing (NH) and hearing-impaired (HI) groups ($N = 121$).

Teenagers with hearing impairments experience a unique reality. On the one hand, they are expected to participate fully in society in terms of social, occupational, and emotional functioning, including living up to the same social obligations demanded of their hearing peers. On the other hand, the limitations engendered by the hearing impairment itself not only erect communication barriers, but also make these young people's sense of social belonging more complex, influencing the quality of their interpersonal relationships and hindering their capacity to pursue standard social roles and behaviors.

In 1964, Myklebust questioned whether hearing-impaired adolescents' social maturity level can reach beyond self-help and self-direction and enter the level of assistance in the care of others. Recent studies have shown significant delays among adolescents with hearing impairments in understanding prosocial concepts such as helping others (Haley & Dowd, 1988; Kusche & Greenberg, 1983), assessing social attributions, and evaluating affect or emotions, all of which are integral to conceptualizing interpersonal relationships (Haley & Dowd, 1988; Happ & Altmaier, 1982; Mertens, 1989).

In a review of mainstreamed hearing-impaired high school students' involvement in school-sponsored activities (Holcomb, 1996), it was found that most of these students reported difficulties becoming integrated. Even when they were active, their reasons were the desire to be accepted and wanted socially, rather than a wish to participate or a personal interest. Moreover, even youngsters attending self-contained special education settings, who were quite involved in co-curricular activities due to the small school size, had limited options and choices with regard to becoming active. The opportunities for social development, interactions, and involvement in school-sponsored activities—which promote self-esteem and enhance identity development—are thus clearly less accessible to teenagers with hearing impairments (Holcomb, 1996).

The hearing-impaired community has been described as seldom expressing interest in world issues such as the environment, pollution, or health concerns. The paucity of political participation among people with hearing impairments has been attributed to school experiences, where few hearing-impaired students are given opportunities for critical thinking, problem-solving, and value identification, and to family life, where decisions made for the hearing-impaired child increase passivity and diminish the sense of responsibility or leadership (Bateman, 1996). Paternalistic home and school environments foster naivete about the possibility of making an impact on the community or of helping oneself and other people with hearing impairments (Vernon & Estes, 1975).

In our study exploring life aspirations among adolescents with and without hearing impairments (Magen, 1990a), only a slight degree of readiness to contribute and devote oneself to others was found among the hearing-impaired adolescents, in contrast to their hearing counterparts (see Figure 9.4). These findings may seem incongruent with the flair for the interpersonal that hearing-impaired adolescents demonstrated in their positive experiences. It appears that these youngsters' ability to fully enjoy mutual relationships has been developed adequately; however, their capacity for the self-transcendent is limited.

It should be noted that, again, care was taken during the judges' training process to eliminate possible variability in rating the responses of the adolescents with hearing impairments due to their communicational difficulties (spelling, grammatical errors, diction, etc.).

Students with hearing impairments most frequently expressed selfish and hedonistic life aspirations compatible with the lowest LAQ level, as in the following excerpts:

To learn how to drive a new motorcycle and car. The motorcycle I want is a new blue Suzuki and the car a new Autobianci or Ford Cortina.

To fulfill my dream of being a dentist and living in a villa or being a veterinarian or pediatrician or working in a dental laboratory for bridges and false teeth. I'd like to live in a villa in a rich neighborhood and to have lots of animals like: two cats, three dogs, four parrots, turtle, fish in an aquarium.

I love a computer manager, because I want very rich and also a beautiful house. And also want to fly out of the country to many place, Europe and America.

The next largest group of adolescents with hearing impairments attained the second level of life aspirations as measured by our study. Their goals continued to demonstrate a predominant level of selfishness, although they did refer to other people or causes:

I want a future, I want to get married because I loved baby very much. Because it's quieter and no problems. Every day I been fight with my parents, I can't stand it I want to get married because I'm jealous that they married and I feel I want quickly age 18 and to marry.

To be a writer or a painter. In water colors—or oils. Which is my favorite hobby. And the second thing that I'm very eager is to travel all over the world. I mean to see all the other different countries on earth while I sail on my little private boat. But I'm not lonely but rather with good friends who are the sailors, and that's what I want to be—a tourist of the world. And these are two the things that are my dreams.

I really want to see Europe and I also really like to fly airplane. I'm not scared on the airplane till the sky. I want to see the people of Europe. I want to see that people behave in different manners. I think Europe is a prettier city than Israel. I love to see Europe: Italy, France, Switzerland, Spain, Greece, Rome, Scotland, England.

Unlike the hearing group, only four of the hearing-impaired teenagers exhibited some degree of willingness to contribute of themselves to others. Of these, one lone adolescent fully attained the expression of a genuine interest in prosocial commitment (Level 4). Her life aspirations, although still not finely honed, were directed toward contributing to society at large:

To do good and to contribute something to the world, and to give everything good to my parents who invested in me so very much of what they could. I'd like to be a kindergarten teacher and to make something of my life and to give something to society and to the world. I still don't know, but I know I can do something.

Only three other hearing-impaired youngsters demonstrated a willingness to contribute of themselves to others, at least to some extent (Level 3). These few students showed no indication of a higher tendency to dedicate themselves to either hearing or hearing-impaired people. Only one of these adolescents mused upon the vision of giving to hearing-impaired society in particular. When asked what was the best thing they wanted to do with their lives, the three students responded with the following life aspirations, which included only some elements of a desire for transpersonal commitment (Level 3):

To work in the vocational work of mechanics. It seems to me that it would be a good job for me. And also to go to the army and to the army I really want to go.

To finish school and immediately to fly overseas with my friends, to travel all over the world. After that I want to learn the teaching profession, I want to be a teacher of deaf first-grade students.

I really want to continue experiences with my friends, trips, parties, etc. To travel to places overseas with friends or with my parents. After school I want to volunteer for the army, to meet lots of people, get to know myself . . . and I want to be a soldier like any other in the country.

Two possible explanations for a lack of readiness for prosocial commitment among these young people suggest themselves. One harks back to descriptions of the hearing-impaired in the literature, where they are seen as more egocentric and lacking in the ability to empathize with others (Kusche & Greenberg, 1983; Selman, 1980) because of communication difficulties with their parents as a result of the impairment (Schlesinger & Acree, 1984).

A second explanation derives from the controversial professional approaches taken to help socialize hearing-impaired children. In recent years, considerable progress has been made in the introduction of innovative training methods to prepare these youngsters for independence and for coping with the demands of life and society. However, it appears that most of the fostering of the hearing-impaired child has remained at the stage of self-help or self-direction. A second and more advanced stage—promoting the ability to feel a sense of caring for others and to act on that feeling—continues to be neglected or almost totally ignored, despite its critical role for developing social maturity in adolescents (as defined by Myklebust, 1964). It is not an unreasonable assumption that what works with impoverished youths should work with hearing-impaired ones as well. If helping, rather than always being helped, was shown (on pages 134-136) to have been an efficacious psychodynamic for the culturally disadvantaged, then why not here as well?

REFLECTIONS ON A
MULTIFACETED PHENOMENON

As we've seen throughout the literature, psychologists representing many schools of thought believe that self-interest is the major motivation for an individual's actions and behavior. Yet, it is never simple, or even psychologically correct, to pigeonhole behavior as stemming from one source alone. Humanness is a complex amalgam of drives, ambitions, motivations, emotions, actions, reactions, and intellectual reasoning, operating on a number of planes of awareness. In practice, many individuals are also motivated by their emotions to behave in ways that contradict their own interests (Frank, 1989). Paradoxically, these people, whom Frank (1987) calls "shrewdly irrational," reap more benefits and self-satisfaction than those who consistently pursue self-interest.

In examining the phenomenon of prosocial behavior, about two thirds of the teenagers we studied disclosed selfish aspirations for their future. Almost one third (31%) of teenagers across cultures in our research did at least refer to the presence of other people in their self-centered dreams (Level 2), but more than another third (36%) of these youngsters expressed completely hedonistic longings that involved only themselves (Level 1). These selfish preoccupations, with meager or no aspirations for commitment to other people or causes, mirrored descriptions in the literature of adolescent egocentricity (e.g., Conger & Petersen, 1984; Kohlberg, 1971; Smilansky, 1991).

However, the fact that about one third of the young populations studied did in fact manifest the ability to transcend self (13% fully at Level 4 and an additional 20% at least to some degree at Level 3) deserves special scrutiny. If, as suggested, human nature requires a sense of purpose and a larger meaning in life beyond that of routine existence (e.g., Adler, 1964a, 1964b; Mosak & Dreikurs, 1973), then these youths expressed wishes that included some indication of their desire to go beyond their own needs and gratifications and give of themselves to others. Many of them fully acknowledged inner strivings to contribute their talents or aptitudes toward the betterment of other human beings and social causes:

> The best thing I'd like to do is to help people so they will have it good in life and so they'll be happy. And that's the same thing that I also wish for myself.

> I'd like to be a pianist and to grant my listeners a momentous experience each time they hear me. For me too, a good concert is an unforgettable experience. But I know that it won't happen because from responses I've heard about my playing I'm talented but not enough. So I think I'll volunteer to perform for people who can't go to concerts. And that will give them genuine happiness.

> The best thing I want to do is:

> I want to gather all the stray animals and to care for them with warmth and love.

> To care for sick people (not as a doctor or nurse), to lighten their hearts, and on the holidays to perform for them and to do charity drives and . . . to send them care packages.

> To work in an institution for orphaned children and to give them the feeling of home, warmth, and love.

The same pattern appeared in all cultures; and our study of disadvantaged youth who were actually involved in activities dedicated to the benefit of others and/or society particularly reinforces the universal appeal of prosocial activity. Such involvement perceptibly enriched these underprivileged youngsters' lives, exerting an impact on their self-perceptions and on their ability to extract meaning and satisfaction from life events and interpersonal interactions. The phenomenon of commitment has been widely mentioned for its impact on healthy adolescent development. Yet, there are questions about youngsters' actual capacity to transcend basic selfish needs in order to make the commitment to others. The current exploration of teenage egocentrism/selflessness suggests that the same clear divergence appears in the literature as manifested in the population itself. The majority of adolescents do seem to aspire only to a selfish devotion toward themselves, thus substantiating one direction purported in the literature. The sense of emptiness in modern society has been imputed as a major cause, as well as a result of, young people's reported hedonism and absorption in momentary pleasures. Several theorists (Frankl, 1967; Jourard & Landsman, 1980; Klein, 1972; Rogers, 1977) have discussed the difficulty of establishing commitment in our morally fatigued, "existentially empty" society.

The widespread malaise noted in the literature should not, however, suggest total incapacity for self-transcendence among younger people. Quite to the contrary, the modern *Weltschmerz* is dangerous enough for us to redouble our efforts. We must discover the different roads leading our young people to a sense of meaning, especially by enhancing their understanding and appreciation of the joy of giving, which links inner happiness to our own role in augmenting the happiness of those who surround us. Commitment to others is not solely the prerogative of an elite group of righteous, pious, seasoned do-gooders but rather deeply pervades the human family.

Part III

Reflections on Concepts and Applications

10

Adolescent Happiness and Commitment: Are They Mutually Exclusive or Interrelated?

All who joy would win must share it—happiness was born a twin.

Lord Byron, *Don Juan* (1824)

Commitment to prosocial causes and a search for personal happiness are two motifs that may seem to conflict, especially in adolescence, when young people are described as egocentric and as absorbed in their own desires, self-image, and immediate needs and satisfaction (Conger & Petersen, 1984; Kohlberg, 1971). At such a time, an interest in the welfare of others, a preoccupation with social goals or global human ideas, and engagement in altruistic, prosocial activities may appear incongruous with the teenager's self-centeredness. The question that we have attempted to unravel is whether the adolescent search for self, the urge for personal enjoyment, and the yearning to explore what makes one happy necessarily run counter to self-dedication and commitment to causes beyond self. In other words, we endeavored to discover whether commitment to self and commitment beyond self are mutually exclusive or in some way interrelated.

At this point, it would seem useful to once again examine some of the material we've already presented and to restate a few of the points we've already made, to reinforce one fundamental theme: The underlying direction of our work, and its validity as a basis for a therapeutic and educational model, hinges on the connection between personal fulfillment and social commitment.

On the one hand, we must tread carefully. No doubt contemporary society needs nothing less than one more excuse for navel-gazing and self-preoccupation. On the other hand, the nexus between self and others is ineluctable; the command from on high, to love our neighbors as ourselves, demands that we begin by loving ourselves too. What we're suggesting in this chapter is that it is preferable to err on the side of the Maslows, who broadly equate personal fulfillment with moral responsibility, than by too circumspectly avoiding anything that smacks of subjectivism.

While the culture of narcissism may jumble self-love with self-indulgence, an existential aspect of our culture points in another and, from a moral standpoint, equally undermining direction. This is the either/or approach—either one is happy and selfish or unhappy and giving. Statements such as, "Every man's happiness is built on the unhappiness of another" made by one of Turgenieff's characters (1860/1923), or "Point me out a happy man and I will point you out either egotism, selfishness, evil—or else an absolute ignorance," from a character in Graham Greene's (1948) *The Heart of the Matter,* have a familiar ring. The generosity and freshness of Marcel Proust's (1896/1948) "Let us be grateful to people who make us happy. They are the charming gardeners who make our souls blossom" are, to the ears of this culture, rather more surprising.

The search for one's self and the quest for identity became conspicuously, and sometimes annoyingly, prevalent among youth during recent decades. Yet the search for one's potential and "true self" and the enhancement of one's individuality, autonomy, and freedom have always been perceived as the deepest values driving mental health professionals. In psychotherapy or counseling, we often strive to enable human beings to explore genuine needs and desires. In so doing, they become free of those outside forces that may keep them in bondage to others, and to the pressures and expectations of others.

Self-realization, as described by Maslow, implies: discover your species, learn what you particularly are, how you are you, what your potentialities are, what your style is, what your pace is, what your tastes are, what your values are. It is a journey to achieve humanness through an intense relationship with the self.

In many cases, however, individuals only make contact with their own selves and can only embark toward self-fulfillment by detaching themselves from their closest bonds, abandoning family obligations and commitments. It doesn't usually work out the way these people intended. In many cases these "free" people have found it very difficult, and sometimes impossible, to achieve their cherished goal of self-realization and fulfillment. Paradoxically, a common concern expressed by those of them who become involved in therapy is the desire for meaningful relationships.

Oftentimes, in the search for real identity, one may achieve a pseudo-identity, an identity that is restricting rather than freeing. Indeed, as I discussed earlier (in Chapter 1), Maslow's concept of self-actualization as a self-centered process came under attack in the literature. Most significantly, perhaps, Victor Frankl objected to the emphasis on subjective fulfillment of the self as a criterion for self-actualization.

Frankl raised profound opposition to the tenet that human beings basically operate in a closed system with the end goal of maintaining or restoring an inner equilibrium and of reducing tensions. According to this homeostasis theory, creating values and accomplishing objectives can only be secondary to the person's primary striving to secure pleasure and satisfaction. Frankl (1988) countered that "a sound amount of tension, such as that tension which is aroused by a meaning to fulfill, is inherent in being human and is indispensable for mental well-being" (p. 48). As Frankl (1967) uses Nietzsche's motto: "He who knows a (why) for living, will surmount almost every 'how' " (p. 103).

In response to the waves of criticism, Maslow (1971) described a person's higher values as transcending many traditional dichotomies, such as flesh and soul, religiousness and secularism, or selfishness and unselfishness.

If you are doing the work that you love and are devoted to the values that you hold highest, you are being as selfish as possible, and yet are also being unselfish and altruistic. . . . The boundaries of yourself in that sense now extend far beyond your personal sphere of interests to include the entire world. (p. 187)

Yet the question still stands: Is it an either-or proposition? Society, as opposed to the individual? Meaning outside the world, as opposed to self-meaning? Commitment beyond self, as opposed to self-realization and fulfillment? Or could the two be deeply interrelated within the human psyche?

THE SELF-BEYOND-SELF LINK _____

In our studies from 1980 through 1993, we examined how commitment to self (i.e., intense happiness) and commitment beyond self (i.e., prosocial behavior) are interrelated. We sought empirical support for the tenet that individuals who commit themselves to activities and projects beyond basic need fulfillment—who live for a purpose, who desire to fulfill a meaning beyond self, who act compassionately and show devotion to a cause—are also those very same people who are exceptionally capable of experiencing moments of deep joy, happiness, and inspiration.

We were keenly interested in determining whether this willingness to look outward and do things for the benefit of others comes at a price of investing in oneself. Or do the two processes intertwine to create a full identity, with the capacity for caring and giving to others as well as caring and giving to oneself? Our series of research studies presented in this book, as well as a substantial number of studies not included here, demonstrated across the board, with only one exception (adolescents with hearing impairments), a powerful relationship between the intensity of young people's happy moments and their readiness to commit themselves to others. In each of these research undertakings, a comparison of PEQ and LAQ data confirmed that the higher the intensity of the adolescent's positive experience, the higher was his or her readiness to be devoted to a purpose beyond self.

In our large-scale cross-cultural study of American Christians and Israeli Jews and Arabs (Magen, 1983a, 1983b, 1985), this finding first evidenced itself and was confirmed for all three cultures. Regardless of cultural background, adolescents who described themselves as experiencing happy, enlightening experiences were also moved, significantly more than others, to express strong readiness to serve the benefit of people and causes beyond themselves ($r = .24, p < .01$).

For example, a 14-year-old boy, who related an intensely joyous experience with nature, also expressed specific goals aiming toward achieving peace:

PEQ: I went on an annual school trip to the mountains and rivers at the Dead Sea and Ein Gedi. I saw things that were astonishing in their beauty, even though it was all barrenness there. Here was a small spring with an assortment of plants, and there was a mountain with a special contour! The more I walked in the barrenness, I saw that this very place was the most beautiful and that there were more colors and animals than in the city! I saw a sunset by the Dead Sea. It was simply an experience. There were colors all mixed up with the sun in the sky, and then the sun was swallowed up by the water. It was just wonderful. The sun in all its glory floated into the sky, and its image reflected on the water!

LAQ: My life aspiration is for there to be peace, and not just any peace between neighbors or friends! But rather that there should be peace between all peoples (and especially with the Arabs) because I don't think that there should be wars all the time. And even before that, there should be unity within our nation, and only later can there be peace with everyone. Afterward, I would talk with people and only later would I take action. And if at one time, I become a teacher or a counselor, I will guide toward peace and patience and love.

In examining the possible correlation between readiness for commitment beyond self and the nature of positive experiences, we had likewise expected that, because experiences of an interpersonal nature were found to be most intense, those young people whose most meaningful experiences were with other people would be differentiated by their expression of a greater readiness for prosocial commitment. We indeed confirmed that adolescents who reported interpersonal relationship experiences scored highest on the LAQ (expressing more often than others a desire for commitment beyond self) in each of the three cultures as well as in the total sample.

The following responses typify the connections between adolescents' joyous interpersonal experiences and their desire to contribute to other human beings as part and parcel of their life aspirations:

PEQ: The experience I mean to describe is a very important experience for me, where I felt wonderful. It happened not long ago during our last summer vacation, when I flew to visit my father who is remarried. . . . I felt excellent because, finally, I felt like I knew my father in a way I never knew him before, and he didn't treat me like the 7-year-old girl he remembered, but rather as an adult. Our relationship was very special, his wife made me feel needed, the relationship between the two of us developed into something very strong. I finally felt that I have another home where I can go to, without any mixed feelings. It's hard for me to define the feeling, I just was on a high. . . . I just felt wonderful and I'm sure that I've changed more than a little because of the experience.

LAQ: The best thing I want to do in my life is to succeed. I really want to succeed in the field that I choose. I personally want to study business and succeed in that field. . . . Of course, following that, I want to help whoever I can, in everything related to helping others. That is an important and significant part that I think will make me happy as well as others.

In conclusion, the findings of this study suggested a complex pattern of relations between the expression of a desire for commitment beyond self, on the one hand, and the critical dimensions of positive experiences—their nature and intensity—along with the personal attributes of the experiences, on the other hand. Because many of these variables have been included in the etiology of the high-functioning person, the uncovering of their interrelationships may further the understanding of the formation of such a person. The contribution of these findings to the process of human growth is all the more promising in view of the fact that these results were found to be universally applicable and not restricted to a particular sample studied.

THE JOY OF GIVING

Our study examining the actual involvement of adolescents in prosocial activities and its relationship to happiness (Magen & Aharoni, 1991)

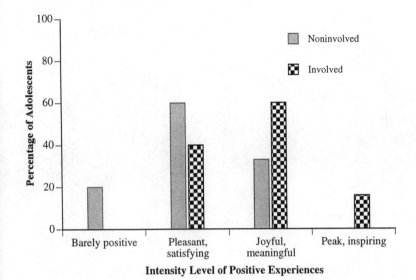

Figure 10.1. Frequency of experience intensity for involved and noninvolved adolescents (N = 260).
SOURCE: Magen (1991). Copyright © 1985 by the American Psychological Association. Reprinted by permission.

compared two groups: involved and noninvolved adolescents. As can be seen in Figure 10.1, those adolescents who were involved reported a greater capacity to experience joyous, exhilarating events in their lives: Involved, M = 2.64, Noninvolved, M = 2.13; $F(1, 256)$ = 37.14, p < .001. The interaction between involvement and gender was not significant, indicating similar patterns for males and females within each group. The involved, committed group of adolescents and the group of their noninvolved peers likewise differed significantly in their expressed life aspirations.

In fact, only those youngsters who were actually involved in giving to others described joyous moments of a peak intensity, whereas none of these involved adolescents reported an experience that was just barely positive in nature. The spirited moments of these involved adolescents were also more frequently of an interpersonal nature, as can be seen from the following sets of responses concerning their remembered positive experiences and their life aspirations:

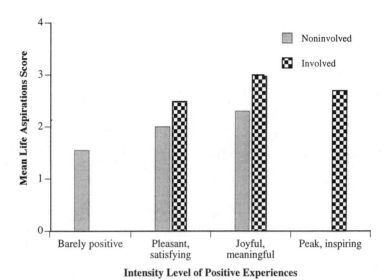

Figure 10.2. Relationship between the desire for commitment beyond self and the intensity of positive experience in involved and noninvolved adolescents ($N = 260$).

SOURCE: Magen (1985). Copyright © 1985 by the American Psychological Association. Reprinted by permission.

PEQ: Within our active citizenship/community involvement program, I chose to become a class representative for cheering up the elderly at an old age home on the Purim holiday. My class organized a short skit, and with some other girls, I organized a singing-aloud program. We got into the mood really quickly and started dancing. When I succeeded in getting some of the old women to get up and be happy and dance with me, I felt that I had achieved an extraordinary achievement. It was only then that I felt how much we were helping. At the ceremony that took place later in our school, I was given the honor of lighting the beacon, and I felt great pride in truly helping the elderly. It gave me a good feeling about myself.

LAQ: The best thing I'd like to do is if I have an opportunity to save someone from dying. That would be, in my eyes, the greatest, the best thing one could possibly do.

PEQ: During the last Olympics, I was sure that we would win a large number of medals. Day after day, I watched until the wee hours of the night, and I saw how my "heroes" fell, one after the other. But on the day of the sailing competition, Israel won the bronze medal by Gal Friedman the savior. At the very moment that I saw that, all of my patriotic feelings and pride rose up, and I was the happiest person in the world.

LAQ: I would want to win or get or earn a large amount of money so that I could help my parents and others who need it like me.

As was suggested by our earlier cross-cultural study, we found a direct relationship between the expressed desire for prosocial commitment and the intensity of remembered positive experiences for both the involved group, $r(134) = .21, p < .01$, and the noninvolved group, $r(126) = .34, p < .01$. However, more than their noninvolved peers, involved adolescents expressed less egocentric life aspirations and a greater desire to contribute of themselves to others and to society (see Figure 10.2). The capacity to experience happiness and meaning was also greater among these adolescents, substantiating the earlier research linking peak experiences with values that emphasize helping those in need and contributing to society.

The highest levels of reported expressions of transpersonal commitment were found among adolescents whose positive experiences were most intense, suggesting that the type of personality who has intense, peak experiences is not necessarily a hedonistic, self-seeking individual. Rather, it may be speculated that this person appreciates the more positive aspects of life and is driven by a willingness and desire to increase others' well-being. Individuals with specific personality traits correlated with highly intense positive experiences: These individuals were more warm-hearted, sensitive to others, resourceful, intelligent, and humble (Magen, 1985). Apparently, then, meaningful positive experiences do not only cause subjective personal satisfaction but also relate to the distinct identity of a human being willing to become involved in causes beyond his or her own skin.

These findings were explicitly substantiated yet again by the comparative study (see Chapter 9) of disadvantaged adolescents who were beginning volunteers, experienced volunteers, or not involved at all (Magen et al., 1992). As recalled, the adolescents who had experienced a full year of helping those less fortunate demonstrated a higher level of verbally expressed transpersonal commitment and a stronger capacity to fully and intensely experience happy moments in life, as well as a greater sense of coherence (see Figure 9.2).

The following essays written by involved students seem particularly important at this juncture because they suggest how the entire connection between personal gratification and prosocial activity gets carried to the next level. Here, we're no longer just listening to young people feeling better by behaving sensitively and helpfully. We're beginning to see a larger pattern of collective responsibility emerge. These youngsters are beginning to sound like the people who actually keep society up and running, the ones who do their part to help humanity struggle from Point A to Point B.

WITH A LITTLE LOVE

The school in which I'm active is for exceptional children up to age 12, with different levels of mental retardation. I decided to choose one of the girls with Down's syndrome. Ronit [pseudonym] is an 11-year-old girl who acts like she's 6. A typical appearance for children with this illness. Every time I come on Thursday, her eyes tell me that she's happy that we're going into town again. At first, I didn't have patience for her, because a lot of things that a normal child would do once, I had to explain to her at least 10 times. With a little determination and patience, I could see that it was easy and pleasant because the reward comes later, at the end of the year, when you feel how hard it is to leave because you're so attached to these children.

I felt that I was doing good for Ronit in her heart and also developing something that didn't exist before, or that existed but hadn't been exposed enough. Only then did I understand that love, patience, and different stimuli expose the magic hidden within these children. Beyond the stares and the repulsive external appearance, there's a warm soul, needing someone to awaken it. Every one of us has a need to contribute. A little listening ear, feeling, and interest and then these children are given the ability to grow up. I enjoyed the duration of my activity in the special school and I want to encourage youth to continue this activity.

(Israeli Jewish girl)

WILL I SUCCEED?

At last, our first meeting transpired. I chose to care for a 6-year-old boy who learns at the Akim school. He suffers from mental retardation and difficulties in walking, hearing, and general functioning. The next day, I told my friends about my meeting at Akim, and one of the girls said, "Forget it! Why should you get involved—what for? It's draining, and you'll never get anything out of it." . . . I was deeply upset. I tried to explain to her that it just wasn't true. You have to look at each person as a person. God created him that way and he shouldn't be humiliated for it. During my activities, I ran into a few more problems. Time—it's hard to find the right time for this activity. Patience—I feel that the activity at Akim requires much patience and strength and I was a little scared. I would have wanted our teachers to prepare us more (films, lectures, etc.) so that the fears wouldn't interfere with our work.

The activity at Akim influenced the course of my life, my personality, and my relationships in society. Now I am more involved and feel myself to be a part of our society. It has given me the right to exist. I feel proud and I have a sense of satisfaction and well-being.

(Israeli Arab girl)

One final note to our findings: In contrast to the substantial body of research on normally hearing adolescents described previously (and, we should mention, again corroborated by the findings for the normally hearing peers in the study of adolescents with hearing impairments), no relationship between degree of readiness for prosocial commitment and intensity of experiences was found in the hearing-impaired group (Magen, 1990a). It appears that, on the one hand, the ability to experience intense positive moments among hearing-impaired adolescents has been facilitated through the growing concern of educators and counselors for these youngsters' well-being. On the other hand, their readiness for commitment beyond self has not developed to the level achieved by their normally hearing peers, as it has not been a sufficient focus of adequate concern in the eyes of educators and professionals working with hearing-impaired youth.

The gradual and quite extraordinary emergence of a mature collective responsibility from private gratification has been well articulated in the literature. For example, Violato and Travis (1995) described the reciprocal connections between harmonious social relations and a sense of beauty and pleasure, as well as between exhilarated spirits and the strength to continue making efforts to act in socially productive ways:

When social experience gives rise to a sense of fellowship, a sense of concordance, or a sense of intimacy or love, we feel or have the sensation of beauty. . . . When we sense that our efforts will be fruitful, we have a sense of control, a sense of optimism, a sense of viability. When we sense that our experiences are good . . . they also buoy our spirits; they evoke a sense of potency or sergeancy; they give a sense of balance that seems right and good. We sense that we have strength and can choose, strive, act, and so on. (p. 58)

The interrelationship between these phenomena of personal gratification and collective responsibility remains imponderable in terms of how they act on and bring each other into being. It might be guessed that even further empirical studies will not necessarily pinpoint if, say, adolescents who are fortunate enough to interact successfully and meaningfully with other people develop a general desire to contribute to their fellow human beings—or if the desire for commitment beyond the self, whatever its source, acts continuously as an independent agent.

The direction of causality is not well-defined; in one construct, a young person is able to build upon a happy experience of joy involving another person or the external world. That experience or experiences then form a basis for positive personality development. In a second construct, an inherent openness on the part of adolescents to the meaning and depth of their experience is reinforced by that experience. In this scenario, the act itself of contributing to another person leads to further openness and sensitivity. The remembered positive experiences reported by some adolescents reflect the obscure connection between happiness and giving of themselves, as is evident in the following two descriptions:

> I volunteered at an old age home where we helped the elderly . . . to eat, to get dressed, and sometimes we told them stories that warmed their hearts. It was a wonderful week. . . . I really enjoyed it . . . and each day I waited for the next so we could start over. . . . It was an experience that made me feel really good.

> The first thing that comes to mind is when I went to an institution for the blind before the holidays, where we students sang and cheered them up. . . . When we left I felt that we had really made a contribution to them, and this deed and the happiness we sparked in those people gave me a feeling that life is really wonderful.

11

Recapping Our Research Findings

Men are wise in proportion, not to their experience but to their
capacity for experience.

George Bernard Shaw, *Man and Superman* (1903)

Spanning over a decade and encompassing different cultures and
adolescent populations, our body of research studies presents over-
whelming testimony to the healthy, positive, and optimistic capacities of
adolescents. A significant number of these adolescents demonstrate the
vital capacity to experience life's joyous moments and thereby discover
the best of themselves, the world, and the meaning of experience. Many
of these teenagers also show an ability to transcend selfish needs, reach
out their hands to help another, or dedicate themselves to a worthy
cause.

The importance of adolescence as a time of potential incipient joy
cannot be overestimated, particularly because such demonstrable joy

occurs in the context of the normal adolescent turmoil and self-doubt with which researchers and psychologists are more accustomed to grapple. The double bind of adolescence is almost a cliché: that, at the very time adolescents are beset with rapid physical changes and emotional revolutions, they must make unrelenting choices and commitments that are of long-range significance for their adult lives. The formidable potential of joy must, then, not only be recognized as a profoundly fortunate compensatory factor, it must also be exploited for its salutary impact on development.

The major finding of our research was indeed the recurrent pattern of relationships between the capacity for joyous self-fulfillment, on the one hand, and, on the other, those life goals oriented toward other people's needs. The two critical dimensions of remembered positive experiences (i.e., their intensity and content), the progressive steps that lead to commitment beyond self (i.e., verbal involvement and the different stages of actual involvement), and the personal attributes of the experiencer (i.e., personality traits and sense of coherence) were found to interconnect in subtle complex patterns. These interconnections were found to transcend cultural and demographic boundaries, even in a political context where one might have expected those boundaries to be impenetrable.

The many reports in our studies on the happiest of life's moments experienced by adolescents ages 14 through 16 included critical moments of illumination and self-revelation that changed perspectives on the world and other people. Yet, only about one third of the respondents depicted experiences of self-realization that correspond with the Aristotelian view of happiness: not limited to hedonistic pleasure but encompassing the greatest fulfillment and meaning in living. In fact, two thirds of the participants recounted experiences of mere satisfaction or simple pleasure, and some youngsters were only able to recall life events that were barely positive in nature.

Educators and therapists may do well to respond to such disappointing results among the majority of the adolescents, for it implies the need to explore ways to strengthen the adolescent's capacity to fully experience life. The quest for happiness has perhaps never been more challenging, and more elusive, than for adolescents entering the twenty-first century. Can interventions enhance the ability in young people whose experience of their world is colorless, bleak, or dull, and whose life events seem to offer no peaks or inspirations? Our research seems to indicate that some interventions can be effective, as we will explore in the next chapters.

Among the many experiences assessed as highly intense were exhilarations solely of the self. Other happy life experiences, however, related to a feeling of connection with the surrounding world. Yet, the majority of the adolescents in different parts of the world who depicted intensely positive moments experienced these joyous occasions within their relationships with other human beings: helping others, sharing, or being encouraged by or believed in by others. It appears that a climate of intimacy in the family, feelings of being trusted, and responses by others to one's accomplishments all lead to a special sense of excitement, joy, and happiness. These sensations amid interpersonal exchanges may ultimately change some young people and how they view the world.

Understandably, the interpersonal component holds special significance in the lives of young people. Positive experiences that contain a strong element of interpersonal encounter, or an "I-Thou" relationship (Buber, 1961), constitute the most frequent as well as the most intense source of delight, happiness, and meaning for adolescents in all of the different groups studied. Being wanted, being trusted, being believed in, relating and connecting to other human beings, belonging to a family with warm and cohesive interrelationships, pursuing a frank and open friendship, experiencing love and romance—these are the experiences that contribute more meaning to the world of most adolescents than do any accumulation of material or physical external events. Even the moments of self-discovery, a sense of accomplishment, or the experiences of achievement that were described by many young people as a source of illumination and joy still do not, as a whole, compare in intensity and frequency to experiences with other human beings.

The drive toward a connection with others was further communicated by the desire of adolescents to "do something" that would change or improve the world, or render transformations in society or in their country. They expressed hopes of striving for the sake of others, whether for their families or friends, for needy children or other unfortunate people in their surroundings, for their ethnic or national group, or for the human race as a whole.

The issue of peace holds a central place in the strivings of adolescents living in Israel; they wished for it and sought to work in that direction, yet, they often acknowledged with regret their own limitations in bringing about this revered goal. The Middle East turned out to be a poignant environment for our studies for several reasons. As we have observed, any demonstration that joy is an intrinsic part of human striving without regard to Arab-Jewish delineations takes on powerful added significance. Yet, the regional struggle added another dimension as well. It emerged that Israel, despite its stereotypical atmosphere of strife and hostility, also arouses a particularly stubborn hunger to help. Adolescent hands reach out even to their own people's long-time foes.

The question of cultural specificity versus universality of human values has been repeatedly considered by writers concerned with the study of the healthy personality. Diener et al. (1995) and Veenhoven (1991) found marked variations between how representatives of different cultures find well-being or happiness. In our cross-cultural investigation, American teenagers in particular reported experiences with the external world as frequently as they did interpersonal experiences, implying the more materialistic and individualistic character of the American culture. In *all* cultures, however, including the American, interpersonal experiences remained the most intense.

Such common data patterns among our different subject groups have implications for the general question of cultural relativity and for defining the positive values often sought by researchers (e.g., Diener et al., 1995; Veenhoven, 1995). Because the dimensions of significant adolescent experiences transcend major cultural differences, psychologists can reevaluate the role of culture in their search to define and encourage the "healthy personality."

Although the specific and ultimate purpose of our research was to use the seemingly universal links of positive experience and commitment beyond self to bind diverse populations, our findings were also significantly affected by unique cultural factors. For example, an unmistakable other-directedness infuses the life aspirations of Jewish boys in particular because, even as the divisions within Israel deepen, a simultaneous wedding of Jew and Jewish state has maintained and accelerated momentum. That the specific personality of culture should come into play in our work is hardly surprising. After all, in the largest sense, our research tapped into the personality of the participants in ways that were bound to reveal both sharp differences and unexpected similarities. Yet, the differences between cultures were less impressive than the total collapse of cultural barriers when certain experimental tools were brought to bear, including a personality test used to compare the traits of the adolescents with the nature of their positive experiences and the degree to which they expressed commitment beyond themselves.

Again, the adolescents who shared positive experiences shared personality traits, and the correlations were as one would expect: experiences with the self corresponded with introversion; fixation on the external world with aggressiveness and frequent coldness; and interpersonal experience with warmth and sensitivity. Less predictable were the personality traits of adolescents reporting high intensity; the surprising result was that the self-absorption one might expect from "peaking" teenagers was not in evidence. To the contrary, they were remarkably tender-minded, less domineering, and less aggressive.

These findings further stimulate specific causative questions bearing on the relationship between experience and personality: Does the positive relationship found between adolescents' personality traits and the intensity and content of the positive experiences imply that certain personality attributes predispose a young person toward certain types of experience? Or, is the experiencer's personality shaped in a particular manner by the kind of positive experiences he or she undergoes? Oscar Wilde (1968) summed up this cause and effect dilemma: "When we are happy, we are always good, but when we are good, we are not always happy." Educators, parents, and mental health professionals should, in any event, not allow such conundrums to discourage opportunities for pleasant and joyous experiences among adolescents.

By responding to the surrounding world with a vibrant longing to participate in it, young people may discover unique meaning from experiences in different environments. Their lives may be enriched, their sense of membership renewed, and their sensitivity to self and others intensified.

In general, our studies showed that, not only does commitment to oneself not contradict commitment beyond self, it may even be a prerequisite for it. A conventional view holds that only an openness to experiences of pain and anguish allows awareness and sensitivity to the needs and misfortunes of others. Yet, we find that *any* openness of individuals to themselves, and their capacity to experience their own world fully, likewise outfits them with the qualities of sensitivity and openness to other human beings—and may also grant them the ability to transcend and become involved in higher causes and purposes.

Over a century ago, the existential philosopher Soren Kierkegaard (1974) drew attention to the intertwining links between one's subjective experiencing, a concern for the self, and the underlying need for an ethical basis on which to live and make choices. An ethical person, following this conception, is one who experiences but is not controlled by changing moods; rather, he or she is able to transcend them in pursuit of the self and in defining life's goals (Dopson & Gade, 1981). Only the individual who is committed to self can take an active role in life.

At certain points over the decade of our studies, it was surprising not to be surprised; after a while, in other words, neat correlations became suspect. More often, the data suggested a profound variance from conventional expectations. It is not the marginal, intensely afflicted population who, as a result of their suffering, necessarily experience self-transcendence and love or exhibit warmth and tenderness more deeply. Remarkably, it is the young, the vibrant, the souls unburdened with the weight of the centuries, who are able to reach beyond themselves toward the tenderness of the interpersonal. There is every reason to believe that deep joy, not just misery, leads to the heartfelt yearning toward others and to keen sensitivity to the needs of the world.

The trend toward the universal continued to be manifest through our final correlations. High intensities corresponded with the interpersonal—again, across cultures. The self is soon exhausted as a source of pleasure, and the external world erodes its stimuli with no adequate replacements in gear. Because high intensity is not synonymous with self-absorption, it is not surprising to find a further connection between high intensity and readiness to seek beyond the self. The prescience of Maslow in realizing that peak experiences, far from being solipsistic, are actually fillips to self-transcendence seems demonstrated in our empirical data. A definite nexus was finally established between the desire for self-transcendence and positive experience in interpersonal relations. This reciprocity implies that a romantic or sexual attachment can be generalized and transformed into an analogous relationship with a mass or culture or cause.

Such connections warrant reconsideration of the whole issue of values and value systems. No doubt, Frankl was able to upbraid Maslow for amorality because Maslow was really too scrupulous to glibly attach ethical ratings to whole types of experiences. One naturally assumes that self-transcendence and the realm of the interpersonal are, as traditional moral thinking allows, the safely traveled routes to the good and the just and the beautiful. To a supreme degree they are, because they allow us to get beyond traditional Cartesian or other dualistic culs-de-sac. Relationship as a mode of transcendence commingles flesh with spirit and allows for the great acts of private love and public benefaction. Yet, there are moral dangers here, too. Consider this response, cited in full earlier (p. 86), by an Arab boy on our PEQ, which was classified by all judges as interpersonal:

> When all Arab villages went on strike, workers didn't work and all the young people were crowded in the streets, pupils refusing to go to their classes. . . . On that day, coming back from school, I had a strange and special feeling. I was happy to see all the young people together as if they were one strong body nothing could separate but death.

What is at issue is the inner structure of his almost mystical identification with the throng in the street. This certainly illustrates the extension of the boy's emotional inner life into a relational dimension. It could also be the very basis of fascism—the symbolic *fasces* is, of course, the ancient binding together that "nothing can separate"—just as the other-directedness of a Jewish boy can be mirrored and reinforced by a militaristic ethos that's potentially numbing and soulless. Neither the self nor pure externality can produce as angelic a form or as horrific an evil as can interpersonal relations. The lesson, then, is to not be glib with assumed moral categorizations.

As we've interpreted our empirical findings, we've learned to value a humbler, less grandiose style of self-transcendence. Indeed, most of our adolescent voices spoke a simpler language than the macrocosmic unity that produces a messiah Christ one minute and a Nazi the next. Yet, their homelier joys did uncover, no less than their despairs, those universals that lead from and go beyond personal experience.

12

Facilitating Happiness: Implications for Education, Counseling, and Psychotherapy

We cannot always build the future for our youth, but we can build our youth for the future.

Franklin D. Roosevelt, Speech,
University of Pennsylvania, Philadelphia (1940)

As adolescents move from one stage of the life cycle to the next, they encounter many tasks, including formation of a sense of self, consolidation of ethical and moral values, establishment of intimate relationships, and achievement of a place in a community that engenders a sense of belonging. The task of the counselor and of the educator is to form a bond with the young person and to use this bond to promote

168

resolution of these psychosocial tasks. One practical means to this end will now be elaborated: the discovery of the self through a positive outlook. In the next chapter, I will emphasize the practical development of a prosocial orientation that provides benefit to self and others.

By introducing interventions aimed at promoting adolescents' well-being, the critical mass is shifted from negativity to positivity. The crux of activity is displaced from a focus on difficulties to a focus on growth-directed patterns that aim toward enrichment and personal development. This is not to say that adolescent difficulties and distress should be ignored or put aside, or that traumatic experiences have no impact on a person's life. However, our assumption is that people want more from their lives than just to "manage" or "get along," or to simply achieve or exist. The main focus of intervention is thus not on curing pathology but rather on the enhancement of human dignity and strength, the expression of higher levels of one's humanity, and the manifestation of a higher state of consciousness as evolving adults.

Psychological wellness (Cowen, 1991, 1994) is thus considered a crucial objective for social intervention and policy planning. It is more acknowledged today that a need exists to study both natural routes to wellness and engineered conditions or interventions that promote well-being. Social systems, including the educational structure to which children are exposed for many hours of every day, can thus be modified to incorporate experiences that accentuate the value of self-transcendent and prosocial activities.

The identification and reconstruction of positive experiences and opportunities for prosocial commitment may aid educators, therapists, and counselors in facilitating adolescents' experience of moments of happiness and growth. Whether the point of departure is pinpointed behavior change, process-oriented amelioration of developmental deficiencies, or dynamic facilitation of self-actualizing peak experiences (see Otto, 1967), such specific knowledge should serve to enrich the insight both of counselor and counseled.

In these concluding chapters, I will be suggesting very specific programs that, following on our research findings, can be practically adapted to encourage adolescents' self-realizing and self-transcending potential.

Educators and mental health professionals are not the only ones who share the burden, and the reward, of reinforcing the optimistic facets of adolescents as they interact with each other and with adults, and in their experiences with themselves. Parents naturally assume a lifelong responsibility to provide those opportunities for their child as well. From what parents offer their children as role models for experiencing happiness and undertaking a commitment to others, children in turn develop their own images.

An overall climate may be established which fosters self-exploration, spontaneity, and readiness to be in open touch with one's experiences and the needs of others—both for adolescents and the adults who people their lives. Positive role models among parents and educators are crucial to achieving such an environment. Numerous studies have demonstrated that nurturing, competent adults can buffer children from the stresses in their lives (Viadero, 1995). Few studies, however, have actually traced the *positive* impact on adolescents of positive adult self-image.

INTERVENTIONS EMPOWERING ADOLESCENTS THROUGH IMPARTING ACCESS TO PERSONAL JOY

Throughout our studies, we have related positive and joyous experience to personality types and, at this point, the question is begged, can positive experiences—any positive experiences—be used to positively influence personality development and perception? In one sense, we're back to a larger question, which our material has already raised in a variety of contexts. Just as we queried whether involvement in a helping activity promoted further self-transcendent proclivities, and just as we saw, at the end of Chapter 10 (p. 160), how acts that contribute to others promote further openness, so too we can now ask, in a therapeutic context, whether someone's positive experience, even a repressed one, can be used to promote his or her further growth.

Some of these positive experiences may indeed be latent or hidden, yet, one of our underlying moral assumptions is that there must be at least one fact of life that instills joy for every individual. As we find in the *Ethics of the Fathers* (Chapter 4, Mishnah 3), "Do not be scornful of any person and do not be disdainful of any thing, for you have no person without his hour and no thing without its place."

The adolescent's positive "hour," to use the Talmudic phrase, can be recalled from some crevice of memory to instill a sense of hope when the future seems bleak or trigger new perceptions and emotional interpretations to counter depression. The techniques described below, because they're based on a premise that certain kinds of experience are universal, can thus be applied to all populations, including deeply antagonistic or antisocial youth. Meanwhile, a sharper microscopic lens focused on remembered positive experiences may also help well-adjusted teenagers identify or reinforce inner strengths.

The inclusion of positive aspects of one's life is a well-accepted part of many therapeutic approaches and, in and of itself, is not innovative. Here, however, we propose a new emphasis on joys and strengths that is appropriate in a range of settings and situations. For example, interventions with a positive emphasis can be developed to target entire classrooms, as in the following very simple intervention by a school counselor:

> During weekly meetings with a class which was having problematic social relations, including individual students being teased and ostracized, the school counselor introduced a competitive game; the student who obtained the most points would win.
>
> One student would exit the room and all of the students would then suggest, discuss, and reach agreement as to three or four qualities they liked or appreciated about the absent student. Upon the student's return, his or her guesses regarding his or her own qualities would be compared to those of the class. Several students would participate during each such meeting and, after several such games, the school counselor led a discussion of what happened and what each student had learned.
>
> For a few rare moments, the focus of the entire class, and of each individual, was on the positive. It appeared from the classroom discussions that this objective was achieved. Yet, perhaps more significant was the experience of the teenagers who participated by leaving the classroom. They described the importance of hearing their classmates' appraisal and recognition, especially for those who were less confident in themselves. Even the more assured youngsters often discovered things that they never knew about themselves, such as the fact that their peers valued their courage or appreciated their honesty.

The most frequent sources of meaningful and joyful experiences for adolescents are those involving other people. This may provide a clue for parents and educators to consider the creation of conditions conducive to interpersonal contact involving love, trust, mutual help, and intimacy. At home, as we gleaned from young people's responses in our studies, such conditions may most commonly revolve around shared leisure activities, nighttime talks, or oftentimes festive family meals.

As a complement to encouraging adolescents' focus on the positive in their lives, counselors can therefore incorporate positive experiences in their work with parents of teenage children. The beneficial effect of exploring with parents their own remembered positive experiences in parenthood was observed during a research study on parents in group counseling (Magen & Stauber, 1992). These parents were troubled by their relations with their teenage children and sought counseling. Within the groups, the parents were given a questionnaire in which they were asked to describe their most positive experience as parents: "Recall an event or experience when, as a parent, you felt extremely good; an incident between you and your child that made you feel that, at that moment, being a parent is wonderful." The mothers and fathers, who generally were extremely distressed by their parenting experiences, at first hesitantly but then eagerly provided just such joyous or gratifying parenting illustrations:

One mother described how she had confided a serious family matter to her teenage son. His response moved her deeply. He was so sensitive and understanding, caring, involved, and showed so much maturity. She was also stirred by his gratitude to her for sharing the matter with him, for allowing him to be a part of this important discussion, for the trust she placed in him. The mother experienced the warm intimate feelings of being a mother, and realized how wonderful it is to see what kind of person her son was growing up to be, how wonderful it was to have such a son.

A father described the experience of discovering the deep humanity within his daughter, expressed toward a blind classmate. While the other students had been teasing him, she not only showed compassion but influenced her classmates to change their behavior. She aroused their sensitivity, without moral superiority or arrogance. The father felt a swell of pride, a sense of gratification in being her father, and a feeling that being a parent was wonderful.

Another mother recounted how prior to a family trip, with so much tension hanging between herself and her teenage daughter, she was apprehensive as to how everyone would get along in the car and during the vacation. The trip turned out to be a remarkable experience for this mother. She was witness to her daughter's enthusiasm for nature, her athletic ability, her genuine interest and curiosity in seeing artifacts and sites. During this short period of 4 days together, so much became clear for the mother; she suddenly saw what kind of good relations her daughter had with her siblings, just how much responsibility for them the girl shouldered, and how much joy she inspired. The mother, discovering all these facets of her teenage child, felt this family trip was one of her best parenting experiences.

In these counseling groups, parents expressed mounting excitement and later reported that this focus on the positive moved them to remember a different kind of experience and to see things they hadn't seen earlier or had forgotten. Later counseling sessions revealed a significant change in atmosphere, with positive remarks interspersed from time to time, in contrast to the usual accumulation of complaints and problems. One group continued to generate more remembered positive experiences, and the parents were able to acknowledge the extent to which their positive parenting experiences had affected them and had, apparently, similarly affected the relationships with their teenage children as well.

In working with parents, this positive focus can serve to enrich counseling groups, adding a heightened dimension to the discussions, and offering a new channel to improve problematic parent-child relations. The approach is reminiscent of Virginia Satir's objectives: to try to transform the home into a happy place by shifting from negativity to positivity, growth-directed patterns; to accentuate the dignity, strength, sense of worth, and self-esteem of the family members; and to help individuals and families use all their inner resources to grow and become more fully human (Satir, Bammen, Gerber, & Gomori, 1991).

Another way to implement a positive approach in counseling the parents of adolescents is to share the young people's own positive experiences with their parents:

One counselor (despite skepticism from staff coworkers) administered the Positive Experience Questionnaire to her adolescent students with cerebral palsy, encouraging them to describe several positive experiences. She was so impressed and touched by the results that she decided, with the students' permission, to use their experiences as a focus in her counseling of their parents. One incident shows the effectiveness of her approach:

Upon meeting with the distressed and overwhelmed parents of one teenage boy who had cerebral palsy, the school counselor shared with them the positive experiences their son had described. These parents were extremely dedicated to their son and invested much time, money, and energy visiting doctor after doctor and involving him and themselves in any number of treatments and interventions for their son.

The young man had recalled a particularly joyous day in the park where his parents had taken him to a show that he had been looking forward to. That day, he so much enjoyed being in the park, the nature, the kids, the atmosphere, but especially the music concert, with two singers he admired. Seeing these singers was "amazing"—such a thrilling experience. He had an exhilarating, wonderful day.

Another experience he described was one with a physical therapist who used a certain technique that the boy liked, and the physical therapy was always so much fun. He always really enjoyed the sessions, especially because he could raise himself up and sit, which was great fun. In fact, he was disappointed he wouldn't be meeting with this therapist anymore.

The emphasis on the young man's joyous experiences created a pleasant mood during the session and instigated a change in the parents' attitude. They said they couldn't remember how to laugh together with their son and commented that they had been so busy trying to make him well that they hadn't given much thought to making him happy. The counselor's unadorned focus on the positive, dramatizing for the parents their son's simple pleasures, enabled them to escape their vicious circle of searching for an impossible cure and to just enjoy him and his company. They returned to the next counseling session reporting that now they laughed more together, noting what a turning point can be achieved when one just thinks a little differently.

The actual interaction with the parent or, for that matter, educator, counselor, or therapist who can thus emphasize healthy personality features should in itself reinforce the value of interpersonal interaction and thus constitute a positive, happy experience: sharing oneself with another human being, for example, or revealing personal feelings in a nonthreatening and nonjudgmental atmosphere.

The crucial possibilities for such healthy joy are often simple ones. We found, for instance, that a frequent source for adolescents is a trip taken with a school or youth group. Often, this type of experience lends itself to positive or even exhilarating interactions with both peers and adults, to a sense of affinity with the external world in a stimulating new environment, or to an experience of self-disclosure and self-discovery:

The enjoyable trip . . . It was an unforgettable experience. In the beginning, I mean before the trip, I felt my life was boring with no joys. After that trip and some others we had, I felt that if you can take advantage of *life,* life is *wonderful,* it's all up to the person whether he spends his life bored or in activities that make life *wonderful* and full of experiences.

We went for a nature walk in class, and I did the work alone without a partner. I finished it quickly and went walking alone in the field. Everything was so colorful and blooming. The flowers were pretty and free, like you always dream of being. I had this wonderful feeling that the flowers love me, and I walked without noticing anyone, just the colorful flowers. The fragrance was fantastic, all of the things in the world were inside that fragrant color. When I walked inside it, it was really really fun. It was something good for me that I did alone and enjoyed alone without sharing it or other people's advice. I was free to be with myself and all of my responsibility was on myself.

When we went last year on a school trip, we climbed a high mountain and someone came down the mountain at a high speed right in front of me and I stopped him. I felt I'd saved somebody's life.

It seems to me that, as educators, we should reexamine our attitudes and rethink the importance we attribute to what we call extracurricular activities. They are not simply hygienic diversions. The adolescent voices here make us appreciate the wonder and deep significance of such experiences for our students. We need to be aware that a school trip, for example, can be a stressful and distressing experience for some students or an opportunity to explore personal and social problems from a different perspective. With the appropriate support from educators, adolescents who have difficult academic or social experiences in the classroom may benefit most. In any event, by being able to deal with and examine special positive events that once occurred in a teenager's life, including affirmative facets of home and school experiences, it then becomes possible to recognize what it is that brings joy, good feeling, change of mood, and a higher quality and greater extent of involvement in the world.

THE JOY OF LEARNING

Another important source of inspiration and delight that can be achieved within the classroom—the learning experience itself—has not gotten sufficient attention in curriculum planning or the instructional training of teachers. Substantial common ground clearly exists between the characteristics of intense positive experiences and the characteristics of a significant learning experience. Students are unquestionably capable of moments of transcendence while learning, which leave an enduring and positive mark. In our research, for example, teenagers have reported their joy upon discovering their own intellectual potential or sense of accomplishment when succeeding in achieving a desired goal.

Scientists and inventors have described powerful exhilaration at moments of discovery or connection. It is the moment when Archimedes cries "Eureka." In studies by Maslow and his followers, famous scientists and artists conceded that they live for such peak experiences, for the sense of elation they feel upon solving a problem, suddenly creating a new idea, or discovering an unknown fact. These moments were defined as the most significant in their lives. Unfortunately, most schools do not provide enough context for such experiences within their walls. Classrooms filled with 30 or 40 pupils, great masses of curricula that must be taught, and discipline problems all contribute to the covert assumption that experiential learning or the art of inquiry cannot and will not happen. It is as if teachers believe that conscientious teaching—to effectively prepare young people for the technology and competition of our modern society—forbids a sense of happiness and excitement while learning, or an emphasis on stimulating experience. What ensues is often a learning experience that lacks emotional meaning or an interpersonal frame of reference for the student, who then feels bored, restless, or indifferent. It is the task of educators to conquer the disengagement dogging youth in today's classrooms. History, geography, and mathematics can become arenas for experiences of wonder, discovery, perfection, and achievement. Within the right climate, the subject matter itself becomes the objective and reward for learning.

One specific item on the agenda of positive experience merits separate attention. As we saw in Chapter 6 (pp. 77-78, 82), musical experiences were a frequent theme in adolescents' responses to our questionnaires. At times the musical experience constituted a joyous self-revelation of one's talent and accomplishment among performers, or a sense of emotional exhilaration and inspiration. For others, the listening experience provided a feeling of being one with the melody. Particularly germane, music afforded an interpersonal experience of happiness for some:

> The first time I played together with someone, I really felt good, and whenever I play together with someone, I feel a "togetherness" feeling, harmony, and it really gives me a feeling, also afterward, that "the world is good," that I'm creating something pleasant to hear and to listen to. That I'm creating something of myself.

Musical motifs were even related by young people to their life aspirations (e.g., p. 45), whether emphasizing a coveted goal of performance achievement or describing the wish for an uplifting, gratifying connection between performing and giving joy to another human being, as in the following adolescent's objective for commitment beyond self:

> I would like one day to teach music. Because I feel that music makes the world more beautiful. In addition, I feel that everyone has the right to experience music and to feel what it says and does. And I also think that music is a good way to express feelings. I would choose to teach children or the needy, who usually don't get such an opportunity.

A link has indeed been established between a musician's intentions, in terms of the emotions he or she wishes to communicate, and the listener's experience of the musical piece (e.g., Gabrielsson & Juslin, 1996). Compositions and instruments naturally vary in their suitability to the expression of different feelings, and musicians' individual differences also have an impact on the listener's experience. An Eastern or African music might be temporarily inaccessible to an American or European listener, but only temporarily. Open-souled listeners soon learn to transcend culture in their experience of another culture's musical joy. As an intervention, music would then seem to have the advantage, not only of opening up the adolescent to his or her own capacity for joy and self-transcendence, but to universalize and therefore further humanize that experience.

INTERVENTIONS USING POSITIVE EXPERIENCES FOR ADOLESCENTS AT RISK

The emphasis on positive experience can be applied in a wide variety of settings and circumstances, limited only by the imagination and creativity of the counselor, educator, or parent. The following small-group intervention (Magen, 1980) is a case in point. It was a focused intervention to improve the performance of distressed soccer team players in late adolescence.

One of the national soccer teams in Israel had a good performance record but entered a disturbing five-game losing streak at the start of a new season, which resulted in low team and player morale. The team was at risk of being removed from the national league. Varied attempts by the team and its coach, manager, backers, and ardent fans (including the offer of bonuses as an extra incentive, a weekend team retreat, and even a range of religious and superstitious rituals) were of no avail. At the goalie's suggestion, they finally turned to a trained counselor-psychologist for a sensitivity group discussion. The 3-hour session included not only the team members but also, in a significant modification of customary relations, the coach and manager and one of the team backers as equal participants.

The group leader's approach accentuated the positive aspects of the soccer team and its performance in order to enhance the individuals' self-awareness and to increase positive regard and cohesiveness between teammates. Particular stress was placed on reconstructing past positive experiences, specifically, a time when the team excelled, when the individual young men performed as one streamlined, cohesive unit.

After initial explanations about group dynamics and the presentation of ground rules, each of the group participants was asked to introduce himself and to explain his unique function in the team. (For details, see Magen, 1980). During the next stage—an attempt to identify and discuss the group's current difficulties and feelings—much distress as well as mutual accusations and recriminations erupted. It was at that point that the group leader moved the discussion toward previous successes and abilities. The participants were asked to recall and describe specific incidents and feelings from times when the team achieved an impressive victory, when individual members "really showed their stuff," when their team was outstanding in its performance and displayed its strengths. Then, each participant was asked to recall and give detail on what he personally had contributed to the successful team performance, including his actions and emotions at the time.

The elation and exhilaration that emerged stimulated a wealth of warm feelings and goodwill between the teammates and staff, replacing the earlier hostility and censure. In addition, the participants began not only to recall moments of self-confidence and competence, but also to accept responsibility for their own behaviors in order to try to win the upcoming game that weekend.

Following this vivid reminder of the individuals' and team's positive capacities and strengths, each group participant was then asked to consider one thing which he could change, or do differently, one new behavior or attitude that could contribute to a win in the next game. The group won the next soccer game, 3:0, against the first-place team in the country. Media attention focused on the metamorphosis, which the group attributed to the positive encounter and the encouraging spirit they had experienced in the group session. The team continued to meet with the group leader three more times and continued to win.

This specific intervention maximized the value of positive experience and inner strengths for a group of talented but discouraged late adolescents whose self-esteem and team spirit depended on their ability to interconnect emotionally and functionally through positive channels. Interjecting a positive approach that emphasized a search for constructive means to bringing about change appeared to be helpful in improving performance as well as interpersonal relationships.

At times this immersion in pleasurable topics can in itself produce some change in mood. In an individual who is accustomed to being reminded of his or her limitations and problems, scrutinizing remembered joyous experiences could enable the recognition of inner strengths that had been ignored, denied, or overlooked; healthy, vibrant aspects of one's personality may seem to suddenly emerge. This type of self-examination, with its positive overtones, facilitates a deeper level of self-searching and self-exploration; even processes that are primarily geared toward prevention can thereby have a therapeutic effect on seriously distressed individuals, no less than on discouraged but essentially healthy soccer players.

Distressed adolescents are perhaps too accustomed to analyses, of one sort or another, of their own pathology. The implicit assumption in therapy, at school, or at home that they are "sick" reinforces the very negative self-evaluation that produced the depression or alienation or destructive behavior in the first place. For these adolescents, interventions based instead on positive experiences and memories could at least begin to reverse the inexorable vicious circle.

The more positive therapy does not merely extinguish symptoms, but also enables these youngsters to find meaning in life, even in their pain and sorrow, and allows them to fully experience the depth of their pain instead of isolating them from their own feelings. Depressed individuals may be viewed as experiencing their pain and sorrow at a blunt, shallow level of emotion rather than deeply and intensely. The anguish and sadness are most often not sensed as a meaningful part of one's existence that could contribute to self-understanding and appreciation of one's place in the world (Frankl, 1992; Jourard, 1971a; May, 1969).

In our recent study conducted in Israel (Magen, Birenbaum, & Pery, 1996), we examined the question of whether individuals who experience joy and happiness at high levels of intensity also experience pain and sadness to the same extent. Conversely, do those who experience sorrow in a shallow manner also lack depth in their experiences of happiness? Our findings demonstrated a consistency between the intensities of the most joyous and the most sorrowful remembered experiences. This correspondence lends support to the contention that the ability to experience life events in their entirety and the capacity to attribute to them their fullest level of meaning are related to the same personality components of the individual, regardless of the joyous or sorrowful nature of the experience.

The person who fails to experience intensely happy or sorrowful events can be described as a defensive individual; his or her identity growth will be limited to the safe and the familiar, thus reduced in scope and thwarted in potential (Jourard, 1971a). Such a person tends to experience only fragments of the environment and of himself or herself, rather than seeking a sense of wholeness or completeness. He or she may attempt to avoid intense experience through mediators such as drugs or through the operation of psychic defenses that block development. In turn, the stronger the barriers to realizing one's deeper potentials, the more dominant the sense of meaninglessness and emptiness.

With troubled youth, facilitation of strong emotional arousal and responsiveness to the surrounding world and the discovery of a personal sense of meaning are key strategies toward increasing the sense of belonging and sharpening sensitivity to self and others. However, we emphatically recommend that, in addition to encouraging the young person to experience pain and sorrow, we should try in our interventions to shift the emphasis from negativity to positivity.

One example of this approach in counseling interventions involves a teenage girl who had serious social and academic problems and was referred to her high school counselor:

This 14-year-old lived in a disadvantaged neighborhood and was being abused in her family. Removal from her home was being considered. At school, she was always in a bad mood and, when she came to the counselor's office, she appeared very sad and distressed. She expressed indifference about her future plans, accepting whatever the authorities would decide. It was difficult to penetrate this melancholy air. Each intervention on the part of the counselor seemed to elicit reminders of her pain and disappointment from everyone in her life. The counselor listened and was very empathetic to her sadness and loneliness, and the girl did talk. Yet, although some relationship was formed, she still felt distant, in a bleak and desolate world.

It was not until the counselor took a different direction—encouraging the girl to try and recall one event that made her feel good, one time in her life when things seemed different—that the girl could remember and describe an experience that brought some joy into her life. This connection usually happened when she would go for a walk in a field, when so many flowers were in bloom, flowers of all colors. She would pick some flowers, one of each color: red, yellow, blue, purple, orange, and make up a little bouquet. She related that at those times, "I feel like I'm having a little fun. Sometimes I even hum a tune. I really like it out there."

After she was encouraged to describe more of her feelings in detail, the girl was able, together with the counselor, to uncover additional moments when she felt good. They tried to examine what, in essence, "feeling good" meant to her ("What do you feel, do, think, and look at?"). To determine the effect these positive experiences may have had on her, the girl was asked how she behaved afterward, and she was able to reveal that something that usually irritated her was no longer so annoying when she had just had a good experience.

Following this intervention, a change was evident in the girl's capacity to discuss and describe positive aspects of her life. Together with her counselor, she found ways to use her own abilities to enjoy certain events and objects in her life. It later emerged that she also liked to draw occasionally and to care for the family dog. For this teenage girl, whose relationships with others were clouded by anger, danger, and pain, interpersonal channels to happiness were blocked. She seemed to find solace and pleasure in experiences with the external world and with self. These areas for happy experiencing were more accessible and easier for her, yet, the counselor's intervention did not allow her to avoid the main problems in her life. Rather, such positive experiences in the noninterpersonal contents were first steps to foster her self-concept, which could later facilitate her coping with interpersonal issues.

It seemed that, for this abused girl, a shift in emphasis from negativity to positivity thus led to self-revelations that contributed to a less despondent outlook on life. The shift in focus also helped forge a bond with an adult—the school guidance counselor—after experiencing pain and mistrust inflicted by the other adults closest to her.

A second example of focusing on the positive as a major resource in intervention, with an adolescent at high risk of delinquency and chronic drug abuse, consisted of informal intervention with a therapist:

A well-adjusted teenager believed that one of his contemporaries in an extracurricular activity was in trouble but showed promise and potential. The distressed 17-year-old responded to his friend's overtures and accepted the suggestion that he meet informally with a therapist of his friend's acquaintance. This troubled young man had a low socioeconomic background, was involved in a neighborhood gang, was a drug user, and was facing indictment in court on charges of harassing a taxi driver. Yet, as his open and benevolent friend had appreciated, this youngster was at the same time a positive leader among his peers, was trying to learn English, and replaced his father at work when the latter was called up to the army reserves.

An initial exploration of his feelings and perceptions revealed that this teenager felt his world was "a mess" and that he had "screwed up everything." Guiding him in changing the focus of his outlook, the therapist helped him identify those strengths and capacities that enabled him to carry out the responsible and positive behaviors he exhibited. He was encouraged to revive memories of successes and achievements, even small ones. This process resulted in a crucial first step on his part: identifying those personal abilities that could serve him in his desire to quit drugs.

The continued emphasis on this young man's obvious strengths and positive capacities within the therapeutic relationship served as a springboard for a number of ensuing improvements, such as his holding down a regular job and getting closer to his parents. Especially noteworthy was his desperate desire to become eligible for army duty, despite the army's rejection of him due to his record and impending trial. Significantly, this young man was very different indeed from many at-risk peers, who would do anything to be exempted from army service. Eventually, the trial date arrived, with the therapist as a character witness, and it was evident that the three formerly drowsy and distant judges were impressed when they heard about the positive aspects of this teenager's character, and they acquitted him.

He found a steady job, got married and started a family. As if inspired by the teenage friend and the therapist who helped extricate him from his vicious circle of defeat and self-destruction, he developed into a kind, generous, and self-confident person. It seems his case demonstrates how the faith placed in the goodness within a person—by peers, parents, therapists, and even judges—can reinforce and strengthen young people's humanity.

HELPING ADOLESCENTS WHO
FACE SOCIAL REJECTION

Interventions that foster the capacity for deep and intense experience of joyous moments in life have additional potential in a variety of other problematic situations. Socially rejected youngsters are often referred or refer themselves to a therapist or counselor for individual counseling. These teenagers are very sad and lonely, often on the verge of despair (Asher & Coie, 1990; Caplan & Weissberg, 1989; Evans & Eder, 1993; Parkhurst & Asher, 1992). At times, even the therapist or counselor feels repulsed by some aspect of the youngster's appearance or demeanor. Usually, in therapy, an attempt is made to help the teenager see that his or her social problems are reciprocal, and to help identify what he or she does that contributes to rejection.

Along with these individual interventions, group discussions are usually conducted with peers, friends, or the entire class to facilitate change in the individual's social condition. Sometimes there is improvement, but in most cases, it is a more resistant, long-lasting difficulty. Another possible approach begins with the assumption that the negative social situation arises because these youngsters do not believe in their ability to establish relations with other human beings. They fail to recognize in themselves those capacities that are essential for establishing bonds and connections with other people.

Most often, rejected adolescents do not trust that others will accept or like them. They usually develop considerable anger and defensiveness and tend to blame others. To establish some understanding of the adolescent's distress, therapists and counselors need to listen empathically to the adolescent's descriptions of painful rejection and declarations of anger: "Everyone's been invited to a school party except me," "No one wants to sit next to me or be my lab partner," "Everybody hates me," and "Who needs them? I hate everybody anyway!"

Based on the assumption that every human being must have at least one other soul that he or she cares about or that means something to him or her, one specific technique may be recommended that emphasizes the search for socially valuable personal attributes through the naming of a positive person in one's life. We may ask the youngster, "Could you think of someone with whom you have felt good at some time or another? Or maybe an occasion when you had a nice feeling with another person—it could be a family member or a neighbor, or whatever."

Most adolescents will exclaim that there is no such person, yet with enough encouragement, the technique achieves results; the teenager is able to find someone. Most of the time, this "discovery" is accompanied by a new brightness, an optimism. We then request elaboration. "Try and describe this person and what it's like when you're together. What are the things that make being with him feel good? What happens to you then? What do you feel? What does he find in you? What makes him enjoy your company?" From here, certain incidents with the person are explored, highlighting the youngster's personal characteristics that people are attracted to and can even love.

Whether the attribute mentioned is a good sense of humor, helpfulness, physical agility, or fun companionship when fishing, meaningful relations and inner strengths have come to the fore. The intervention may continue: "Perhaps there are others who see this quality in you. On what other occasions have you seen this quality come out?" Finally, the adolescent can be helped to generalize these positive qualities and interpersonal feelings to other people and other situations. This method can help the process of self-change to begin. Sometimes the recall itself has its own value, causing a change in mood, opening a door to further hope and exploration.

Such interventions thus attempt to help socially deficient youngsters rediscover those elements and qualities within themselves that enable favorable relations with other people, freeing them from the vicious circle of loneliness and alienation. Self-examination of their own positive qualities may enable even severely disturbed teenagers to realize the healthy, formative aspects of their lives, to reflect on and better appreciate the parts of experience that render a feeling that life is worthwhile. Conversely, the agonizing reappraisals and therapeutic immersions in vast pools of personal failure and pain will not, as we have suggested, encourage confident new beginnings. Thus, the tendency of most therapists to avoid psychoanalysis with adolescents may indeed be well-advised.

A similar intervention can likewise be applied with the extremely frustrating and challenging group of delinquent youth. The positive approach may seem ironic for cynical, hostile, and suspicious adolescents, who generally encounter much difficulty establishing a therapeutic alliance with educators or mental health professionals. Yet, my experience supervising counselors who were involved with juvenile offenders shows that the same approach described above offers much potential, not only in expanding the youngsters' access to positive facets of themselves, but also in breaking the impasse between themselves and the counselors who wanted to help but found it extremely difficult to do so.

One particularly vivid example occurred at a U.S. community center that juvenile offenders were required to attend and where the youngsters, typically filled with self-hate and hate for others, often exhibited a worldview based on pessimism and negativity, with no trust in anyone. Despite strong motivation and an empathetic approach, the counselors and other mental health professionals felt a growing hopelessness and weariness in the face of the youngsters' persistently hostile, angry, and desolate expressions. It was the introduction of the same positive orientation described above—directing the young people's attention to a search for one person who meant something to them—that rendered some change in the community center's atmosphere. When the youngsters finally could identify someone, the next stage consisted of inquiring, "What do you find in this person? What does he or she do or have that means something to you?" Remarkably often, the quality found in the person was goodness or trustworthiness. Many times, the youngsters would even state, "I'd give my life for her/him."

This shift in approach simultaneously strengthened the therapeutic bond, enabling the therapist to connect to these "unreachable kids," to find something to like or identify with in the youngsters. For both counselor and client, this approach often fostered a more op-timistic perspective about the world and the future, establishing the beginnings of a foundation for the therapeutic working relationship.

By learning more about themselves and their place in the world around them, even young people at risk can thus become attuned to the creative impact of intrinsically rewarding and fulfilling moments and relationships. Teenagers on the verge of crime, who were neglected by their families, have also been a recent target of affirmative interventions in Israel.

In one mandatory residential institution for these youngsters in Israel, a positive approach emphasizing the trusting and listening attitude of the counselors and their special relationship with the students has shown clear results. While it appears that delegating tasks, guiding behavior, and clarifying past and present diffi-

culties were effective, counselors and educators have also attributed much importance to a focus on these youngsters' reasons
for hope and optimism, on the things they enjoy in life, however
few and uncommon these may be. In interviews, these students
recalled times when they felt trusted or respected, when others
showed interest in what they were feeling, and when it seemed that
someone truly cared about them. These experiences, they reported,
were very important in their personal growth, influencing their
view of themselves and the world. (For more, see Ronen, Magen,
& Zabar, 1996)

A recent exhibition of photography by at-risk adolescents demonstrated impressively both the difficulties in their lives as well as their
dreams of a better future. One 16-year-old boy described his preference
for taking photos of optimistic sights, explaining that, "In photography,
I find the joy of life, the joy I would want for myself" (Regev, 1997,
p. 19). Another boy of the same age said, "I most like to photograph
birds because they're always free, like I dream of being" (p. 19). In many
of the teenagers' night photographs, a beam of light passes through the
image, or a central source of light appears. They easily interpreted this
as their desire to search for light in the dark gloom of their lives.

Educators, through their encouragement and by providing access to
such a symbolic art form and means of expression, have facilitated in
these youngsters an opportunity to seek out and identify some brightness
in life, to acknowledge that the positive sights for which they yearn are
indeed a part of their world. A large number of these teenagers went on
to complete high school, staying clear of criminal activity, and some even
took their matriculation exams and later enlisted for military service. It
was an opportunity that changed the meaning of their existence.

Our findings suggest an additional important reason for creating
conditions that promote intense and meaningful positive experiences. If
the adolescents who reported intense positive experiences expressed
greater readiness for commitment beyond self, then meaningful positive
experiences not only cause subjective personal satisfaction, but seem to
make the adolescent a better person at least in terms of his or her
willingness to contribute to others and to get involved in causes beyond
oneself. As will be elaborated in the next chapter, it is a particularly happy
marriage of therapeutic intervention with social engineering.

13

Nurturing the Soil: Interventions to Encourage Transpersonal and Prosocial Focus

The need for devotion to something outside ourselves is even more profound than the need for companionship. If we are not to go to pieces or wither away, we all must have some purpose in life: For no man can live for himself alone.

Ross Parmenter, *The Doctor and the Cleaning Woman* (1949)

Once we understand the dynamic relationship between commitment beyond self and happiness, we understand, really, that our job has just begun. The transcendent moment is a fragile experience; its memory may linger, and the consciousness of it still nurture, but our obligation as therapists, teachers, and parents is to create a social situation that will encourage more such transcendent moments. In other words, we have to take the best positive experiences of our subjects and build a world around them.

In this chapter, we will discuss ways to guide and to encourage the proliferation of prosocial commitments in order to foster positive identity formation and self-acceptance. Various projects can be planned to help youngsters learn more about the world and the direct rewards of involvement with its people. Each project forges new links between the self and world. Eventually, the repetition of positive giving or helping experiences creates an innate assumption in the individual that the link between self and commitment to others is indissoluble. Once learned, the value to self of commitment beyond self cannot be forgotten.

As a road map to these strategic experiences, let's turn again to the actual voices of our adolescent subjects. The following essays, written by adolescents who were involved in our Personal Commitment Project, suggest how potently these factors play out, and how the moral values implicit in such commitment represent both new directions for curricula and a therapeutic tool to use in our schools, institutions, counselors' offices, and homes.

TO BE A FRIEND

For several months now, I have been a counselor for "Rachel" who's a 16-year-old needy student from a very large family of Indian descent. Socially, Rachel is disconnected and closed. She has no girlfriends her age, she has no one to share her thoughts with. Her parents don't allow her to get involved with kids her age so that she won't get "ruined." In her home, she has to help a lot, doesn't go out, doesn't enjoy herself. Despite all that, Rachel has good potential—she wants to learn and to know. When the counselors' coordinator told me about her, I was apprehensive. I thought we had nothing in common, that we wouldn't have anything to talk about, and I planned to help her only with her studies. Yet to my surprise we found common topics for conversation, about school, home, her parents, beauty, fashion, adolescence, and singers. It's fairly obvious that my contact with her has helped her be more open with me, to express her opinion, to ask and be interested, and even also to help her with peers at her school and in her neighborhood. Although my commitment to the counseling ends at the end of the school year, I think we'll continue to stay in touch.

From this experience I learned a lot about preconceptions about a disadvantaged population, that even a girl who is a poor student and comes from a disadvantaged family can have beautiful sides to her. And about myself I learned that I have the self-ability to help as a counselor even though I didn't learn how to do it, and that the investment of time isn't great compared to the benefit you reap.

(Israeli Jewish girl)

COACHING FOOTBALL
IN THE YOUTH CENTER

The sports coordinator at the youth center advertised an announcement about the possibility of registering for a football club, and my name was listed as the team's coach. When I saw my name prominently on the announcement, a very good feeling arose in me; I felt the responsibility placed upon me. I received an explanation that I wouldn't only be coaching football, but rather I'd also be working with young students, and my job would be to awaken their interest in the subject, and to handle the team's social problems. I started to coach the team, and then the worries started. I had to take an interest—how should I coach the students? I found out that in addition to football, there are so many beautiful things about these children—they're very talented. The activity gave me a clear picture of the significance of working with children, and I learned to understand the real meaning of "responsibility" and "personal commitment."

(Israeli Arab boy)

THE SOLDIERS' MEMORIAL CENTER

One of the areas in which I work is editing memorial albums on people who fell in Israel's wars, through the "Remembrance of Our Sons" Center. . . . This work has not a few difficulties, but it contributes a lot to those who perform it. The main problem is in gathering material on the fallen from the War of Independence: Many of the people I want to interview in order to get material and information are no longer living. And time takes its toll, and people get older. They forget and can't tell us a lot. So it's very hard to coordinate enough material to put out a memorial album.

But along with the difficulties, this work gives much to the person doing it: I've been greatly enriched as a person and as an Israeli. I learned about battles, about events, and about places. Mostly, I learned to appreciate people, I learned to respect people—the "silver platter" of our country, those who gave their lives for our lives. This appreciation and respect for the living and the dead has made me into a better person, a more educated person, and a better patriot. My activity grants me intense satisfaction and a good feeling, that I am memorializing heroes, people who are very important in this country's history. Also older parents, who thank me tearfully after I've published a memorial album and memorialized their son who gave his life for the country, and no action was taken to memorialize him—until now.

(Israeli Jewish boy)

In light of such testimony, I propose that social skill intervention in the schools be broadened to include the value of commitment beyond self, with its accompanying benefits for the youngster's self-esteem, sense of purpose and worth, feeling of accomplishment and mastery, and satisfying interaction with other human beings. We thereby strengthen teenagers' identity formation and self-acceptance, while fostering their capacity to experience moments of real joy and definition in their lives.

One of the familiar ways to draw upon and enhance the growth-promoting effects of the interpersonal encounter within the existing educational setting is peer counseling. Here, young people aid their contemporaries, support them, and undergo the mutual interpersonal experience of helping and being helped. It has been shown, for example, that adolescents who become involved in peer tutoring activities that benefit their at-risk schoolmates (e.g., Martino, 1994) may likewise benefit themselves in the process. We would like to strongly emphasize the importance of this reciprocity in the helping relationship, as in the illustration below from the work of a high school counselor. Such interventions, by definition, are not then limited to at-risk students receiving help. Being on the helping end of a relationship can also boost the self-image of the young person with social deficits, as opposed to his or her consistently being on the receiving end, with incumbent feelings of neediness and incompetence. Many such opportunities for prosocial involvement with peers arise regularly in the school system.

In one instance, a dispute arose among teachers and parents regarding a ninth-grade class with six students who demonstrated low academic performance and disruptive classroom behavior as they neared the second term of the school year. It was feared that these six students would lower the level of education for the remainder of the class, and it was suggested that they should be transferred. Instead, a reciprocal peer tutoring intervention was initiated. The school counselor presented the problem to the class—that some students were academically weak and others were not—and that this was a problem for the entire class. She enlisted the students' help, according to the following rule: All students should envision what they could offer classmates and also the area in which they could benefit from the help of others. Together with the teacher, the reciprocal assignments were determined. The academically weak students were assigned tutors in their areas of need—biology or math, and so on—and, at the same time, gave help to their tutors in various ways, such as coaching an athletic skill.

At times, the identification of areas of need was difficult, as when students excelled in both academics and other spheres. One well-rounded adolescent prepared to tutor a classmate in academic subjects but could not find an area of need for himself. Eventually a solution was found: The classmate accepted the responsibility of helping his tutor modify chronic tardiness to school, taking it upon himself to awaken the tutor every morning before school and to make sure that he arrived on time.

Reports were presented weekly in small groups and every 2 to 3 weeks to the entire class. Despite occasional sluggishness and some residual lack of motivation, the students in this classroom began to comment on the feelings of gratification and satisfaction they enjoyed while performing their assignments. In fact, when some students were found to be avoiding their duties, peer pressure got them back on track. Some even reported enjoying new relationships with peers who had formerly not been in their circle of friends.

As a result of this intervention, the class was extraordinarily active for a period of several months, and the academically weak students, rather than suffering the destructive effects of being transferred, even improved their performance. Most important, these adolescents were enabled to discuss their difficulties and problems in the classroom, to accept them and find ways to cope with them, rather than giving up in the face of challenges.

PROJECTS PROMOTING
YOUTH INVOLVEMENT _____

Our research studies indicated that, even in disadvantaged neighborhoods, the healthy aspects of at-risk adolescent personalities may be empowered through prosocial involvement.

Children in these neighborhoods often develop a fatalistic attitude affecting their cognitive system such that neither success nor failure is believed to be related to their own actions. An externally oriented "culture of poverty" in such environments has been described. External factors are felt to control all needs, feelings, and interactions, and external conflicts supplant complex affects and internal tensions (Coleman, Kelly, & Moore, 1975; Frankenstein, 1970, 1979; Spiro, 1988). Disadvantaged individuals are described as typically expecting events to lead to failure, as not believing in a logical, rule-based order for the world, as having difficulty mastering abstract concepts, and as tending to attribute the fulfillment of needs or expectations to chance. Youngsters in these neighborhoods, consequently, tend to establish manipulative and impersonal relations with others.

Much research has highlighted various means for intervening in the vicious circle of this culture of poverty. In the past, the severe deprivation in these communities often led to the introduction of simple, quick, concrete changes in physical surroundings, in order to improve residents' sense of pride and self-image. However, the very limited results of comprehensive programs focusing on physical rehabilitation via legislative, economic, and housing conditions has led to the difficult recognition that such modifications, without adequate emphasis on internal social changes, are doomed to failure (Churchman, 1987; Churchman, Alterman, & Law-Yong, 1985; International Committee, 1984; Spiro, 1988).

Our research on happiness and commitment beyond self in disadvantaged adolescents (Magen et al., 1992) demonstrated that students who were involved in activities dedicated to the benefit of others clearly surpassed similarly underprivileged youths in terms of their willingness to commit themselves to others, their sense of life coherence, and the intensity of their positive experiences. In other words, such activities triggered a correction of the imbalance in some aspects of their lives created by their cultural and social deprivation.

Our findings corroborated previous research (Alterman et al., 1982; Churchman, 1988) establishing that a heightened sense of manageability over one's destiny and life circumstances through increased involvement in the community can reduce social distress in culturally disadvantaged situations. Our study thus highlighted the crucial importance of fostering the involvement of underprivileged adolescents in activities dedicated to the benefit of others and/or society. The tendency in Western nations has usually been to "help" the poor by "helping them help themselves." As a corrective to that tendency, the data here would seem to open up a wholly different new vista of social intervention.

The deprived adolescents' responses to volunteer activity may be explicated both from an environmental approach, with regard to modifications engendered in the culture of poverty, and from a developmental approach in terms of age-related malleability. According to the environmental perspective, the involved youngsters were exposed to opportunities for experiencing their actions as directly producing results, rather than viewing outcomes as grimly inevitable or coincidental. A happy corollary was a perceptible improvement in the attitudes of these adolescents toward institutionalized authority, because those authority figures were the ones who had introduced or supported the youngsters' pursuit of the volunteer activities that had proved so satisfying and purposeful.

From a developmental standpoint, social supports have been cited elsewhere as having a strong beneficial role in the lives of disadvantaged youth (DuBois, Felner, Meares, & Krier, 1994; Milgram & Palti, 1993; Rosenthal, 1995). The three components of adolescents' sense of coherence were strengthened: understanding that reality is governed by predictable rules, feeling that one possesses adequate resources for coping with life events, and achieving personal meaning from daily challenges and difficulties. These processes appear to effect some reversal in the culture of poverty, which is passed on through the generations. Although scarce, other studies have also indicated the potential usefulness of a sense of caring, the forging of interpersonal connections, and community concern among poor urban youth (Romer & Kim, 1995; Way, 1995).

On the basis of these findings, new directions in social rehabilitation programs may be proposed. It has already been found that volunteer involvement in extracurricular programs in Israeli school settings (e.g., community service, companionship to residents in homes for the aged, peer counseling, and assistance to younger students with various social and academic difficulties) has been successful in fostering commitment beyond self among a wide range of adolescents (e.g., Magen & Aharoni, 1991).

An additional word on the hearing-impaired adolescent is warranted here. Recorded successes among the general adolescent population are instructive for educators, counselors, and rehabilitation workers who plan curricula and interventions for this more special handicapped population. Failure to foster and strengthen the desire for prosocial commitment (as demonstrated in Magen, 1990a) may well be one of the reasons why this population—or any population, for that matter—can still maintain a sense of being disadvantaged, despite the considerable support received from society. Or, perhaps, the very support and assistance given to people with hearing impairments are in themselves factors that encourage a sense of entitlement or a feeling of being underprivileged, thereby generating a focus on self-centered needs, with less openness and sensitivity to the needs of others.

Our studies conducted in school settings also underscore the importance of *guiding* young people who become involved in various sorts of prosocial activities. Although at one level they point to the potential value of introducing such projects into schools during adolescence, the results of our studies suggest the need to proceed with caution. We studied a high school that requires all tenth graders to participate in mandatory prosocial activities and permitted eleventh graders to continue this volunteer involvement (Magen & Offek, 1993). Whereas students required to engage in prosocial activities did not show pre-post differences on the examined variables, those who later volunteered did show such differences. These findings document the importance of two factors, that is, personal inclination to volunteer for prosocial activities and involvement in such activity itself.

It appears that adolescents most benefit from discussions and meetings with professionals who follow and encourage their community services. I suggest that any prosocial activities where youth are involved as givers should be accompanied by a supportive professional framework that encourages self-monitoring and self-evaluation to clarify the significance of the activity, and to bring into awareness the feelings, thoughts, and sensations within oneself that arise during such interactions.

To help others is often not a simple task emotionally; we may feel guilt, helplessness to make a change, or anger at the neediness or frequent apathy of our beneficiaries. Such ambivalence is a fundamental part of the human experience of giving, and it demands the patient attention of counselors who have no doubt been wrestling with such shadows in their own careers. The exhilaration of youth who can tough out these frustrations and setbacks of the giving experience speaks, again, for itself.

I ENRICHED MYSELF WITH LIFE EXPERIENCE

I arrived at the Keren Or family club, which is actually a substitute home for children ages 6 to 12 from needy families. I adopted one boy and helped him especially. It was clear to me that, in order to truly help him, I had to establish a warm and trusting relationship with him. At first it wasn't easy, he was reserved and suspicious and strongly rejected my help out of embarrassment. Gradually through improvised attempts on my part to get closer to him, he opened up and enjoyed it, and I felt that I'd begun to gain his trust.

My contact with the club wasn't just with the boy. I also established relationships with all of the other children, I played and talked with them, showered the little ones, and cleaned up after meals. By the way, we received guidance in social studies class through films and social games. . . .

During my activity I felt that I wanted to contribute much more and that I'd only contributed a little. I didn't know how beneficial I was until the separation at the end of the year, which was difficult for me and the children. Then I realized that I'd undergone a full, effective year, that the constant activity with children from difficult homes had matured me. I discovered within myself competence and capabilities that I didn't know existed before, and I enriched myself with life experience.

(Israeli Jewish girl)

BIG SISTER IN THE VILLAGE

As part of the "Personal Commitment" project, I worked in a psychoeducational school for children located in my village. The principal asked me to help one of the children who had just arrived and to escort him to the club. I turned to the boy and saw him crying. I went closer to him affectionately and I stroked him until he calmed down. I asked him the reason for his crying, and he answered me with a stifled voice:

"I want Mommy." I continued sitting next to him until I felt he would trust me, and during this, he fell asleep. When I arrived the next day, it seemed like the boy was eagerly awaiting my arrival, and he smiled at me. From that day, our relationship grew close, and he would ask them to call me at home and remind me of the date of my next visit.

This relationship was in question when the institution was going to close down, and the boy would be returned to his home. The boy's parents did live in the village, but I was afraid my parents wouldn't let me visit him. I am a daughter in a traditional family that wouldn't easily let me leave the house to go visit an unknown family. But my parents showed understanding toward me. That weekend, I decided to visit the boy's house. An older woman, in shoddy clothes, opened the door and told me her son didn't need help. Even so, I asked her if I could see her son, and when the boy saw me, he ran to me and hugged me innocently. His mother said that there was no need for me to come. I was insulted and said I wouldn't come anymore.

At home, I deliberated a lot about it. It's true that I was insulted by the mother's behavior, but the boy wasn't to blame for that, and I couldn't punish him. That same week, there was a school trip planned, and I remembered that the boy's birthday was on the same date. I debated with myself what to do—to join in his celebration or go on my trip? I preferred the boy and went to visit him. His mother apologized to me for her behavior, and he came running and happy toward me. I discovered that sometimes you have to give up certain things for the sake of something more important. I also discovered that this activity contributed a lot to me and changed something inside me. It gave me first of all self-confidence that I can help others and contribute of my strength and energy so that they will be happier.

(Israeli Arab girl)

THE FAMILY ROLE AS A CONTEXT
FOR PROSOCIAL BEHAVIOR _____

In designing interventions, it is crucial to identify the social processes within the family unit and the community that may enhance resilience and contribute to the development of healthy attributes in adolescents. Influences on empathic feelings, moral commitment, and prosocial behavior include modeling and socialization, as well as conventional norms of social responsibility and reciprocity (Clary, 1994; Mansbridge, 1990).

Schulman and Mekler's (1994) book, *Bringing Up a Moral Child,* offers sorely needed guidance for parents who face adolescents' disparaging attitudes, disregard for others' feelings, and even cruelty at times. Enhancing empathy and simply teaching the Golden Rule, they stress, is more important for today's youth than it has ever been. This simple morality is easier to inculcate in younger children who already feel empathy for other human beings. In such cases, parents can encourage good works benefiting others through role modeling and by stressing that helping others feels good, or, alternatively, that not helping can make one feel bad.

The relationship between feeling good and helping others as a moral lesson has been demonstrated throughout our own research and by previous studies. Reminding children of previous incidents when their actions created certain feelings is a good way to identify emotions that equate with moral values: "Remember how sad you felt when you knocked Johnny down and hurt him?" or "Remember how good you felt when you saw how happy Nancy was the time you let her join your game?" (Schulman & Mekler, 1994, p. 101).

When youngsters are less inclined to feel empathic toward other people, the task of instilling a prosocial orientation is more challenging. Yet, fundamentally, almost every child has had the experience of making someone else happy. Youngsters are capable of giving much love and even "love to give love" (Schulman & Mekler, 1994, p. 101). According to these authors, who developed an actual moral training program for parents to implement, the natural moral capacities of each child can be brought to bear. One way to enhance the development of empathy or conscience would be to encourage youngsters to focus on the feelings of other people as they listen to others.

One concern often voiced by parents is whether encouraging their children to be kind, caring, and just will put them at a disadvantage in today's aggressive, competitive society. Parents fear that "nice," giving children will be pushed around, ridiculed, or ignored. Yet, research evidence points to the contrary. Those youngsters who have strong moral principles tend to stand their ground and are not easily coerced; and those who treat people compassionately because of their sensitivity to others' feelings do not constitute an easy target because they know how to read others' motives (Schulman & Mekler, 1994). Such youngsters are usually recognized and appreciated for their principles and behavior, and their popularity is often linked to their sensitivity to other people's feelings and their willingness to help. The type of youngster described here must be differentiated from "pleasers," who lack confidence and act nicely to win friends. Adolescents want their friends to be truthful, cooperative, encouraging, and trustworthy, as well as fun.

The interventions I am suggesting, and the potential impact of the family, must naturally be measured against the immense modifications to social standards, norms, and expectations that have occurred over recent decades. Today's generation of young people are far more exposed from a younger age to a wider variety of behaviors, choices, and information. Especially with respect to sexuality and the legitimacy of unusual lifestyles, youngsters receive mixed messages. Even healthy adults often find it challenging to distinguish today between nonconformism and dysfunctional behavior. In one sense, previous generations had an easier task because parental prohibitions were generally clear and were rigidly upheld, in keeping with societal expectations. Any deviation from these strict rules could be interpreted either as rebellion or as doing something wrong.

Today, in recognition of adolescents' perceived maturity and desire for independence, we expect them to choose their own paths. Having encountered teenage anger and resistance, having recognized the vast impact of their children's peer culture, adults are more reluctant to interfere or to set limits on appearance, demeanor, and decision making. Thus, teenagers are now given more "space" in which to experiment and define themselves.

Yet, often this new parenting mode does not enable more autonomy nor does it enhance identity formation. Whether in the guise of tolerance, permissiveness, or indulgence, when external limits are not set appropriately, teenagers face an increasing inner confusion and insecurity. As they have told us directly in our research (Magen, 1994), adolescents *need* guidance and involvement from their parents. They may have a world of choices and information at their fingertips, but they still are confused by sexual challenges. They may be extremely attracted to new social situations, but they still have inhibitions and hesitations about their own social behavior. They may want to be treated with the same trust and respect as adults, yet emotionally, they feel immature and unready to face the adult world with all its tasks and demands.

Parents can play a dual role. On the one hand, adolescents want and need their parents to help them look inward. Encouraging youngsters to do so can be initiated by asking the questions, "Who are you? What do you want to do with yourself? What makes you happy?" Offering guidance and opinions about information the teenager possesses or about choices teenagers face can help them to understand the full significance of decisions and to find direction when exposed to new opportunities (Magen, 1994).

On the other hand, actually introducing new experiences and suggesting ideas for positive alternatives can be another important function for parents. While encouraging youngsters to become involved, for example, in volunteer work or to take some action that would benefit others, parents are, perhaps, drawing on their own experience, or at least remembering the depth of connection between selfless acts and self-satisfaction in their own lives. While suggesting ideas for how best to handle a situation with a classmate, the parent doesn't limit, direct, or choose for the adolescent, but rather broadens the repertoire of responses.

Epilogue

Throughout my work, I have been impressed over and over again both by the depth and by the dazzling variety of ways in which young people from such diverse backgrounds express joy. The complexity of their expressions is often fascinating and challenging. At other times, it is their very simplicity that amazes.

To a great extent, it is, as I have suggested, a moral exhilaration. The capacity of adolescents for self-understanding, their willingness to share and reveal their inner struggles, convince me that the capacity for self-transcendence is something that adolescents—perhaps like everyone—are just waiting to exercise. All they need is the faith of others.

It's easy, really, to find a way to end this book. My empirical study—of adolescent joy and transcendence, and the potential for guiding adolescents toward a personal fulfillment promised by the recognition of their intrinsic penchant for positive experience—has relied throughout on the eloquent personal testimony of the adolescents themselves.

It behooved me to simply find one such passage that could stand for all, and one youngster who, eloquent but not grandiose, could speak for all. It would have to be a direct and coherent narrative that would yet connect all our themes of personal joy through personal giving. Not surprisingly, I did find one, who happened to be an Israeli Jewish girl.

"AYELET"—A SILENT REQUEST FOR FRIENDSHIP

After the 3 days of presenting the different areas of activity we could choose, including the "Service for Others" setting, I found myself facing worlds which I had only encountered in the newspapers, literature, and cinema—people who truly need help. . . . After several meetings with the volunteer coordinator, the social worker took me to my first meeting with the family. She introduced me to them and left me to deal with the new situation on my own. For a moment, I stood embarrassed. My fears—that I wouldn't know how to approach them, that I wouldn't know what to say—came true. All that passed in an instant. The children—hungering for warmth, for conversation, for attention—surrounded me with their curiosity, questions, and a silent request that I be their friend. . . .

The time passed more quickly than I expected. We spent a lot of time together and our closeness was mutual. I couldn't believe how hard the separation was. I left knowing that the "Ayelet" I'd met in the beginning was not the same girl when I left. And I am not the same girl I was when I arrived either. "Ayelet" changed from an insecure girl who hid herself in the house, ashamed of her own existence, into a dynamic girl who isn't afraid to express her opinion. Her grades went up and her face smiled more and more—all of this gave me a lot of satisfaction. "The satisfaction in giving"—this abstract pedagogical concept became tangible and familiar. I left with the feeling that all the difficulties I dealt with had strengthened me for dealing with other difficulties, my own difficulties.

(Israeli Jewish girl)

References

Adams, J. F. (Ed.). (1973). *Understanding adolescence*. Boston: Allyn & Bacon.

Adler, A. (1917). *The neurotic constitution: Outline of a comparative individualistic psychology and psychotherapy*. New York: Moffat, Yard.

Adler, A. (1964a). *Social interest: A challenge to mankind*. New York: Capricorn.

Adler, A. (1964b). *Superiority and social interest*. Evanston, IL: Northwestern University Press.

Ajzen, I., & Fishbein, M. (1977). Attitude-behavior relations: A theoretical analysis and review of empirical research. *Psychological Bulletin, 84*, 888-918.

Allport, G.W. (1961). *Pattern and growth in personality*. New York: Holt, Rinehart & Winston.

Alterman, R., Carmon, N., & Hill, M. (1982). Integrated evaluation: A synthesis of approaches to the evaluation of broad-aim programs. *Social-Economic Planning Sciences, 18*, 381-389.

Alvarez, A. (1991). Wildest dreams: Aspiration, identification, and symbol-formation in depressed children. *Psychoanalytic Psychotherapy, 5*, 177-189.

Andrews, F. M., & Withey, S. B. (1976). *Social indicators of well-being: America's perception of life quality*. New York: Plenum.

Antonovsky, A. (1979). *Health, stress, and coping*. San Francisco: Jossey-Bass.

Antonovsky, A. (1987). *Unraveling the mystery of health*. San Francisco: Jossey-Bass.

Argyle, M. (1986). *The psychology of happiness*. London: Methuen.

Aristotle. (1925). *The Nicomachean ethics* (David Ross, Trans.). London: Oxford University Press. (Original work 4th century B.C.).

Aron, A. (1977). Maslow's other child. *Journal of Humanistic Psychology, 17,* 9-24.

Aron, A., & Aron, E. N. (1986). *Love and the expansion of self.* New York: Hemisphere.

Asher, S. R., & Coie, J. D. (Eds.). (1990). *Peer rejection in childhood.* New York: Cambridge University Press.

Aubrey, J. (1982). *Brief lives* (R. Barber, Ed.). Totowa, NJ: Barnes & Noble. (Original work published 1697/1813)

Barber, B. L., & Eccles, J. S. (1992). Long-term influence of divorce and single parenting on adolescent family- and work-related values, behaviors, and aspirations. *Psychological Bulletin, 111,* 108-126.

Bar-Tal, D. (1982). Segmental development of helping behavior: A cognitive learning model. *Development Review, 2,* 101-124.

Bateman, G. C. (1996). Attitudes of the deaf community toward political activism. In I. Parasnis (Ed.), *Cultural and language diversity and the deaf experience* (pp. 146-159). Cambridge, UK: Cambridge University Press.

Batson, C. D. (1990). How social an animal? The human capacity for caring. *American Psychologist, 45,* 336-346.

Batson, C. D., Dyck, J. L., Brandt, J. R., Batson, J. G., Powell, A. L., McMaster, M. R., & Griffitt, C. (1988). Five studies testing two new egoistic alternatives to the empathy-altruism hypothesis. *Journal of Personality and Social Psychology, 55,* 52-77.

Batson, C. D., & Shaw, L. L. (1991a). Encouraging words concerning evidence for altruism: Authors' response. *Psychological Inquiry, 2,* 159-168.

Batson, C. D., & Shaw, L. L. (1991b). Evidence for altruism: Toward a pluralism of prosocial motives: Target article. *Psychological Inquiry, 2,* 107-122.

Baum, S. K., & Stewart, R. B. (1990). Sources of meaning through the lifespan. *Psychological Reports, 67,* 3-14.

Becker, H. S. (1971). Personal change in adult life. In B. R. Cosin, I. R. Dale, G. M. Esland, & D. F. Swift (Eds.), *School and society: A sociological reader* (pp. 129-135). London: Routledge & Kegan Paul.

Bell, J., Grekul, J., Lamba, N., Minas, C., & Harrell, W. A. (1995). The impact of cost on student helping behavior. *The Journal of Social Psychology, 135,* 49-56.

Binswanger, L. (1963). *Being-in-the-world: Selected papers of Ludwig Binswanger* (J. Needleman, Trans.). New York: Basic Books.

Blaney, P. H. (1986). Affect and memory: A review. *Psychological Bulletin, 99,* 229-246.

Blass, N. (1982). The evaluation of the educational reform in Israel. *Studies in Educational Evaluation, 8,* 3-37.

Blos, P. (1967). The second individuation of adolescence. *Psychoanalytic Study of the Child, 72,* 182-186.

Blos, P. (1979). *The adolescent passage: Developmental issues.* New York: International Universities Press.

Borke, H. (1971). Interpersonal perception of young children: Egocentrism or empathy. *Developmental Psychology, 5,* 263-269.

Boss, M. (1963). *Psychoanalysis and daseinsanalysis* (L. B. Lefebre, Trans.). New York: Basic Books. (Original work published 1957)

Bosworth, K. (1995). Caring for others and being cared for: Students talk caring in school. *Phi Delta Kappan, 76,* 686-693.

Bower, G. H., Gilligan, S. G., & Montiero, K. P. (1981). Selectivity of learning caused by affective states. *Journal of Experimental Psychology: General, 110,* 451-473.

Bradburn, N. M. (1969). *The structure of psychological well-being.* Chicago: Aldine.

Bradburn, N. M., & Caplowitz, D. (1965). *Reports on happiness: A pilot study of behavior related to mental health.* Chicago: Aldine.

Breen, D. T., & Quaglia, R. J. (1991). Raising student aspirations: The need to share a vision. *School Counselor, 38,* 221-228.

Buber, M. (1961). *Between man and man.* London: Collins.

Bugental, F. T. (Ed.). (1967). *Challenges of humanistic psychology.* New York: McGraw-Hill.

Bullis, M., & Reiman, J. W. (1989). Survey of professional opinion or critical transition skills for adolescents and young adults who are deaf. *Rehabilitation Counseling Bulletin, 32,* 231-242.

Call, K. T., Mortimer, J. T., & Shanahan, M. J. (1995). Helpfulness and the development of competence in adolescence. *Child Development, 66,* 129-138.

Callan, V. J., & Noller, P. (1986). Perceptions of relationships in families with adolescents. *Journal of Marriage and the Family, 48,* 813-820.

Campbell, A. (1981). *The sense of well-being in America.* New York: McGraw-Hill.

Campbell, A., Converse, P. E., & Rodgers, W. L. (1976). *The quality of American life.* New York: Russell Sage.

Caplan, M. Z., & Weissberg, R. P. (1989). Promoting social competence in early adolescence: Developmental considerations. In B. H. Schneider, G. Attili, O. Nadel, & R. P. Weissberg (Eds.), *Social competence in developmental perspective* (pp. 371-385). London: Kluwer.

Carlson, R. (1965). Stability and change in adolescent self-image. *Child Development, 3-4,* 659-666.

Cattell, R. B. (1969). Comparing factor trait and state across ages and cultures. *Journal of Gerontology, 24,* 348-360.

Cattell, R. B. (1973). *Personality and mood by questionnaire.* San Francisco: Jossey-Bass.

Cattell, R. B., & Cattell, M. D. L. (1975). *Handbook for the high school personality questionnaire: HSPQ.* Champaign, IL: Institute of Personality and Ability Testing.

Cattell, R. B., Eber, H. W., & Tatsuoka, M. N. (1970). *Handbook for the 16 personality factors questionnaire: HSPQ.* Champaign, IL: Institute of Personality and Ability Testing.

Chang, E. C. (1996). Cultural differences in optimism, pessimism, and coping: Predictors of subsequent adjustment in Asian American and Caucasian American college students. *Journal of Counseling Psychology, 43,* 113-123.

Churchman, A. (1987). Can resident participation in neighborhood rehabilitation programs succeed: Israel's project renewal through a comparative perspective. In I. Altman & A. Wandersman (Eds.), *Neighborhood and community environment* (pp. 113-162). New York: Plenum.

Churchman, A. (1988). Shituf hatoshavim baproyect shikum hashchunot: Matarot vehesegim (Resident involvement in Project Renewal: Goals and achievements). *Megamot Behavioural Sciences Quarterly, 31,* 342-362. (Hebrew)

Churchman, A., Alterman, R., & Law-Yong, H. (1985). Public participation in Israel. *Participation, 8,* 3-5.

Cialdini, R. B., Baumann, D. J., & Kenrick, D. T. (1981). Insights from sadness: A three-step model of the development of altruism as hedonism. *Developmental Review, 1,* 207-233.

Cialdini, R. B., Schaller, M., Houlihan, D., Arps, K., Fultz, J., & Beaman, A. L. (1987). Empathy-based helping: Is it selflessly or selfishly motivated? *Journal of Personality and Social Psychology, 52,* 749-758.

Clark, D. M., & Teasdale, J. D. (1985). Constraints on the effects of mood on memory. *Journal of Personality and Social Psychology, 48,* 1595-1608.

Clary, E. G. (1994). Altruism and helping behavior. In *Encyclopedia of human behavior* (Vol. 1, pp. 93-102). New York: Academic Press.

Coan, R. W. (1974). *The optimal personality: An empirical and theoretical analysis.* London: Routledge.

Coleman, J. C., & Hendry, L. B. (1990). *The nature of adolescence* (2nd ed.). London, New York: Routledge.

Coleman, J. S., Kelly, S., & Moore, J. (1975). *Trends in school segregation: 1968-1973.* Washington, DC: Urban Institute.

Combs, A. W. (1969). *Perceiving, behaving, becoming: A new focus for education.* Washington, DC: ASCD Yearbook.

Comte, I. A. (1875). *System of positive policy* (Vol. 1). London: Longmans, Green. (Original work published 1851)

Conger, J. J., & Petersen, A. C. (1984). *Adolescence and youth.* New York: Harper & Row.

Costa, P. T., Jr., & McCrae, R. R. (1980). Influence of extraversion and neuroticism on subjective well-being: Happy and unhappy people. *Journal of Personality and Social Psychology, 38,* 668-678.

Cottle, T. J., Pleck, J., & Kakar, S. (1968). Time and content of significant life experiences. *Perceptual & Motor Skill, 27,* 155-171.

Cowen, E. L. (1991). In pursuit of wellness. *American Psychologist, 46,* 404-408.

Cowen, E. L. (1994). The enhancement of psychological wellness: Challenges and opportunities. *American Journal of Community Psychology, 22,* 149-179.

Csikszentmihalyi, M. (1975). *Beyond boredom and anxiety: The experience of play in work and games.* San Francisco: Jossey-Bass.

Csikszentmihalyi, M. (1984). *Being adolescent: Conflict and growth in the teenage years.* New York: Basic Books.

Csikszentmihalyi, M. (1990). *Flow: The psychology of optimal experience.* New York: Harper & Row.

Csikszentmihalyi, M., & Larson, R.W. (1984). *Being adolescent: Conflict and growth in the teenage years.* New York: Basic Books.

Danziger, S. K., & Danziger, S. (1995). Child poverty, public policies, and welfare reform [Special double issue: Child poverty, public practices, and welfare reform]. *Children and Youth Services Review, 17,* 1-10.

de Oliveira, W., Baizerman, M., & Pellet, L. (1992). Street children in Brazil and their helpers: Comparative views on aspirations and the future. *International Journal of Social Work, 35,* 163-176.

Diener, E. (1984). Subjective well-being. *Psychological Bulletin, 95,* 542-575.

Diener, E. (1994). Assessing subjective well-being: Progress and opportunities. *Social Indicators Research, 31,* 103-157.

Diener, E., & Diener, M. (1995). Cross-cultural correlates of life satisfaction and self-esteem. *Journal of Personality and Social Psychology, 68,* 653-663.

Diener, E., Emmons, R. A., Larsen, R. J., & Griffin, S. (1985). The satisfaction with life scale. *Journal of Personality Assessment, 49,* 71-75.

Diener, E., Sandvik, E., & Pavot, W. (1990). Happiness is the frequency, not the intensity, of positive versus negative affect. In F. Strack, M. Argyle, & N. Schwarz (Eds.), *Subjective well-being: An interdisciplinary perspective* (pp. 119-136). New York: Pergamon.

Diener, E., Sandvik, E., Pavot, W., & Gallagher, D. (1991). Response artifacts in the measurement of subjective well-being. *Social Indicators Research, 24,* 35-56.

Diener, E., Suh, E. M., Smith, H., & Shao, L. (1995). National differences in reported subjective well-being: Why do they occur? *Social Indicators Research, 34,* 7-32.

Dopson, L., & Gade, E. (1981). Kierkegaard's philosophy: Implications for counseling. *The Personnel and Guidance Journal, 60,* 148-152.

DuBois, D. L., Felner, R. D., Meares, H., & Krier, M. (1994). Prospective investigation of the effects of socioeconomic disadvantage, life stress, and social support on early adolescent adjustment. *Journal of Abnormal Psychology, 103,* 511-522.

Eagly, A. H., & Crowley, M. (1986). Gender and helping behavior: A meta-analytic review of the social psychological literature. *Psychological Bulletin, 100,* 283-308.

Ebersole, P. (1972). Effects and classification of peak experience. *Psychological Reports, 30,* 631-635.

Eccles, J. S., Buchanan, C. M., Flanagan, C., Fuligni, A., Midgley, C., & Yee, D. (1991). Control versus autonomy during early adolescence. *Journal of Social Issues, 47,* 53-68.

Eisenberg, N. (1986). *Altruistic emotion, cognition, and behavior.* Hillsdale, NJ: Lawrence Erlbaum.

Eisenberg, N. (1991). Values, sympathy, and individual differences: Toward a pluralism of factors influencing altruism and empathy. *Psychological Inquiry, 2,* 128-131.

Eisenberg, N., Carlo, G., Murphy, B., & Van Court, P. (1995). Prosocial development in late adolescence: A longitudinal study. *Child Development, 66,* 1179-1197.

Eisenberg, N., Fabes, R. A., Miller, P. A., Fultz, J., Shell, R., Mathy, R. M., & Reno, R. R. (1989). Relation of sympathy and personal distress to prosocial behavior: A multimethod study. *Journal of Personality and Social Psychology, 57,* 55-66.

Eisenberg, N., McCreath, H., & Ahn, R. (1988). Vicarious emotional responsiveness and prosocial behavior: Their interrelations in young children. *Personality and Social Psychology Bulletin, 14,* 298-311.

Eisenberg, N., & Miller, P. A. (1987). The relation of empathy to prosocial and related behavior. *Psychological Bulletin, 101,* 91-119.

Eisenberg, N., Miller, P. A., Schaller, M., Fabes, R. A., Fultz, J., Shell, R., & Shea, C. L. (1989). The role of sympathy and altruistic personality traits in helping: A reexamination. *Journal of Personality, 57,* 41-67.

Eisenberg, N., Miller, P. A., Shell, R., McNalley, S., & Shea, C. (1991). Prosocial development in adolescence: A longitudinal study. *Developmental Psychology, 27,* 849-857.

Eisenberg, N., Shell, R., Pasternack, J., Lennon, R., Beller, R., & Mathy, R. M. (1987). Prosocial development in middle childhood: A longitudinal study. *Developmental Psychology, 23,* 712-718.

Eisenberg-Berg, N., & Neal, C. (1979). Children's moral reasoning about their own spontaneous prosocial behavior. *Developmental Psychology, 15,* 228-229.

Elkind, D. (1967). Egocentrism in adolescence. *Child Development, 38,* 1025-1034.

Elster, J. (1990). Selfishness and altruism. In J. J. Mansbridge (Ed.), *Beyond self-interest* (pp. 44-52). Chicago: University of Chicago Press.

Emmons, R. A., & Diener, E. (1985). Personality correlates of subjective well-being. *Journal of Personality and Social Psychology, 11,* 89-97.

Erikson, E. H. (1963). *Youth: Change and challenge.* New York: Basic Books.

Erikson, E. H. (1967). *Childhood and society.* New York: Norton.

Erikson, E. H. (1968). *Identity, youth, and crisis.* New York: Norton.

Evans, C., & Eder, D. (1993). "No exit:" Processes of social isolation in the middle school. *Journal of Contemporary Ethnography, 22,* 139-170.

Feinstein, C. B., & Lytle, R. (1987). Observations from clinical work with high school aged, deaf adolescents attending a residential school. *Adolescent Psychiatry, 14,* 461-477.

Feiring, C. (1996). Concepts of romance in 15-year-old adolescents. *Journal of Research on Adolescence, 6,* 181-200.

Felner, R. D., Brand, S., DuBois, D. L., Adan, A. M., Mulhall, P. F., & Evans, E. G. (1995). Socioeconomic disadvantage, proximal environmental experiences, and socioemotional and academic adjustment in early adolescence: Investigation of a mediated effects model. *Child Development, 66,* 774-792.

Florian, V., Mikulincer, M., & Weller, A. (1993). Does culture affect perceived family dynamics? A comparison of Arab and Jewish adolescents in Israel. *Journal of Comparative Family Studies, 24,* 189-201.

Flum, H. (1993). The evolutive style of identity formation. *Journal of Youth and Adolescence, 23,* 489-498.

Flum, H. (1994). Styles of identity formation in early and middle adolescence. *Genetic, Social, and General Psychology Monographs, 120,* 437-467.

Ford, M. E. (1979). The construct validity of egocentrism. *Psychological Bulletin, 86,* 1169-1188.

Fordyce, M. W. (1988). A review of research on the Happiness Measures: A sixty-second index of happiness and mental health. *Social Indicators Research, 20,* 355-381.

Forgas, J. P., Bower, G. H., & Krantz, S. E. (1984). The influence of mood on perception of social interactions. *Journal of Experimental Social Psychology, 20,* 497-513.

Foster, S. (1988). Life in the mainstream: Reflections of deaf college freshmen on their experiences in the mainstream high school. *Journal of the American Deafness and Rehabilitation Association, 22,* 27-35.

Fox, D. J. (1969). *The research process in education.* New York: Holt, Rhinehart & Winston.

Frank, A. (1952). *The diary of a young girl.* Garden City, NY: Doubleday.

Frank, R. H. (1987). Shrewdly irrational. *Sociological Forum, 2,* 21-41.

Frank, R. H. (1989, October). Social commitment: Beyond self-interest. *Current,* pp. 4-13.

Frankenstein, C. (1970). *Impaired intelligence.* New York: Gordon & Breach.

Frankenstein, C. (1979). *They think again.* New York: Van Nostrand Reinhold.

Frankl, V. (1963). *Man's search for meaning.* New York: Washington Press.

Frankl, V. (1966). Self-transcendence as a human phenomenon. *Journal of Humanistic Psychology, 5,* 97-106.

Frankl, V. (1967). *Psychotherapy and existentialism: Selected papers on logotherapy.* New York: Simon & Schuster.

Frankl, V. (1988). *The will to meaning: Foundations and applications of logotherapy.* New York: Meridian.

Frankl, V. (1992). Meaning in industrial society. *The International Forum for Logotherapy, 15,* 66-70.

Freud, A. (1958). Adolescence. *Psychological Study of the Child, 13,* 255-257.

Freud, S. (1920). *Beyond the pleasure principle.* London: Hogarth.

Freud, S. (1982). *Civilization and its discontents* (J. Strachey, Ed., J. Riviere, Trans.). London: Hogarth. (Original work published 1930)

Fuerst, R. E. (1967). *Turning point experiences.* Unpublished doctoral dissertation, University of Florida, Gainesville.

Gabrielsson, A., & Juslin, P. N. (1996). Emotional expression in music performance: Between the performer's intention and the listener's experience. *Psychology of Music, 24,* 68-91.

Gibson, J. W., & Lanz, J. B. (1991). Factors associated with Hispanic teenagers' attitude toward the importance of birth control. *Child and Adolescent Social Work Journal, 8,* 399-415.

Gibson-Cline, J. W. (1996). *Adolescence from crisis to coping.* Oxford: Butterworth-Heinnemann.

Gibson-Cline, J. W., Dikaiou, M., Haritos-Fatouras, M., Shafrir, B., & Ondis, G. (1996). From crisis to coping: Theories and helping practices. In *Adolescence from crisis to coping* (pp. 3-12). Oxford: Butterworth-Heinnemann.

Gilligan, C. (1982). *In a different voice.* Cambridge, MA: Harvard University Press.

Giora, Z., Esformes, Y., & Barak, A. (1972). Dreams in cross-cultural research. *Comprehensive Psychiatry, 13,* 105-114.

Greene, G. (1948). *The heart of the matter.* New York: Viking.

Grygielski, M. (1984). Meaning in life and hopelessness: Interrelationships and intergroup differences. *Polish Psychological Bulletin, 15,* 277-284.

Haley, T. J., & Dowd, E. T. (1988). Responses of deaf adolescents to differences in counselor method of communication and disability status. *Journal of Counseling Psychology, 35,* 258-262.

Hall, G. S. (1904). *Adolescence.* New York: Appleton.

Hampden-Turner, C. (1977). Comment on "Maslow's other child." *Journal of Humanistic Psychology, 17,* 25-31.

Happ, D. A., & Altmaier, E. M. (1982). Counseling the hearing impaired: Issues and recommendations. *Personnel and Guidance Journal, 60,* 556-559.

Havinghurst, R. J. (1965). *A cross-national study of Buenos Aires and Chicago adolescents.* New York: Krager.

Headey, B., Holmstrom, E., & Wearing, A. (1984). The impact of life events and changes in domain satisfaction on well-being. *Social Indicators Research, 15,* 203-227.

Heidegger, M. (1962). *Being and time* (J. Macquarrie & E. Robinson, Trans.). New York: Harper & Row. (Original work published 1927)

Hernandez, A. E. (1995). Do role models influence self-efficacy and aspirations in Mexican American at-risk females? *Hispanic Journal of Behavioral Sciences, 17,* 256-263.

Hobbes, T. (1947). *Leviathan.* London: J.M. Dent; New York: Dutton. (Original work published 1651)

Hoffman, M. (1991). Is empathy altruistic? *Psychological Inquiry, 2,* 131-133.

Holcomb, T. K. (1996). Social assimilation of deaf high school students: The role of school environment. In I. Parasnis (Ed.), *Cultural and language diversity and the deaf experience* (pp. 181-198). Cambridge, UK: Cambridge University Press.

Hornstein, H. A. (1991). Empathic distress and altruism: Still inseparable. *Psychological Inquiry, 2,* 133-135.

Hume, D. (1896). *A treatise of human nature* (L. A. Selby-Brigge, Ed.). Oxford, UK: Oxford University Press. (Original work published 1740)

Inglehart, R. (1990). *Culture shift in advanced industrial society.* Princeton, NJ: Princeton University Press.

International Committee. (1984). *Annual report to assess the project renewal program.* Tel Aviv, Israel: Author.

Isen, A. M., Daubman, K. A., & Nowicki, G. P. (1987). Positive affect facilitates creative problem solving. *Journal of Personality and Social Psychology, 52,* 1122-1131.

Isen, A. M., & Levin, P. E. (1972). The effect of feeling on good helping, cookies, and kindness. *Journal of Personality and Social Psychology, 21,* 384-388.

Ivey, A. E., Ivey, M. B., & Simek-Morgan, L. (1993). *Counseling and psychotherapy: A multicultural perspective.* Boston: Allyn & Bacon.

Jencks, C. (1990). Varieties of altruism. In J. J. Mansbridge (Ed.), *Beyond self-interest* (pp. 53-67). Chicago: University of Chicago Press.

Jones, E. E., & Pittman, T. S. (1982). Toward a general theory of strategic self-presentation. In J. Suls (Ed.), *Psychological perspectives on the self* (pp. 231-262). Hillsdale, NJ: Lawrence Erlbaum.

Jourard, S. M. (1969). The effects of experimenters' self-disclosure on subjects' behavior. In C. Spielberger (Ed.), *Current topics in clinical and community psychology* (pp. 109-150). New York: Academic Press.

Jourard, S. M. (1971a). *Self-disclosure: An experimental analysis of the transparent self.* New York: John Wiley.

Jourard, S. M. (1971b). *The transparent self.* New York: Litton Educational Publishing.

Jourard, S. M. (1972). Some notes on the experience of commitment. *Humanitas, 8,* 5-9.

Jourard, S. M., & Landsman, T. (1980). *Healthy personality: An approach from the viewpoint of humanistic psychology.* New York: Macmillan.

Jung, C. G. (1959). *The archetypes and the collective unconscious.* Princeton, NJ: Princeton University Press.

Jung, C. G. (1961). *Memories, dreams, reflections.* New York: Random House.

Jurich, A. P., Schumm, W. R., & Bollman, S. R. (1987). The degree of family orientation perceived by mothers, fathers, and adolescents. *Adolescence, 15,* 119-128.

Kammann, R., & Flett, R. (1983a). Affectometer 2: A scale to measure current level of general happiness. *Australian Journal of Psychology, 35,* 257-265.

Kammann, R., & Flett, R. (1983b). *Sourcebook for measuring well-being with Affectometer 2.* Dunedin, New Zealand: Why Not? Foundation.

Kamptner, N. L. (1991). Personal possessions and their meanings: A life-span perspective. *Journal of Social Behavior and Personality, 6,* 209-228.

Kelly, G. A. (1969). *Clinical psychology and personality: The collected papers of George Kelly.* New York: John Wiley.

Kenrick, D. T. (1991). Proximate altruism and ultimate selfishness. *Psychological Inquiry, 2,* 135-137.

Kierkegaard, S. (1974). *Concluding unscientific postscript.* Princeton, NJ: Princeton University Press.

Klein, G. (1972). Fostering commitment in today's world. *Humanities, 8,* 37-54.

Koch, S. (1971). The image of man implicit in encounter group theory. *Journal of Humanistic Psychology, 11,* 109-128.

Kohlberg, L. (1971, Fall). The adolescent as a philosopher. *Journal of the American Academy of Arts and Sciences,* pp. 1051-1086.

Kohlberg, L. (1981). *The philosophy of moral development*. San Francisco: Harper & Row.

Kohlberg, L., & Candee, D. (1984). The relationship of moral judgment to moral action. In W. M. Kurtines & J. L. Gewirtz (Eds.), *Morality, moral behavior, and moral development* (pp. 52-73). New York: John Wiley.

Kohlberg, L., & Gilligan, C. (1971, Fall). The adolescent as a philosopher: The discovery of the self in a postconventional world. *Journal of the American Academy of Arts and Sciences*, pp. 1051-1086.

Kolaric, B., & Galambos, N. L. (1995). Face-to-face interactions in unacquainted female-male dyads: How do girls and boys behave? *Journal of Early Adolescence, 15*, 363-382.

Kozma, A., & Stones, M. J. (1980). The measurement of happiness: Development of the Memorial University of Newfoundland Scale of Happiness (MUNSCH). *Journal of Gerontology, 35*, 906-912.

Kozma, A., Stones, S., Stones, M. J., Hannah, T. E., & McNeil, J. K. (1990). Long- and short-term affective states in happiness. *Social Indicators Research, 22*, 119-138.

Krebs, D. L. (1991). Altruism and egoism: A false dichotomy? *Psychological Inquiry, 2*, 137-139.

Kubovy, D. (1977). *Ben moreh latalmid: Hamoreh hatov be'enay talmidav* [The good teacher in his pupils' minds]. Tel Aviv: Kibbutz Haarzi, Hashomer Hatzair.

Kusche, C. A., Garfield, T. S., & Greenberg, M. T. (1983). The understanding of emotional and social attributions in deaf adolescents. *Journal of Clinical Child Psychology, 12*, 153-160.

Kusche, C. A., & Greenberg, M. T. (1983). The development of evaluative understanding and role-taking in deaf and hearing children. *Child Development, 54*, 141-147.

Landsman, M. (1995). *High-level human functioning and its relation to life experiences.* Unpublished doctoral dissertation, Bar-Ilan University, Israel.

Landsman, T. (1967). One's best self. In S. M. Jourard (Ed.), *Existential studies of the self* (Social Science Monograph, Vol. 34, pp. 37-49). Gainesville: University of Florida.

Landsman, T. (1969). The beautiful person. *The Futurist, 3*, 41-42.

Landsman, T. (1974). The humanizer. *American Journal of Orthopsychiatry, 44*, 345-352.

Landsman, T., & Landsman, M. (1991). The beautiful and noble person: An existentialist-phenomenological view of optimal human functioning. *Journal of Social Behavior and Personality, 6*, 61-74.

Lapsley, D. K., & Murphy, M. N. (1985). Another look at the theoretical assumptions of adolescent egocentrism. *Developmental Review, 5*, 201-217.

Larsen, R. J., & Diener, E. (1985). A multitrait-multimethod examination of affect structure: Hedonic level and emotional intensity. *Personality and Individual Differences, 6*, 631-636.

Larsen, R. J., & Diener, E. (1987). Affect intensity as an individual difference characteristic: A review. *Journal of Research in Personality, 21*, 1-39.

Larson, R. W. (1989). Is feeling "in control" related to happiness in daily life? *Psychological Reports, 64*, 775-784.

Larson, R. W., Csikszentmihalyi, M., & Graef, R. (1980). Mood variability and the psychosocial adjustment of adolescents. *Journal of Youth and Adolescence, 9*, 469-490.

References   213

Latten, J. J. (1989). Life-course and satisfaction, equal for every-one? *Social Indicators Research, 21*, 599-610.
Lecoroy, C. W. (1989). Parent-adolescent intimacy: Impact on adolescent functioning. *Adolescence, 23*, 137-147.
Lewin, K. (1939). *Field theory in social science*. London: Tavistock.
Lewin, K., Dembo, T., Festinger, L., & Sears, P. (1944). Level of aspirations. In J. McV. Hunt (Ed.), *Personality and behavior disorders* (Vol. 1, pp. 333-378). New York: Ronald.
Lewy, A. (1988). *Issues in curriculum evaluation*. Jerusalem: Ministry of Culture.
Lynch, S. (1969). *The relationship between self-concept and the reported effects of intense experience*. Paper presented at the annual convention of the Southeastern Psychological Association, Roanoke, VA.
Magen, Z. (1972). Havayot hiyuviyot shel mitbagrim [Positive experiences of adolescents]. In A. Ziv (Ed.), *Psychology and counseling education* (translated from Hebrew; pp. 368-385). Tel Aviv: Tel Aviv University.
Magen, Z. (1980). Encounter group effects on soccer team performance. *Small Group Behavior, 11*, 339-344.
Magen, Z. (1983a). Re-forming the boundaries: A trans-cultural comparison of positive experiences among adolescent males and females. *Adolescence, 18*, 851-858.
Magen, Z. (1983b). Transpersonal commitments in adolescence: A cross-cultural perspective. *Journal of Humanistic Psychology, 23*, 96-112.
Magen, Z. (1985). Cross-cultural personality correlates of intensity and content category of positive experience. *Journal of Personality and Social Psychology, 49*, 1631-1642.
Magen, Z. (1990a). Positive experiences and life aspirations among adolescents with and without hearing impairments. *International Journal of Disability, Development, and Education, 37*, 57-69.
Magen, Z. (1990b). *Prosocial commitments of Jewish and Arab adolescents in Israel: A follow up study*. Unpublished manuscript, Tel-Aviv University.
Magen, Z. (1994). Good parents: Comparative studies of adolescents' perceptions. *Current Psychology: Developmental, Learning, Personality, Social, 13*, 172-184.
Magen, Z. (1996). Commitment beyond self and adolescents: The issue of happiness. *Social Indicators Research, 37*, 235-267.
Magen, Z., & Aharoni, R. (1991). Adolescents' contributing toward others: Relationship to positive experiences and transpersonal commitment. *Journal of Humanistic Psychology, 31*, 126-143.
Magen, Z., Birenbaum, M., & Ilovich, T. (1992). Adolescents from disadvantaged neighborhoods: Personal characteristics as related to volunteer involvement. *International Journal for the Advancement of Counseling, 15*, 47-59.
Magen, Z., Birenbaum, M., & Pery, D. (1996). Experiencing joy and sorrow: An examination of intensity and shallowness. *The International Forum for Logotherapy, 19*, 45-55.
Magen, Z., & Offek, V. (1993, February). *Personal commitment in high schools: A comparison of voluntary versus mandatory involvement*. Paper presented at the annual conference of the Israel Educational Research Association (AYALA), Haifa. (Hebrew).
Magen, Z., & Stauber, E. (1992). *Positive experiences in parenthood*. Unpublished manuscript, Tel-Aviv University, Israel.
Mahrer, A. R. (1978). *Experiencing: A humanistic theory of psychology and psychiatry*. New York: Brunner Mazel.

Mansbridge, J. J. (Ed.). (1990). *Beyond self-interest.* Chicago: University of Chicago Press.

Marcia, J. E. (1993). The status of the statuses: Research review. In J. E. Marcia et al. (Eds.), *Ego identity: Handbook for psychosocial research* (pp. 22-41). New York: Springer-Verlag.

Margoshes, A., & Litt, S. (1966). Vivid experiences: Peak and nadir. *Journal of Clinical Psychology, 22,* 175.

Mar'i, S. K. (1982). Cultural and socio-political influences on counseling and school guidance: The case of Arabs in the Jewish state. *International Journal for the Advancement of Counseling, 5,* 247-263.

Marjoribanks, K. (1991). Adolescents' learning environments and aspirations: Ethnic, gender, and social-status group differences. *Perceptual and Motor Skills, 72,* 823-830.

Marjoribanks, K. (1994). Family and school environments, adolescents' aspirations, and young adults' status attainment: Ability-attitude group differences. *European Journal of Psychology of Education, 9,* 215-223.

Marsh, H. W. (1991). Failure of high-ability high schools to deliver academic benefits commensurate with their students' ability levels. *American Educational Research Journal, 28,* 445-480.

Martino, L. R. (1994). Peer tutoring classes for young adolescents: A cost effective strategy. *Middle School Journal, 25*(4), 55-58.

Maslow, A. H. (1961). Peak experiences as acute identity experiences. In *Personality theory and counseling practice.* Material Diffusion Project, University of Florida, Gainesville.

Maslow, A. H. (1963). Further notes on the psychology of being. *Journal of Humanistic Psychology, 3,* 120-135.

Maslow, A. H. (1964). *Religions, values, and peak experiences.* Columbus, OH: Imprint State University Press.

Maslow, A. H. (1965). *Toward a psychology of being.* Princeton, NJ: Van Nostrand.

Maslow, A. H. (1970). *Motivation and personality* (2nd ed.). New York: Harper & Row.

Maslow, A. H. (1971). *The farther reaches of human nature.* New York: Viking.

Maslow, B. G. (Ed.) (1972). *Abraham H. Maslow: A memorial volume.* Montery, CA: Brooks/Cole.

Massimini, F., Csikszentmihalyi, M., & Carli, M. (1987). The monitoring of optimal experience: A tool for psychiatric rehabilitation. *Journal of Nervous and Mental Disease, 175,* 545-549.

Mathes, E. W., & Jerom, M. A. (1982). Peak experiences tendencies: Scale development and theory testing. *Journal of Humanistic Psychology, 22,* 93-106.

May, R. (1958). Contributions of existential psychotherapy. In R. May, E. Angel, & H. H. Ellenberger (Eds.), *Existence: A new dimension in psychiatry and psychology* (pp. 37-91). New York: Basic Books.

May, R. (1969). *Love and will.* New York: Norton.

McClain, E. W., & Andrews, H. B. (1969). Some personality correlates of peak experiences: A study in self-actualization. *Journal of Clinical Psychology, 25,* 36-38.

McKenzie, D. H. (1967). *Two kinds of extreme negative human experiences.* Unpublished doctoral dissertation, University of Florida, Gainesville.

Meadow, K. P., & Trybus, R. J. (1979). Behavioral and emotional problems of deaf children: An overview. In L. J. Bradford & W. G. Hardy (Eds.), *Hearing and hearing impairment* (pp. 395-403). New York: Grune & Stratton.

Mertens, D. M. (1989). Social experiences of hearing-impaired high school youth. *American Annals of the Deaf, 134,* 15-19.

Michalos, A. C. (1985). Multiple discrepancies theory (MDT). *Social Indicators Research, 16,* 347-376.

Michalos, A. C. (1991). *Global report on student well-being: Vol. 1. Life satisfaction and happiness.* New York: Springer-Verlag.

Mikulincer, M., Weller, A., & Florian, V. (1993). Sense of closeness to parents and family rules: A study of Arab and Jewish youth in Israel. *International Journal of Psychology, 28,* 323-335.

Milgram, N. A., & Palti, G. (1993). Psychosocial characteristics of resilient children. *Journal of Research in Personality, 27,* 207-221.

Montemayor, R. (1983). Parents and adolescents in conflict: All families some of the time and some families all of the time. *Journal of Early Adolescence, 3,* 83-103.

Mook, D. G. (1991). Why can't altruism be selfish? *Psychological Inquiry, 2,* 139-141.

Mosak, H., & Dreikurs, R. (1973). Adlerian psychotherapy. In R. Corsini (Ed.), *Current psychotherapies* (pp. 35-83). Itasca, IL: Peacock.

Moustakas, C. E. (1972). *Loneliness and love.* Englewood Cliffs, NJ: Prentice Hall.

Moustakas, C. E. (1977). *Turning points.* Englewood Cliffs, NJ: Prentice Hall.

Myers, D. G. (1993). *The pursuit of happiness.* New York: Avon.

Myers, D. G., & Diener, E. (1995). Who is happy? *Psychological Science, 6,* 10-19.

Myklebust, R. H. (1964). *The psychology of deafness.* New York: Grune & Stratton.

Nakleh, K. (1975). Cultural determinants of Palestinian collective identity: The case of Arabs in Israel. *New Outlook: Middle East Monthly, 18,* 31-40.

Newman, B. M. (1989). The changing nature of the parent-adolescent relationship from early to late adolescence. *Adolescence, 96,* 915-924.

O'Connor, B. P., & Nikolic, J. (1990). Identity development and formal operations as sources of adolescent egocentrism. *Journal of Youth and Adolescence, 19,* 149-158.

Offer, D., Ostrov, E., & Howard, K. I. (1981). *The adolescent: A psychological self-portrait.* New York: Basic Books.

Offer, D., Ostrov, E., Howard, K. I., & Atkinson, R. (1988). *The teenage world: Adolescents' self-image in ten countries.* New York: Plenum.

Olson, J. M., Roese, N. J., Meen, J., & Robertson, D. J. (1995). The preconditions and consequences of relative deprivation: Two field studies. *Journal of Applied Social Psychology, 25,* 944-964.

Otto, H. A. (1967). The Minerva experience: Critical report. In F. T. Bugental (Ed.), *Challenges of humanistic psychology* (pp. 119-124). New York: McGraw-Hill.

Overmier, K. L. (1990). Biracial adolescents: Areas of conflict in identity formation. *Journal of Applied Social Sciences, 14,* 157-176.

Paffard, M. K. (1970). Creative activities and peak experiences. *British Journal of Educational Psychology, 40,* 238-290.

Parasnis, I. (1996). On interpreting the deaf experience within the context of cultural and language diversity. In I. Parasnis (Ed.), *Cultural and language diversity and the deaf experience* (pp. 3-19). Cambridge, UK: Cambridge University Press.

Pardeck, J. A., & Pardeck, J. T. (1990). Family factors related to adolescents' autonomy. *Adolescence, 98,* 311-319.

Parkhurst, J. T., & Asher, S. R. (1992). Peer rejection in middle school: Subgroup differences in behavior, loneliness, and interpersonal concerns. *Developmental Psychology, 28,* 231-241.

Parsons, T. (1960). *Structure and process in modern societies*. London: Cass.

Patterson, J. M., & McCubbin, H. I. (1987). Adolescent coping style and behaviors: Conceptualization and measurement. *Journal of Adolescence, 10,* 163-180.

Pavot, W., Diener, E., & Fujita, F. (1990). Extraversion and happiness. *Personality and Individual Differences, 11,* 1299-1306.

Perry, L. C., Perry, D. G., & Weiss, R. J. (1986). Age differences in children's beliefs about whether altruism makes the actor feel good. *Social Cognition, 4,* 263-269.

Piaget, J. (1967). *Six psychological studies*. New York: Vintage.

Piaget, J. (1972). Intellectual evolution from adolescence to adulthood. *Human Development, 15,* 1-12.

Privette, G., & Landsman, T. (1983). Factor analysis of peak performance: The full use of potential. *Journal of Personality and Social Psychology, 44,* 195-200.

Proust, M. (1948). *Pleasures and regrets*. London: Dobson. (Original work published 1896).

Punamaki, R.-L. (1988). Historical-political and individualistic determinants of coping modes and fears among Palestinian children. *International Journal of Psychology, 23,* 721-739.

Puttick, W. (1964). *A factor analytic study of positive modes of experiencing and behaving in a teacher college population*. Unpublished doctoral dissertation, University of Florida.

Quaglia, R. J., & Perry, C. M. (1995). A study of underlying variables affecting aspirations of rural adolescents. *Adolescence, 30,* 233-243.

Rabichow, H. G., & Sklansky, M. A. (1980). *Effective counseling of adolescents*. Chicago: Follett.

Rapoport, T., & Lomsky-Feder, E. (1988). Patterns of transition to adulthood: A comparative study of Israeli society. *International Sociology, 3,* 415-432.

Regev, D. (1997, February 4). Cholmin Ymetzalmim [Dreaming and photographing]. *Maariv Daily News,* p. 9.

Riley, T., Adams, G. R., & Nielsen, E. (1984). Adolescent egocentrism: The association among imaginary audience behavior, cognitive development, and parental support and rejection. *Journal of Youth and Adolescence, 13,* 401-417.

Rogers, C. R. (1961). *On becoming a person: A therapist's view of psychotherapy*. Boston: Houghton Mifflin.

Rogers, C. R. (1977). *Carl Rogers on personal power*. New York: Delacorte.

Rogers, C. R. (1980). *A way of being*. Boston: Houghton Mifflin.

Romer, D., & Kim, S. (1995). Health interventions for African American and Latino youth: The potential role of mass media. *Health Education Quarterly, 22,* 172-189.

Ronen, Y., Magen, Z., & Zabar, N. (1996). *The relations between staff and adolescents in institutional care*. Unpublished master's thesis, Tel-Aviv University, Israel.

Rosenthal, B. S. (1995). The influence of social support on school completion among Haitians. *Social Work in Education, 17,* 30-39.

Rushton, J. P. (1991). Is altruism innate? *Psychological Inquiry, 2,* 141-143.

Rutter, M., & Garmezy, N. (1983). Developmental psychopathology. In E. M. Hetherington (Ed.), *Handbook of child psychology: Social and personality development* (Vol. 4, pp. 321-387).

Rutter, M., Graham, P., Chadwick, D. F. D., & Yule, W. (1976). Adolescent turmoil: Fact or fiction. *Journal of Child Psychology and Psychiatry, 17,* 35-56.

Sandvik, E., Diener, E., & Seidlitz, L. (1993). Subjective well-being: The convergence and stability of self-report and non-self-report measures. *Journal of Personality, 61,* 317-342.

Santrock, J. (1993). *Adolescence* (5th ed.). Madison, WI: Brown and Benchmark.

Satir, V., Bammen, J., Gerber, J., & Gomori, M. (1991). *The Satir model: Family therapy and beyond.* Palo Alto, CA: Science and Behavior Books.

Schlesinger, H. S., & Acree, M. C. (1984). The antecedents of achievement and adjustment: A longitudinal study of deaf children. In G. B. Anderson (Ed.), *The habilitation and rehabilitation of deaf adolescents* (pp. 48-59). Norman, OK: Oklahoma University.

Schroeder, D. A., Dovidio, J. F., Sibicky, M. E., Matthew, L. L., & Allen, J. L. (1988). Empathic concern and helping behavior: Egoism or altruism? *Journal of Experimental Social Psychology, 24,* 333-353.

Schulman, M., & Mekler, E. (1994). *Bringing up a moral child.* New York: Doubleday.

Sebald, H. (1986). Adolescents' shifting orientation toward parents and peers: A curvilinear trend over recent decades. *Journal of Marriage and the Family, 5,* 5-13.

Seginer, R. (1988). Adolescents facing the future: Cultural and sociopolitical perspectives. *Youth & Society, 19,* 314-333.

Seidlitz, L., & Diener, E. (1993). Memory for positive versus negative life events: Theories for the differences between happy and unhappy persons. *Journal of Personality and Social Psychology, 64,* 654-664.

Selman, R. L. (1980). *The growth of interpersonal understanding: Developmental clinical analyses.* New York: Academic Press.

Sen, A. K. (1990). Rational fools: A critique of the behavioral foundations of economic theory. In J. J. Mansbridge (Ed.), *Beyond self-interest* (pp. 25-43). Chicago: University of Chicago Press.

Shulman, S., Seiffage-Krenke, I., & Samet, N. (1987). Adolescent coping style as a function of perceived family climate. *Journal of Adolescent Research, 2,* 367-381.

Silbereisen, R. K., & Todt, E. (1994). *Adolescence in context: The interplay of family, school, peers and work in adjustment.* New York: Springer-Verlag.

Smetana, J. G. (1988). Adolescents and parents: Conceptions of parental authority. *Child Development, 56,* 321-335.

Smilansky, M. (1991). *Between adolescents and parents.* Gaithersburg, MD: Psychological and Educational Publishers.

Smith, D. (1973). On self-actualization: A transambivalent examination of a focal theme in Maslow's psychology. *Journal of Humanistic Psychology, 13,* 17-33.

Smith, S. M. (1973). *Intense experiences of black and white female prisoners.* Unpublished doctoral dissertation, University of Florida, Gainesville.

Spiro, S. E. (Ed.). (1988). Issues in the evaluation of neighborhood rehabilitation programs: Lessons from Israel's project renewal. *Megamot Behavioural Sciences Quarterly, 31,* 269-285. (Hebrew).

Sprinthall, A. N., & Collins, W. A. (1988). *Adolescent psychology: A developmental view* (2nd ed.). New York: Random House.

Staub, E. (1978). *Positive social behavior and morality: Social and personal influences* (Vol. 1). New York: Academic Press.

Staub, E. (1991). Altruistic and moral motivations for helping and their translation into action. *Psychological Inquiry, 2,* 150-153.

Steinberg, L. (1990). Autonomy, conflict, and harmony in the family relationship. In S. S. Feldman & G. R. Elliott (Eds.), *At the threshold: The developing adolescent* (pp. 255-276). Cambridge, MA: Harvard University Press.

Stock, W. A., Okun, M. A., Haring, M. J., & Witter, R. A. (1983). Age and subjective well-being: A meta-analysis. In R. J. Light (Ed.), *Evaluation studies: Review annual* (Vol. 8, pp. 279-302). Beverly Hills, CA: Sage.

Stones, M. J., & Kozma, A. (1991). A magical model of happiness. *Social Indicators Research, 24,* 43-62.

Stones, M. J., & Kozma, A. (1994). The relationships of affect intensity to happiness. *Social Indicators Research, 31,* 159-173.

Szivos, S. E. (1990). Attitudes to work and their relationship to self-esteem and aspirations among young adults with a mild mental handicap. *British Journal of Mental Subnormality, 36,* 108-117.

Teevan, R. C., & Smith, B. B. (1975). Relationship of fear of failure and need achievement motivation to a conforming interval measure of aspiration level. *Psychological Report, 36,* 967-976.

Tolor, A. (1978). Personality correlates of the joy of life. *Journal of Clinical Psychology, 34,* 671-676.

Triandis, H. C. (1989). The self and social behavior in differing cultural contexts. *Psychological Review, 96,* 506-520.

Turgenieff, I. (1923). The novels and stories of Ivan Turgenieff (I. F. Hapgood, Trans). New York: Scribner's. (Original work published 1860)

Tzuriel, D. (1992). The development of ego identity at adolescence among Israeli Jews and Arabs. *Journal of Youth and Adolescence, 21,* 551-571.

Urberg, K. A. (1995). The structure of adolescent peer networks. *Developmental Psychology, 31,* 540-547.

Van-Tassel-Baska, J., Olszewski-Kubilius, P., & Kulieke, M. (1994). A study of self-concept and social support in advantaged and disadvantaged seventh and eighth grade gifted students. *Roeper Review, 16,* 186-191.

Veenhoven, R. (1984). *Conditions of happiness.* Dordrecht: D. Reidel.

Veenhoven, R. (1988). The utility of happiness. *Social Indicators Research, 20,* 333-354.

Veenhoven, R. (1991). Is happiness relative? *Social Indicators Research, 24,* 1-34.

Veenhoven, R. (1993). *Bibliography of happiness.* Rotterdam: Erasmus University Studies in Socio-Cultural Transformation.

Veenhoven, R. (with Ehrhardt, J.). (1995). The cross-national pattern of happiness: Test of predictions implied in three theories of happiness. *Social Indicators Research, 34,* 33-68.

Verkuyten, M. (1986). The impact of ethnic and sex differences on happiness among adolescents in the Netherlands. *The Journal of Social Psychology, 126,* 259-260.

Verkuyten, M. (1989). Happiness among adolescents in the Netherlands: Ethnic and sex differences. *Psychological Reports, 65,* 577-578.

Vernon, M., & Andrews, J. F. (1990). *The psychology of deafness.* New York: Longman.

Vernon, M., & Estes, C. C. (1975). Deaf leadership and political activism. *The Deaf American, 28,* 3-6.

Viadero, D. (1995). Against all odds. *Teacher-Magazine, 6*(8), 20-22.

Violato, C., & Travis, L. (1995). *Advances in adolescent psychology.* Alberta, Canada: Detselig.

Wallach, L., & Wallach, M. A. (1991). Why altruism, even though it exists, cannot be demonstrated by social psychological experiments. *Psychological Inquiry, 2,* 153-155.

Wallach, M. A., & Wallach, L. (1990). *Rethinking goodness.* Albany: State University of New York Press.

Waterman, A. S. (1982). Identity development from adolescence to adulthood: An extension of theory and review of research. *Developmental Psychology, 18,* 341-358.

Waterman, A. S. (1984). Identity formation: Discovery of creation? *Journal of Early Adolescence, 4,* 329-341.

Waterman, A. S. (1990). Personal expressiveness: Philosophical and psychological foundations. *The Journal of Mind and Behavior, 11,* 47-74.

Waterman, A. S. (1993). Two conceptions of happiness: Contrasts of personal expressiveness (eudaimonia) and hedonic enjoyment. *Journal of Personality and Social Psychology, 64,* 678-691.

Way, N. (1995). "Can't you see the courage, the strength that I have?": Listening to urban adolescent girls speak about their relationships. *Psychology of Women Quarterly, 19,* 107-128.

Weisel, A. (1988). Parental hearing status, reading comprehension skills, and social-emotional adjustment. *American Annals of the Deaf, 133,* 356-359.

Weisel, A. (1995). Are there angels in heaven who know sign language? Trends in the education of hearing-impaired Israeli children. In D. Chen (Ed.), *Education toward the twenty-first century* (pp. 503-515). Tel Aviv: Tel Aviv University—Ramot Press.

Weller, A., Florian, V., & Mikulincer, M. (1995). Adolescents' reports of parental division of power in a multicultural society. *Journal of Research on Adolescence, 5,* 413-429.

Wilde, O. (1968). *The short stories of Oscar Wilde.* Burlington, VT: Lane Press.

Wright, B. (1994). *The moral animal: The new science of evolutionary psychology.* New York: Pantheon Books.

Wuthnow, R. (1978). Peak experiences: Some empirical tests. *Journal of Humanistic Psychology, 18,* 59-75.

Yaar-Yuchtman, E. (1983). Expectations, entitlements, and subjective welfare. In S. E. Spiro & E. Yaar-Yuchtman (Eds.), *Evaluating the welfare state: Social and political perspectives.* New York: Academic Press.

Yahel, U., & Ilovich, C. (1985). *Positive experiences and readiness for transpersonal commitment among adolescents from disadvantaged neighborhoods.* Unpublished manuscript, Tel Aviv University, Israel. (Hebrew)

Youniss, J., & Smollar, J. (1985). *Adolescent relations with mothers, fathers, and friends.* Chicago: University of Chicago Press.

Zahn-Waxler, C. (1991). The case for empathy: A developmental perspective. *Psychological Inquiry, 2,* 155-158.

Zajonc, R. B. (1982). Altruism, envy, competitiveness, and the common good. In V. J. Derlega & J. Grezlak (Eds.), *Cooperation and helping behavior: Theories and research* (pp. 417-436). New York: Academic Press.

Zak, I. (1979a). Constancy and variability of the HSPQ across two Israeli cultures. *Multivariate Experimental Clinical Research, 4,* 81-92.

Zak, I. (1979b). Modal personality of young Jews and Arabs in Israel. *Journal of Social Psychology, 109,* 3-10.

Ziv, A. (1984). *Hitbagrut* [Adolescence]. Tel Aviv: Massada.

Index

About the Author

Zipora Magen, Ph.D., is Associate Professor at Tel Aviv University. She is one of the architects of the counseling approach currently followed in the Israeli educational system. As a teacher and school counselor, she helped establish educational policy, developing an innovative humanistic orientation toward work with students, teachers, staff, and school administrations.

Professor Magen's cross-cultural research over a decade is also recognized as a groundbreaking contribution to educational counseling throughout the profession. Her articles have appeared in leading scientific and professional journals and have been presented widely at international conferences. Her main research interests continue to be in adolescents' growth-promoting characteristics, the multicultural implications of ethnic developmental issues, parenting roles in modern society, and counselors' perceptions and function.